The
Mixer and Blender
Cookery Book

THE

Mixer and Blender

COOKERY BOOK

ALISON DENNY
B.Sc.

FABER AND FABER
3 Queen Square
London

First published in 1973
by Faber and Faber Limited
3 Queen Square London WC1
First published in Faber Paperbacks 1977
Photoset and printed in Great Britain
Lowe and Brydone Printers Limited, Thetford, Norfolk
All rights reserved

ISBN 0 571 11073 8 (Faber Paperbacks)
ISBN 0 571 09736 7 (Hard Bound Edition)

For Mother

Acknowledgements

The author is most grateful to the following firms for their considerable help and encouragement and for the loan of equipment and photographs:

    Associated Health Foods Ltd (Alfonal)
    Bosch Ltd
    Hoover Ltd
    Moulinex Ltd
    Sunbeam Electric Ltd
    Thorn Domestic Appliances (Electrical) Ltd (Kenwood)
    Tower Housewares Ltd

and to Mark Gerson who took the photographs for plates 3, 7, 8 and 13.

    She especially wishes to thank Mrs Dryden-Stuart of Kenwood and Mrs Weatherby formerly of Sunbeam for their kind interest and help.

Contents

CONTENTS

Illustrations

Introduction

It is only since the end of the last war that mixers and blenders have been used domestically in this country and probably in the last ten to fifteen years that they have found their way into a large number of ordinary homes. Now, they are owned by many cooks who undoubtedly make great use of them, but it can only be a few who take the fullest advantage of these versatile tools.

It is to those who still do not find them the great asset they anticipated, and to those who have just bought, or who are contemplating buying, a mixer or blender that this book is directed.

First it is important to make quite clear what is meant by a mixer and a blender. Basically both consist of a small electric motor, to which can be fitted various attachments useful in cooking, in exactly the same way as the handyman's electric drill can be made to run a saw, a sanding disc or a polisher. Into the electric motor of the mixer can be inserted whisks, beaters or dough hooks and – provided the motor is powerful enough – many other attachments too, such as a mincer, slicer and shredder, potato peeler, etc. Of these attachments, probably the most useful and most frequently owned is the blender. This is usually a glass or plastic goblet with revolving knives at the bottom, and the speed with which it does its work can be a revelation to the new owner. Another name for a blender is a liquidizer: these two are synonymous, but for convenience in this book the term used will always be 'blender'.

When buying a mixer and/or blender the primary reason is usually to save time and effort, and food preparation time, especially of large quantities, is cut enormously. With the appropriate attachments, they accomplish at high speed such things as cake making, shredding cabbage, grating carrots or cheese, mincing, potato peeling, making breadcrumbs, chopping nuts, parsley and mint, and chopping peel for marmalade. It is only after using the equipment for a while that it becomes apparent that it will also help in many economies, particularly in using up left-over food and in making inexpensive substitutes to stretch the budget (see pp. 54–55).

In order that the maximum use is made of the equipment she has, the reader is strongly recommended to study the preliminary instructional chapters before embarking on the recipes. There is necessarily some overlapping of the advice given in these chapters, largely in the interests of emphasizing some of the more important factors. Chapter 1 shows what equipment is available, and how it should be cared for, and it also suggests the points to look out for when choosing items for a particular household. Chapter 2 advises on how to use the equipment to obtain the best results in cooking. When the recipes are reached, it will be found these have been selected especially to suit the largish household of moderate means, where some entertaining, casual or formal, is done. It is probable that such a family stands to gain most in time and money saved by the use of the equipment described. However, there are many small households where it will prove invaluable, and the quantities given in the recipes can easily be reduced as necessary. The recipe section will show how the mixer and blender can help in a wide range of dishes, and many can be attempted which would normally be too difficult or too time-consuming by hand.

Finally, do please read the notes which appear immediately before the recipes themselves, for in them are collected together for easy reference some of the more important pointers to success which are discussed in Chapters 1 and 2.

PART I

I

The Equipment: What it is and How to Care for it

∽⃝∽⃝∽⃝∽⃝∽⃝∽⃝∽⃝∽⃝∽⃝∽⃝∽⃝∽⃝∽⃝∽⃝∽⃝∽⃝∽⃝

MIXERS

All mixers work on the principle of using an electric motor to drive devices for beating or whisking, but they can roughly be divided into two groups, the large table mixers and the small hand-held mixers. Between these two ends of the scale are a range of mixers including table models which can also be held in the hand if necessary, and light hand-held models which can be fitted with a stand and bowl. Many hand-held mixers have no stand at all; they are basically the same as the larger table models with their fitted bowls, but it is important that they should be light so as a general rule they have less powerful motors. For this reason they do not have the range of attachments available with the more robust table models, but some are equipped with small blenders.

Table Mixers

These are the big, powerful members of the mixer family, which are capable of dealing efficiently with large quantities. (For example: creaming 1 lb. ($\frac{1}{2}$ kg.) fat and 1 lb. ($\frac{1}{2}$ kg.) sugar takes only a few minutes with the table mixer, without any effort, but it would take at least 20 minutes by hand.)

The whisk can either be held downwards into the bowl by an overhead arm which houses the motor, or driven by a spindle which sticks up in the centre of a specially designed bowl. Both are equally efficient in working, but the central spindle tends to make the bowl more awkward to clear out, and harder to use away from the machine for such essentials as folding flour in by hand. One becomes accustomed to this in time, however, so it is no real disadvantage.

In all table mixers there must be an arrangement for seeing that the whisk reaches every part of the mixture, and gets very close to the side of the bowl, so it may be that the whisk itself, besides revolving, moves round the edge of the bowl, or that the bowl rotates round a whisk in fixed position.

It is most unwise to leave any mixer in the kitchen working unattended; however, the table mixer does not need constant attention and while it gets on with the mixing, the cook can be doing a multitude of other jobs in the kitchen, such as preparing cake tins etc.

With its powerful motor and stable base the table mixer is ideal for the attachment of other tools and perhaps this is its greatest advantage. It can run a wide range of kitchen aids, such as a potato peeler, mincer, slicer/shredder, and best of all, a large and powerful blender.

The table mixer is best used with its own bowl, and the fact that there is usually only one size bowl provided can be a great disadvantage. A small quantity is lost in a large bowl, and so the owner of a table mixer sometimes finds herself doing by hand what would be done ideally by a hand mixer. It is, however, sometimes possible to find a small pudding basin which can be held on the mixer and used for small quantities, but a non-standard bowl *must always be held firmly* while the mixer is working in it. It is a great advantage to have at least two bowls for the mixer, even if they are the same size, so that when a recipe has several processes which can be carried out in the mixer there is no necessity to keep transferring the contents from the bowl. To give just one example – in most cold soufflés the yolks and sugar must be whisked till thick, the cream whipped and the egg whites whisked stiff – three processes in all. It would therefore seem no extravagance to purchase an extra mixer bowl and have two in use, and this would certainly allow for more efficient working. In the long run too, a single bowl is sure to need replacing.

A tool which is essential for the owner of a mixer or blender is a plastic or rubber spatula. Some manufacturers give one with their machine, but if not, one should be bought. In the course of mixing or blending the mixture often splashes up the sides and the spatula is ideal for scraping down, easily getting the sides completely clean. In the mixer too, however closely the beaters skim the sides, they always leave a layer of mixture untouched against the bowl, and during the course of mixing the machine must be stopped and this layer scraped down and incorporated ready for further beating. The spatula is even more essential for use with the blender where the sharp blades can easily be damaged and must not be touched with metal utensils. A spatula is a particularly good shape for getting down the sides of the tall jar and round the knives – when switched off, of course!

Hand-held Mixers

These are ideal for preparing small amounts of food but they are not capable of dealing with large quantities, nor of running a multitude of attachments as are the larger mixers; however they have other advantages, for they are light and easy to handle and hence convenient to use and to store – particularly on a clip attached to the wall.

Sometimes the hand-held machine has a beater to be used for dry processes such as rubbing fat into flour, or heavy ones such as creaming fat and sugar, and also a delicate wire whisk for lighter mixtures such as those containing cream, eggs and gelatine. Other machines have one or two multipurpose beaters, rather like a rotary egg beater, which are used for everything.

The great advantage of hand-held mixers is that they can be used in bowls or saucepans, perhaps in two or three during the stages in the preparation of one dish. They can be taken to the stove and used in a saucepan, to mash potatoes or beat a lumpy sauce smooth, or in a bowl over a saucepan of hot water, provided, of course, the power points are suitably situated and care is taken not to trail the flex over the burners.

If the mixer has two beaters, one can be removed and the other used if required for beating in a jug or beaker.

It is obvious that the hand-held mixer does not save as much time as the table mixer for it must be held all the time it is in use, and hence all ingredients and cooking tins should be ready before starting mixing. This also brings with it the problem of the necessity for putting the mixer down at intervals during working, which should be accomplished without much mess. Most manufacturers make provision for this, so that the beaters can be left to drip into the bowl.

No-Flex Equipment

A new development has produced equipment without the need for trailing flexes. A power unit contains nickel-cadmium cells which store electricity and are recharged whenever the equipment is not in use: recharging takes place when the unit is connected to its power base which is plugged into the mains. The machine uses very little power, rather like an electric clock. The power unit is used to drive a hand-held mixer, or a blender, coffee grinder or other attachments, but as the power available is low, it can only take the place of a small conventional mixer. It can be used a number of times before recharging and is very convenient and particularly safe as there is no danger of a flex burning on a cooker.

Another recent introduction is a battery-powered whisk, inexpensive and lightweight and suitable only for whisking cream, eggs, sauces, drinks, etc., but of great advantage where power points may not be conveniently available and, of course, in boats, caravans and so on.

ATTACHMENTS TO MIXERS

The powerful motors of table mixers can be used to drive a number of attachments, though not all attachments are produced by all manufacturers. Some, mainly blenders, *are* produced as machines in their own right, with their own separate motors, but whatever their source of power they function in similar ways. These attachments often require no culinary skill and provided they are used according to the manufacturers' instructions they do their work well. However, it is best to check before buying an attachment that it really will do the job required of it, for the claims made by manufacturers may sometimes be rather exaggerated. In many cases the particular attachment is only useful in a household where large quantities of food are being prepared; in small quantities it is still easier to use a hand tool for many tasks and the expensive mechanical one could become a dust-catching white elephant. However, when large quantities of food *are* being prepared, both the mixer and its attachments are a godsend in time and effort saving.

Blenders – see p. 28

Dough Hooks

These are inserted into the mixer in the same place as the beaters or whisks (but are much stronger than either as they have to work a heavy dough) to be used downwards into the mixer bowl. Dough hooks have several designs, but they are all essentially of strong construction, and all have a flat guard plate, fitted horizontally across the top to prevent the dough creeping up into the motor. Bread dough is very elastic and easily climbs up the dough hook in the course of kneading unless this guard is in position.

Centrifugal Juicer

Basically the juicer consists of a grating disc which, revolving at high speed, breaks up the vegetable tissues. The pulp is then thrown by centrifugal force on to a very fine strainer or a filter which allows the juice through while the dry matter remains on it. The filtered juice is clear and the residue is very dry. In some machines the filter has to be cleaned of dry pulp after a certain quantity (given in instruction booklet) has been juiced, while in others it is thrown off by the centrifugal action and away down a funnel.

The juicer is a useful aid in amateur winemaking (p. 48).

Citrus Juice Extractor

In effect this is the familiar lemon squeezer with the central cone driven by the mixer motor at high speed.

This attachment is particularly useful where large quantities of orange or lemon drinks are required, and it can also be used to extract the juice in marmalade making.

Mincer Attachment

This is another example of using the mixer motor to drive a familiar appliance, the hand food mincer.

In many ways the mincer does the same work as the blender, but it is very powerful and quick, so it is obvious that it is better for dealing rapidly with large quantities. It is invaluable in dealing with meat, both raw and cooked, which the blender does not cope with so well.

Sausage Filler

This attachment is in effect an extension of the mincer, for it is, as it were, a long plastic 'snout' which fits on the front of the mincer, and shapes the extruded mince into sausages.

Once the mincing attachment is purchased, the sausage filler is a very inexpensive addition which can be used with great ease and success to make delicious sausages from home recipes.

Slicer/Shredder

The external appearance of this varies according to the manufacturer, but all models are simply a means of housing interchangeable discs or drums which are driven by the mixer motor and which, as they rotate, shred or slice the food which is fed down a chute and held against them by a pusher. This machine carries out much more quickly and efficiently the functions of a hand grater. The discs or drums usually provided with the slicer/shredder are:

i. *The fine shredder.* This is suitable for finely grated cheese (particularly Parmesan), carrots, suet, nuts, block chocolate and bread raspings.

ii. *Coarse shredder.* Again this grates cheese, more coarsely, and root vegetables including beetroot, apples and onions.

iii. *Slicer.* This will cut fine slices very rapidly, although not quite as neatly as can be achieved by hand with a sharp knife.

The slicer disc is particularly valuable for making potato crisps (p. 117) and as they are so expensive nowadays for families where a large number of crisps are consumed, this can be a real money saver. It is best to make a large batch at a time, as the crisps can be stored very successfully for some while in an airtight tin. The disc is also extremely useful for slicing cabbage, particularly if raw cabbage is to be used for salads in the form of coleslaw, because it is possible to achieve very appetizing fine shreds.

iv. Some manufacturers also provide a thicker slicer which is particularly useful for slicing cabbage to be boiled. Sometimes this coarser slicer may have crinkly cutting edges which can be used to give fancy slices of carrot, beetroot, cucumber and potato and the latter may be deep fried to make crinkly game chips.

Colander/Sieve

This is in reality a powered version of the old-fashioned hair sieve which was used for sieving soups or making purées of fruits or vegetables. The motor of the mixer is used to drive an arm with two paddles which push the food through a sieve, into a bowl.

The colander usually has two sieves, one with a fine mesh, the other with larger holes. Many of the jobs done by the colander/sieve can be done by the blender, but in two stages – the food must be passed through a strainer after blending. Thus, although the blender is quite satisfactory for small quantities, the colander/sieve deals much better with large ones. It is ideal for making purées of fruits with pips and stones, and also much quicker than the blender for making larger quantities of apple purée. It is also excellent for making puréed vegetables, such as peas or spinach, and for sieving soups.

The colander/sieve can only deal with soft food and is not nearly so versatile as the blender as it has no cutting action, although sometimes the sieve has a rough surface which helps to break down stringy parts of the food as the paddles force them round. It is very quick at the jobs for which it is designed and is particularly useful in the kitchen where large quantities of home-grown produce have to be dealt with when they are in season, such as on a farm, or in a home with a large kitchen garden. It can also be helpful in a family where one member needs a low residue or strict gastric diet (p. 57) and where it may be convenient at times to give the whole family this type of food.

Bean Slicer and Pea Huller

Some manufacturers produce attachments which will only slice beans, but others will shell peas as well. As peas and beans are vegetables with a short season it is probably only worth owning this attachment if one has a big kitchen garden and a deep freeze in which one can store large quantities of peas and beans for winter use. If this is the case, and bumper crops must be dealt with quickly, then a bean slicer/pea huller is a real boon.

There are several attachments available and one of the most popular works in this way: the topped and tailed beans are fed through a set of revolving roller knives which slice them lengthways as they pass between them. If the beans are at all tough the stringy sides must be sliced off first with a knife. This machine can also be used to slice the peel for chunky marmalade.

The peas are dealt with by the other end of the rollers which are smooth. They grasp the end of the pod and by squeezing it, open the shucks and force the peas out. The peas are caught in a bowl underneath, while the shucks fall away to the side. Of course the peas must be looked over afterwards to remove any which are discoloured or maggoty.

Potato Peeler

Because potatoes feature so largely in the British diet, the peeling of them can be quite a lengthy chore, and this attachment which also peels root vegetables is a real asset. There are some machines on the market with independent motors, but others can be fitted as attachments to mixers. Because of the weight of the potatoes a powerful motor is required, so potato-peeling attachments are only made for large table mixers. They consist of a drum, usually metal, with well-fitting cover. The bottom of the drum is a disc which is rotated rapidly by the mixer motor. When the potatoes are in the drum the rapid rotation throws them against the sides. The drum, or sometimes only the base, is lined with an abrasive surface, usually carborundum, which is like a very coarse dark sandpaper, but extremely hard. This has the action of rubbing away the skins of root vegetables, and any unevenness of their surface.

Coffee Grinder

Although in an emergency coffee beans can be ground in most blenders, it is not something which manufacturers recommend as a regular practice because the hard beans can damage the knives, so if freshly ground coffee is needed frequently it is best to purchase the coffee mill which many manufacturers make as an attachment to their mixer or blender.

A coffee mill may be like a small blender with knives at the bottom especially suited for grinding the coffee beans. In this case the manufacturer always suggests the maximum amount of beans which can be ground at one time and this should not be exceeded. The size of the grounds is determined by the length of time the beans are in the grinder, and this must be regulated carefully to finish up with the coffee ground fine, medium or coarse, as required. Other grinders work on a continuous running principle – the beans are fed in at the top and ground coffee runs out of the chute at the bottom, having been through a grinding mechanism. This can usually be adjusted to give fine, medium or coarse grounds. This type of machine is more suitable if large quantities of coffee are needed at a time, but as coffee is at its best freshly ground, just before use, it should be prepared in 1–2 oz. (25–50 g.) batches for the average family; thus the blender-type coffee grinder is perfectly adequate.

Tin Opener

This is a mechanized version of the familiar, efficient, wall tin opener which does its work quickly and cleanly.

The tin opener is fixed on to the motor, and the tin grasped and pierced as a handle is pulled down firmly. It is then turned by the motor of the mixer and a very clean cut is made round the rim of the tin, with no jagged edges. In some tin-opening attachments, when the cut is complete the lid is held firmly by a magnetic disc; the tin itself cannot fall until the lever is released.

If you have always used a hand-operated tin opener, the ease and speed with which these mechanical ones operate is a revelation. They are particularly excellent for opening sardine or herring tins which can be turned upside down, so obviating the need to struggle with the key. Meat tins can be quickly opened from both ends and the meat is then easily pushed out.

As the tin-opening attachment will often be required, but only for a short time, it is best if possible to keep it permanently in position on the mixer, ready for use at once.

BLENDERS
(Liquidizers)

In many of the more powerful electric mixers the motor is utilized to run a blender as well, or the blender may be a separate machine. In both cases the principle is the same – that of a tall jar with knives (usually four) at the bottom, motor-driven, which revolve at very high speed; these break down and chop the food in contact with them into very fine particles. All the contents of the jar are drawn down on to the knives by the consequent downward spiralling action.

The blender is an extremely useful tool, in reality a new composite mechanical tool for the kitchen, made possible by the power of its electric motor. It combines the work of a pestle and mortar, hair sieve, hand whisk, mincer, grater, and a sharp chopping knife, and can do the work in a fraction of the time it would take by hand. Because in many ways it is different from the hand tools, it requires new techniques which have been developed to make use of it to the full, and these will be apparent as the recipes in Part II are followed.

Some blenders are made to unscrew at the base of the jar near the knives. This obviously makes it easier to clean the blender, and to scrape out solid foods such as meat pastes. There is a rubber ring/washer which must be placed quite flat and the jar screwed up tightly, or it will leak. The washer should also be renewed when it first shows signs of perishing, again to prevent leaking.

Every blender has a lid, and it is most important that this should always be put on firmly before switching on the motor. Otherwise the contents may fly out, and, quite apart from the mess, it is possible to have a nasty scald from hot liquids. Usually the lid is designed to lock on to the jar, but it is advisable to hold it on as the motor is switched on, for the contents of the jar always make an initial jump. It is for this reason that the jar should never be filled more than three-quarters or two-thirds full of liquid. When using the blender with solid foods it will probably be found to work best if the jar is less than half-full.

Most blender lids have a small central 'cap' which can be removed during working and this is very useful to prevent splashing while adding ingredients when the machine is running – and essential for sauces like mayonnaise and hollandaise where ingredients must be added slowly and continuously. Often too, one must add solid pieces one at a time and drop them on to the fast revolving blades, as for making breadcrumbs, and these can jump very violently. If there is no cap it is possible to manage by tipping one side of the lid carefully, but it is much better to make a lid for the blender from aluminium foil, and then cut a hole in the centre through which the food can be added.

CLEANING THE EQUIPMENT

Modern mixers and their attachments are generally constructed of three materials, plastic, glass and metal, and the cleaning of the machines is largely a matter of common sense, depending on the material of which they are made.

Plastics, although unbreakable, can be damaged in other ways, especially by scratching or by melting, and therefore must be cleaned with soap and water without the help of abrasive powders or scouring pads. Should food be dried on, soaking for several hours often greatly facilitates cleaning. Plastics should never be put to dry on, or in, an oven or in a hot cupboard, or over a gas flame. The high temperatures in dishwashing machines can damage some rubber or plastic parts.

Only warm soapy water, and not abrasives, should be used on glass bowls or goblets, and extremes of temperature should be avoided.

The metals usually used in the construction of mixers are aluminium, and steel, often stainless. These are easy to clean and abrasive powders or pads can be used; however, soda should not be used on aluminium parts. Stainless steel is, of course, the easiest to clean and dry, but ordinary steel, such as found in the mincing attachment, will go rusty if left damp, and must be dried quickly.

Mixer

The power units of the machines discussed in this book are electric motors housed in plastic or painted metal cases (and stands). On no account should these ever be put into water because of the danger of damaging the motor and they must therefore be cleaned by wiping over with a warm, damp cloth and polishing with a dry one. The motor often gets splashed during working, and it is well worth while wiping it over immediately after use before the splashes can dry on. It should always be switched off first because of the danger of touching electrical equipment with damp hands. This is the time, too, to eject the beaters or whisks and put them to soak.

After using a hand-held mixer it can be held upright in a jug of warm soapy water and switched on for a few seconds, taking care not to let the motor get wet. This will clean the beaters without even removing them from the machine.

The No-Flex Mixer

The most important thing is to keep the contact points on the base unit and the power unit clean, dry and bright, so that a steady flow of electricity is maintained from the mains. Switch off before cleaning and use a dry cloth, not abrasives which might damage the points. No part of the system should be immersed in water (except the bowl, beaters, blender jar, etc.) but it should be wiped over with a damp cloth.

Blender

This is a very simple matter as the jar can be immersed in soapy water. A brush or mop is good for getting to the problem area found around the knives, but in some makes the blades unscrew, thus providing an ideal way to clean when food is stuck. In this case the jar, knives (wash these under a running tap) and sealing rubber ring must not be reassembled until dry. Then great care must be taken to ensure that the ring is lying flat before screwing up really tight. Another excellent way of cleaning the blender is to fill it half-full of warm soapy water and switch on at fast speeds for a few seconds to loosen the food, before taking it to the sink. Be careful not to plunge the jar into very hot washing-up water after making iced drinks or icecream.

Centrifugal Juicer

Once juicing has been finished the filter should be put into soak and washed as soon as possible – unless it is a paper one to be thrown away. Some filters are very delicate, but usually a soft brush can be used with effect, and after cleaning the filter must be dried carefully in a warm place. It should then be stored in a place where it will not be damaged. Probably the best solution is to reassemble the juicer loosely, and store it fitted.

Mincer and Sausage Filler

The mincer is usually made of non-stainless steel and therefore stains and rusts easily. It should be dismantled completely after use, and the pieces should be washed separately in warm soapy water. They should then be dried and put in a warm place (over a radiator or on a cooker) until completely dry, when the mincer can be loosely reassembled. The sausage filler is usually plastic and best cleaned with a bottle brush and dried away from heat.

Slicer/Shredder

This is an attachment which is much more useful if it can be kept permanently fitted to the machine, so that small amounts can be sliced, shredded, or grated at a moment's notice. In this case it is usually only necessary to remove the shredding disc or drum and wash it in warm, soapy water, while wiping out the main part of the attachment with a damp cloth. Of course the whole attachment should be dismantled and thoroughly washed after several usings.

Potato Peeler

As can be imagined, the abrasive inside of the drum becomes clogged up with the rubbings of potato peel, and this should be cleaned between each operation. The best way is to hold the bowl under running cold water immediately after use, and brush off any adhering peel, then dry it in the air.

Coffee Grinder

As this is only used for coffee there is no need to wash it, in fact most manufactures recommend that you should not do so. The outside can be wiped over with a damp cloth if necessary and the inside brushed with a dry brush.

CARE AND MAINTENANCE

The vital thing here is to read the manufacturer's booklet very carefully to see what is recommended for maintenance, servicing and general care, and see that the advice given is followed. It is important to find out whether the machine, and particularly the motor, needs oiling or not. Many high-powered machines have their gearboxes packed with grease during manufacture, and need no further oiling for the normal life of the machine. However, there are some machines which do need oiling regularly and there are definite oiling points and holes indicated by the makers. If your machine is one of these, do make sure that you know the oiling procedure and carry it out as frequently as required, to save engine wear. It rarely takes more than a few seconds. Sometimes it is necessary to oil underneath the blender, although more often these bearings are made of nylon and need no lubrication. Naturally the motor should be considered as any other electrical appliance and any electrical fault dealt with immediately. A worn or frayed flex should be renewed at once.

The beaters and whisks of the mixer can easily become bent or badly adjusted during use, and if a fault does occur it must be quickly rectified. If the metal whisks become bent so that they are hitting the sides of the bowl or each other, this is at once obvious from the noise and the machine should be stopped and the whisks straightened again immediately, otherwise they may easily become damaged beyond repair.

There should be a minimal gap between the bowl and the beaters, but this varies with the make of mixer. In some it can be adjusted simply, but if this is so, and the gap becomes appreciably larger than when the machine was new, it should be sent back to the manufacturers for adjustment. If there is too thick a layer of mixture round the bowl which does not become properly mixed, the machine is very inefficient and the results poor. A few machines have a bowl which can be manually moved nearer the beaters.

Mixers and blenders need very little regular maintenance, and the only other point to watch is that parts should be replaced individually as they become worn. This is particularly true of any rubber rings which ensure a tight seal, as at the base of a blender jar which unscrews. If these rings become perished they will cause a leaking joint.

Looking after the Mixer

The mixer and blender, like any other electrical machines, have only limited lives, but these can be greatly prolonged if they are used carefully.

Some mixers are designed for continuous running, and this is usually stated in the instructions, but more often there is a time limit beyond which it is not wise to continue mixing. After this the motor should be switched off and cooled for at least 20 minutes.

Having set a time limit for the machines, the manufacturers usually recommend a maximum amount that should be mixed, and this should not be exceeded. It is usually obvious when a mixer bowl is too full, because the beaters are submerged beneath the mixture, and consequently labour. The kneading of dough is extremely hard work and the weight of flour which can easily be worked by the machine is always given. This weight should not be exceeded. However, as mechanical kneading is very quick, it is not difficult to do several batches. It is possible to hear immediately if the mixer motor is labouring, and something must be done about it at once. Either some of the mixture must be taken out of the bowl, or the mixer can be switched to a higher speed, which gives more power to the beaters. It is the very slow speeds which are a particular strain on the mechanism.

Hand-held mixers are especially easily overloaded as they can be used in any bowl, but the cook will soon become sensitive to overworking.

Looking after the Blender

The action of blending is a particular strain on an electric motor and it should be switched off to prevent unnecessary wear as soon as a job is finished. It is for this reason that the blender should never be left working unattended. Most manufacturers give an upper time limit for the use of the blender, with quite a long recovery time afterwards, but as most blending operations are very short this is normally no hardship. However, it must be considered when there are several batches to be processed, and carefully observed when dry ingredients, such as breadcrumbs, or very solid ones, such as meat paste, are being blended. These operations with solids are particularly wearing on the motor, and if at all possible it is best to add liquid when chopping solids as this makes the work easier. It is possible to hear at once if the motor is labouring when blending, and it must be stopped immediately. Then either more liquid can be added, or some of the mixture can be taken out of the jar. It is also best to use the mixer in preference to the blender in all those recipes where either could be used (e.g. for batters, mayonnaise etc.).

Almost all blender jars are made of glass or plastic and these are easily broken or damaged and expensive to replace. It is wise to check if the jar can be filled with boiling liquids, and sensible to warm the jar before filling it with hot foods.

CHOOSING THE EQUIPMENT

1. For the Cook

From the range of mixers, blenders and their attachments which have been discussed it can be seen that no one household would want all that is available. Probably the greatest single factor which should influence the choice of equipment is the character of the cook and the degree of her enthusiasm for cooking. It might be pointless to give a table mixer with all its gadgets to a housewife, with a family, who is only minimally interested in cooking, and chooses to use ready-prepared and convenience foods – although it *could* arouse her interest in cooking! Much more use of it might be made by an older single woman living alone, if she spent much of her time entertaining, cooking for bazaars, women's institutes' teas, and charity luncheons.

Once that has been said, it is obvious that needs of households vary, and a few are considered here. For instance the average family of, say, parents and two children, will not usually need to cook very large quantities unless they do a lot of entertaining, so one of the smaller table mixers available would be quite sufficient. A blender attachment would certainly prove very useful and also a mincer, as the dishes cooked are likely to be varied.

Once the family has reached a bigger size, with six or more in the household, a large table mixer is indicated, not only for its larger mixing capacity but also for the powerful attachments it can drive – a large blender, mincer, slicer/shredder etc. In this household the vegetable preparation will be a lengthy chore, so the potato peeler, slicer/shredder and bean slicer will prove great assets, especially if there are home-grown fruit and vegetables to be harvested and if jams and marmalades are made.

At the other end of the scale is the flat-dweller, with a small kitchen, where a hand-held mixer, which would clip to the wall and take up the minimum of space, would probably be the most useful. Perhaps this might be supplemented by a small blender with its own motor on which a coffee grinder could also be used. Similarly the small household which does a great deal of entertaining would benefit most from a small table mixer or hand-held mixer. Either would be used to provide exciting dishes for dinner parties, and a blender attachment would be very useful for soups, sauces and drinks.

Finally we come to the family where the cook is elderly or

disabled, particularly in the use of her arms. A mixer becomes almost a necessity for anyone suffering from neuritis, rheumatism, arthritis or partial paralysis, and for anyone in a wheel chair who finds it difficult to get sufficient purchase when beating. For all these people the whisking, beating and creaming action of a hand mixer or small table mixer will help tremendously in overcoming their disability, as it will the weakness of old age. When buying a hand-held mixer it should be tested for weight, for it must be light enough to be held comfortably by the cook for several minutes.

2. For the Kitchen

Once having decided on the purchase of equipment, the kitchen where it is to be used must be considered carefully to find the best place to keep it – if possible in a place convenient for both mixing and food preparation. The word 'stored' has deliberately been avoided, because this implies putting away on a shelf or in a cupboard and fitting up when required, and this is the worst possible thing. Once bought, the single factor most likely to decide how much benefit is obtained from the machines is the place where they are kept. The mixer and blender should be permanently out on the table top, plugged in (switched off of course) and ready to use at a moment's notice. It is possible to get attractive plastic covers which keep them clean when out on the bench top, and they do not look unsightly.

Many table mixers (and large blenders too) seem to live almost permanently in a cupboard and are very rarely used 'because it's such a bother to get it out and fix it up'. If there really is no place where they can live ready plugged in (and they are sizeable pieces of equipment which occupy a considerable amount of space) it is probably better to opt for a smaller mixer or buy a hand-held one which can be clipped to the wall, and a small blender as well. However the top of the refrigerator is often unused and this might be a very good place to stand the equipment, since there is probably an electric socket nearby.

The ideal solution for the mixer's place in the kitchen is to create a mixing centre near the stove with the machine ready on the working surface, together with the scales, while underneath are kept the mixer tools and attachments and baking accessories such as rolling pin, cake tins, pastry cutters etc. Dry goods such as flour, sugar, dried fruit, essences could be in a cupboard above or very near the mixing area. This would ensure that cooking, particularly baking, could be carried out very quickly with a minimum of walking.

The centrifugal juice extraction is bound to be rather a messy business so it is a good idea to plug the machine near the sink or even to stand it on the draining board when this attachment is to be used, for then it is easy to put parts to soak after use.

The siting of the electric sockets is *very* important and if possible there should be one just above the work-top for the mixer and blender. In any case long lengths of trailing flex should be avoided, and it is not a good idea to use a mixer or blender on a table standing in the centre of the room, as the machine may get pulled off by someone not noticing the flex. However the flex of a hand-held mixer *must* be long enough to reach wherever it may be used. This particularly applies to the stove, where the mixer will be used in saucepans. Ideally it should be plugged in near the stove, taking care that the flex does not trail dangerously over the burners.

Finally, having bought your equipment and decided where to place it, make the most of it.

2

Using the Equipment

Having discussed the various kinds of equipment available, and their place in the kitchen, this chapter deals with the practical details of how to use the machines, and how to make them earn their keep by daily use. Remember that you must get used to this equipment like any other tool, and that practice with it makes one increasingly quick. Of course one is slower than by hand the first time, especially if one is very practised by hand, but by about the third time of using the machine one finds the time taken by the two methods is very similar, and at the tenth time of using, the machine is infinitely quicker. Experience will soon teach when the quantities being used are so small that it really *is* quicker by hand. The manufacturers' booklets should also be consulted carefully, for each make of machine is different, and naturally those with more powerful motors can attempt more, but the following general information should help everyone.

THE BASIC MIXER

General Preparations before Mixing

At least one hour before starting, take out of the refrigerator all the ingredients such as eggs and fat which should be at room temperature before beginning mixing. Next, it is important to light the oven at the required setting in good time so that it is steady at the right temperature when the food is ready to go in. If a steamer is needed it must be boiling well, and if icecream is to be made, the refrigerator must be turned to its lowest setting half an hour before needed.

Before actually mixing, any baking tins and trays to be used should be prepared by greasing and lining where necessary, especially if this is a lengthy job. It is sometimes possible to do this while a table mixer is working, but the tins must be fully prepared by the time mixing is finished. Finally, when making preparations one must see that the bowl and beaters are ready for use. The beaters depend on the type or types fitted with the machine and should be chosen according to the manufacturers' instructions.

Creaming fat and sugar is one of the basic cookery processes, used in so many cake and biscuit recipes and one which is a long, hard job by hand. In fact it is safe to say that more cooks use a mixer for creaming than for anything else the mixer can do and that they are very thankful for its help with this particular job. The fat can be butter, margarine, dripping or vegetable cooking fats, although the first two are almost always used. The important thing is that the fat should be soft and workable but not oiled, which in practice means that it should be at warm room temperature, about 70°F (21°C). For this reason it should stand in a warm room for at least one hour before use, but it should not be put to warm rapidly, say in a cool oven where it will become oiled. Caster sugar is the best to use, but if this is not available granulated sugar can always be ground fine in the blender (p. 59). The bowl and beaters should be warmed, and the best way to do this is by filling the bowl half-full with hot water and standing the beaters in it. Pour away the water, dry equipment, and immediately start beating the fat. Some manufacturers recommend using a slow speed for creaming, but it is much more satisfactory to start with a slow speed for a few seconds, just to break down the fat, and then continue at medium speed to complete the creaming. Should the mixture climb up the sides of the bowl it may be that the speed is too high. The solution then is to stop the mixer, scrape down the sides of the bowl and start creaming again at a slower speed.

It is impossible to state here how long creaming will take, because there are so many variants – the type of fat, the room temperature, the size and shape of bowl, the quantity being mixed etc. During the creaming process air is beaten into the mixture to form a fine foam throughout, so the final appearance of the mixture should be aerated, light and fluffy. It will also turn very pale in colour, in many cases almost white. It is this incorporated air which helps a cake to rise, and because a mixer does the creaming so efficiently it may be necessary to reduce by as much as a half the quantity of baking powder given in recipes written for hand methods.

If eggs are to be added they are dropped singly into the bowl when the fat and sugar have been sufficiently creamed, while the beaters continue at medium speed. It is quite all right to add a whole egg at a time provided it is completely incorporated well before the next is added. It is not necessary to put flour in with the eggs, as is suggested in many recipes, though if the proportion of eggs is very high, a little of the flour may be added with the last egg or two to prevent the mixture curdling. The mixer beats so thoroughly that the risk of curdling on adding the eggs is very much reduced. Curdling causes loss of aeration from the mixture, with consequent reduced rising on baking, but is much more likely to occur when the mixture is beaten by hand rather than with a mixer. When the eggs have been beaten in, the mixture should be very smooth, light and creamy and is then ready for the flour to be folded in (p. 44).

A mixer can, of course, be used for making one-stage cakes where all the ingredients, including quick-creaming margarine, are put in the bowl and then combined together, using the mixer at slow speed. In this way a cake can be mixed in two or three minutes. However this method was originally devised to eliminate the labour of creaming by hand, and it does not give such good results as other cake-making methods. The cake does not rise as well unless more baking powder is added, which causes it to go stale more quickly. It is probable, then, that the owner of a mixer will prefer the conventional method of cake-making, using creaming, rather than the one-stage method.

Rubbing in fat to flour is the method used for some pastry and for so-called plain cakes. The proportion of ingredients is usually approximately one part fat to two parts flour.

The flour is put in the mixer bowl and the fat added, cut roughly into lumps, and the mixer switched on, always at slow speed. After about 2 minutes the fat will have been completely dispersed among the flour grains and the whole mixture will resemble breadcrumbs. Some mixers do leave a few larger lumps of fat on the surface but it is best to switch off with those still remaining, for if mixing is continued longer the fat and flour amalgamate as in shortbread, and the cake will become heavy, or the pastry will be difficult to roll and too short. So once the fat and flour reach the breadcrumbs stage, stop and add sugar, dried fruit, nuts etc., and then the liquid and mix slowly for a moment longer, then switch off.

Some people do not use their mixer for rubbing-in for two main reasons. Firstly it is so quick to rub fat into a small quantity of flour by hand that it hardly seems worthwhile fixing up the mixer to do it. However it is much more labour-saving if a large quantity is mixed (p. 63) and the remainder stored dry, ready to be mixed up when needed. Once the liquid has been added, pastry ready to roll out can be kept for only a few days. The other reason is that with some mixers, depending on the shape of the bowl and the speed of the beaters, the flour tends to splatter out of the bowl and make a mess all round. This can be overcome by throwing a cloth over the machine, putting on its plastic cover, or making a stiff card cover to fit over the bowl.

Sponge Cakes are those in which eggs are whisked very thoroughly with the sugar, this making a foam firm enough to hold the flour when it is folded in. The mixture can be baked just like this for a fatless sponge or swiss roll, or melted fat may be folded in too, as in a genoese sponge.

Because the eggs take such a lot of whisking, sponge cakes are a great labour to make by hand, and the bowl is usually stood over a pan of hot water to assist the formation of a stable foam. A mixer completely alters one's attitude to making sponge cakes. The eggs and sugar are simply put in the mixer bowl and whisked at fast speed. This whisking will take some minutes but eventually the mixture will have the consistency of whipped cream, with small bubbles on the surface, and be very pale in colour. The whisk will leave a trail which remains for some moments when it is lifted out of the mixture. At this point the well-sifted flour is folded in, and also the melted butter, if this is being used; this should be done very gently with a metal tablespoon, for the mixer, even at slowest speed, is too vigorous for the very fragile foam. No raising agent is used in these cakes and the air beaten in must be sufficient to make a light cake, so it is important to whisk until the foam is as stable as it can be, and to fold in very gently so as not to destroy it.

Egg Whites are used, whisked stiff, either to make meringue or to give lightness to a cake or a soufflé. This can be a very laborious task by hand, but the use of the mixer does away with all the hard work, though the cook's skill is still needed if the operation is to be a success.

As with whisking by hand, the first and most important point is to see that the bowl and the whisk are scrupulously free from any grease, especially if they have just been used for some other process in the recipe. This is best accomplished by washing in hot water with detergent, and draining, or drying on a clean cloth. Should there be any grease in the bowl, it will prevent the whites becoming stiff however long they are whisked.

The whites should be at room temperature, and the eggs broken individually into a separate cup or basin to avoid any egg yolk getting into the mixer bowl, as this can also prevent the whites whisking properly. Once the whites are in the bowl, start whisking with the mixer, first at slow, then at medium, and finally at fast speed for most of the time, until the whites are opaque and stiff. The most successful meringues and soufflés are made with egg white that has *just* reached the point when if the whisk were taken out of the bowl and the bowl inverted the whites would not slip out. At this 'soft-peak' stage, when the whisks are lifted out the whites are glossy and stand in peaks, not standing up quite straight but bending over at the very top. It is important to watch the whisking

43

as if the whites are over-whipped they will become dry and granular in appearance. If this happens they will not make good meringues, nor will they blend in well to a soufflé mixture or give such good aeration. If sugar is to be added to the egg white it must be done very carefully. It can all be whisked in rapidly adding one teaspoonful after another, but normally it is more satisfactory to whisk in half the sugar and then fold in the remainder; the mixer is not suitable for folding this into the foam and it should be done with a large metal spoon, using a cutting and lifting action. The same is true of any mixing of egg white foam with other ingredients – it should be done gently by hand.

Folding in, that is the mixing together of two sets of ingredients, is a difficult subject on which to generalize, and using the mixer for folding is very much a matter of commonsense. If it is a question of folding a light, aerated mixture, such as egg white foam, into a heavy sauce, as in a soufflé, it is clear that gentle folding by hand is required. However, when mixing heavy fruit and flour into the creamed mixture for a Christmas cake, the use of the mixer is quite suitable. When making cakes it is important to keep the action at this stage to a minimum (i.e. watch the mixer and stop it the moment all the ingredients are mixed), for too much beating makes the flour elastic and the cake tough and unpleasant. In this book the recipes state clearly when the mixer is to be used for folding and when not. The fact that it is often not used is not to the detriment of the mixer: folding in by hand takes very little time and labour, and the mixer can be used much more efficiently for other processes.

Whipping: The mixer is superb for whipping such things as cream, jelly and icecream, a process which is such hard and sometimes lengthy work by hand. Fast speed is nearly always used on the mixer, unless this causes too much splattering.

Cream: Single cream alone will not whip satisfactorily because its fat content is not high enough, but double cream with 48 per cent fat gives a rather dense whipped cream. For dishes where the lightness of the cream is important, such as cold soufflés, mousses etc., it is therefore best to use a mixture of equal parts single and double cream. The cream should be cold before whipping, preferably having been stored in the refrigerator, and it should be put in a clean mixer bowl and beaten with the whisk first at slow speed, increasing to fast speed. As the cream begins to thicken, turn the speed to slow again, and watch carefully, for it must be stopped when the cream is thick and the whisk leaves a mark, before it all turns buttery. If a sweetened cream is desired, one teaspoonful of caster sugar for every quarter of a pint of cream can be added towards the end of whisking.

Jelly: Many dishes containing gelatine can be whisked into a foam most successfully with a mixer, *provided the gelatine is on the point of setting.* Plain water jelly made according to the instructions on the packet can be made much more interesting by whisking it just as it is about to set, to double its volume and form jelly sponge. If the jelly is made with evaporated milk it also becomes more nutritious (p. 151, Mandarin Whip). The jelly should be made and then left until it feels cold, by which time it is probably almost setting. It can then be put in the mixer bowl and whisked at fast speed. If the foam does not appear to becoming thicker and the volume greater after a short time, switch off the mixer and wait a little while for the jelly to reach setting point, before trying again. The mixture can then be whisked at fast speed for several minutes to increase the volume and give a stable foam. Once the jelly is whisked sufficiently it should be poured at once into serving dishes as it will set very quickly.

Icecream: The mixer is an invaluable tool in the making of home-made icecream (p. 159) as it can be used to take over the heavy work of beating the half-frozen mixture and so breaking down the ice crystals and aerating the icecream. This produces a much smoother result than would be achieved by hand.

Batters, Sauces, Gravies, etc.: The mixer is excellent for beating any semi-solid mixture which starts lumpy and needs to be quite smooth, although in some ways the blender is a better tool for this job. When using the mixer for making batter, the flour and other dry ingredients should be put in the mixer bowl and the eggs and half the liquid added. The mixer can then be started at fast speed and the batter thoroughly beaten for 2–3 minutes, by which time it is perfectly smooth. At this stage the remainder of the liquid can be added, using the mixer at slow speed, and the batter is then ready – quite effortlessly. In a similar way the mixer can be used to beat smooth any lumpy sauces or gravies. The sauce is tipped into the mixer bowl and beaten at fast speed until all the lumps have disappeared, and then reheated if necessary. For this rescue operation a hand-held mixer is even more of a boon than the table mixer, for it can be taken to the stove to beat sauces or gravies in the pan. A mixer is also invaluable if a sauce, left over or part of a double batch, is to be rewarmed from cold: if it is beaten first with a little extra liquid (milk, water, stock) it can be made quite smooth and therefore easier to rewarm, if stirred all the while.

Mayonnaise (p. 87) even when made with a mixer requires care, but all the physical effort is removed and the cook can concentrate on establishing and holding a stable emulsion. The egg acts as an emulsifying agent, and if the oil is dropped in very slowly at first an emulsion is formed which gradually becomes thicker and thicker. Once this happens it is certain that the emulsion is well-stabilized and the oil can be added more quickly. Machines which have an oil-dropping attachment are a great advantage in making this sauce, for the oil *must* be added drop by drop in the first stages. However the cook should be around during the whole process for it is possible for the sauce to become too thick and then the mixer labours. If this happens, vinegar or hot water must be added immediately to thin the emulsion. In the recipe section two variations of mayonnaise are given and mixer mayonnaise-making becomes so easy that you should be stimulated to try many others.

Yeast Cookery and the use of the mixer with dough hooks is dealt with very thoroughly in the recipe section (pp. 225–8).

Using the Mixer or Blender with Convenience Foods: this is the age of convenience foods, and although a mixer is such a convenience in itself, there are still some occasions when the modern housewife will find it necessary to use a quick-mix packet. Even here the mixer is often useful, as will be seen from the following examples.

Packet cake mixes: these can be put in the mixer bowl and beaten according to the directions on the packet, at slow speed increasing to medium. Care must be taken not to overbeat, and the mixer should be used for half the time suggested for beating by hand.

Instant Meringue and Icecream Mix: these can be put in the mixer bowl and whisked according to the directions on the packet. The icecream should be beaten halfway through freezing to give a smooth result.

Instant Whip: this quick standby for the busy mother can be made equally well in a mixer or blender. Put the milk in first and then scatter the powder on top, being careful none of it clings to the sides during mixing. It need only be mixed at medium speed or blended at fast speed for about half a minute, and then left to set as usual.

Instant Potatoes: the potato powder is put in the mixer bowl and the required amounts of very hot water, milk and butter are poured in while mixing, first at slow, then increasing to medium speed. Beat just long enough to give fluffy potato, and serve immediately in a hot dish.

Packet Sauces or Soups: these do not normally need a mixer, but it is very convenient to take a hand-held mixer to the saucepan and beat them there. If, however, either soup or sauce should go lumpy, it can be blended at high speed for a few seconds in the blender to make it quite smooth again.

THE ATTACHMENTS

Blender

This is probably the most valuable of the mixer attachments but as it is frequently an entirely separate piece of equipment, it has a section to itself (see p. 53).

Dough Hooks

These are only used when yeast dough mixtures are being mixed. Their powerful action stretches and develops the gluten present in bread flour, thus taking the place of hand kneading.

Centrifugal Juicer

Its main purpose is to provide the fresh juices not only of fruits such as apples, pears, pineapples, rhubarb and melons, but also of many vegetables such as cabbage, beetroot, carrots, celery and spinach.

The fruit and vegetables are washed and cut into suitably sized pieces to be pushed down the chute on to the grater, which will break them up completely. The pieces must be pushed firmly, but not too vigorously, down with the pusher provided – but never with the fingers. The centrifugal juicer can also be used by the amateur winemaker for extracting juice, and if there is a keen winemaker in the family it is well worth purchasing this attachment for the mixer (see below).

The great advantage of these juices is that they carry the minerals and vitamins present in the fruits and vegetables without their bulk. It is so much easier to drink, say, a glass of carrot juice than to eat the original large pile of carrots. This is particularly important to anyone whose intake is impaired for some reason – by illness or by lack of appetite. Since they are largely taken for their health-giving properties, the juices should be made from really fresh fruits and vegetables, for as they become stale some of the vitamin content is lost: this can be replaced to some extent in apple juice, where ascorbic acid (vitamin C) should be added to the juice, which will also prevent it browning. To gain the maximum nutrient content from root vegetables they should be scrubbed but not peeled and the peel should be left on apples, tomatoes etc. when juicing. A few soft fruits such as bananas, peaches, plums and apricots are not suitable for use in a juicer because they give a cloudy juice.

Winemaking: if the centrifugal juicer is to be used for this, naturally the quantities of fruits or vegetables to be processed will be larger than for culinary use, and the type of juicer where the spent residue is continuously ejected is more practical than one where the machine has to be frequently emptied. One of these continuous ejecting juicers can process as much as 1 cwt. (50 kg.) of fruit before any cleaning is required. The advantages to the winemaker of using a juice extractor instead of working by hand are that it saves time and labour when preparing the fruit and also improves the quality of the wines produced, making them more delicate and refined.

Centrifugal juice extractors are especially good for processing fruit and vegetables with firm flesh such as apples, elderberries and oranges (peeled), rhubarb, celery and carrots. Peaches, plums and other soft pulpy fruit can be processed (stoned first) but in general this is not entirely satisfactory as a sludge of pulp and juice can result.

Citrus Juice Extractor

To obtain orange, lemon or grapefruit juice, the fruit is cut in half and pressed firmly over the juicing cone. The motor is switched on, usually at medium speed, until all the juice is extracted and this runs through the strainer into the container below. It is probably not worth fitting up the juicer to squeeze one orange or lemon, here a hand lemon squeezer is a quicker tool, but if there is an invalid in the household it is an excellent idea to leave the juicer permanently fixed up, so that a lemon or orange drink can be freshly made at a moment's notice.

The Mincer

This is usually provided with at least two screens with holes of different sizes, and these must be altered to suit the food to be minced. The fine screen is used for mincing all cooked meats, and for chopping nuts finely. For raw meat, fish, vegetables including onion, and coarsely cut nuts, and for chopping peel and dried fruit for marmalade and puddings, the coarser screen with larger holes is used.

All foods must be cut into suitable sizes to be fed down the hopper, and this means cutting meat into 1 in. (2-3 cm) wide strips. It must be pushed into the hopper, using the tool provided and no other, for the rapidly rotating corkscrew shaft is very powerful, and dangerous if carelessly treated, and would break a wooden spoon or a knife. At the conclusion of mincing it is a good idea to feed through a piece of stale bread to clean out the inside.

Sausage Filler: this very simple attachment is screwed on to the front of the mincing attachment by unscrewing the large ring nut and rescrewing with the sausage filler protruding.

Sausages can be made with a variety of meats, of which fatty pork is the most usual, but beef is also very good. The meat is mixed with breadcrumbs or other cereal, and the percentage of this included can vary enormously; probably the greatest advantage of home-made sausages is that they can have a much higher proportion of meat than is usual in the commercial variety. Sausage skins are usually prepared from beef or sheep guts and must be soaked overnight to soften them. They can be washed by pulling the end over the tap and allowing the water to run right through them. Then the end of the skin is slid over the end of the sausage filler and the whole skin pushed back until it is rucked over the filler. It should be possible to purchase small quantities of sausage skins from a butcher who makes his own sausages, but if this is difficult, perfectly satisfactory skinless sausages can be made by extruding the sausage mixture on to a floured tray and rolling the sausages in flour.

The meats for the sausages are minced once, then mixed with the breadcrumbs or other cereal, seasoning and spice, and everything reminced, using the coarsest screen on the mincer, and extruded down the sausage filler. The softened skins are gently eased over the sausage mixture as it comes out. Finally the one long sausage is pressed and twisted to form individual sausages. A sample sausage recipe is given on p. 111 but it is only intended as a guide to the many variations which can be made.

The Slicer/Shredder

There is little that need be said about the use of this very straightforward attachment, except that the pusher should always be used to feed the food into the machine, never the fingers. It is well worth experimenting with this tool, using different drums or discs to shred different foods. The results can be astonishingly attractive. One thing the slicer/shredder does do extremely quickly is to make raspings from baked stale bread (see also p. 61). The pieces of bread are pushed on to the fine shredding disc or drum, the machine switched on, and the raspings pour out. They must then be sifted as some large lumps tend to get through and should be removed.

When slicing, care must be taken that the food is held in such a position by the slicer/shredder as to give the best shaped cross-section (slice) that can be obtained. This often becomes altered during slicing, so it is good idea to stop the machine halfway through, and rearrange the food, or trim it. (This is particularly so with cucumber.)

If used for large quantities the slicer/shredder is a most worthwhile attachment, but it is sometimes left languishing in a cupboard if it is only required for small amounts. For this reason care must be taken to do as much with it as possible at any one time; for example, if cabbage is to be sliced for lunch, perhaps at the same time carrots and onions can be done for dinner or for next day's casserole. If cheese is to be grated, always do more than is needed immediately and store the remainder in a plastic bag or box in the refrigerator; it keeps especially well in the icebox. Perhaps this cheese can be followed up by making bread raspings. By making so much use of it in this way the assembling and washing up of the slicer/shredder does not seem so onerous. If possible it is a good idea to keep this attachment always fitted to the mixer ready for immediate use.

Bean Slicer and Pea Huller

The method of using this attachment has been described in Chapter 1 when its construction was discussed (p. 26).

Since it will help in the preparation of large quantities of the vegetables very quickly, it is obvious that it is particularly useful in the kitchen which has a deep freeze and which is linked to a productive vegetable garden. Here the pea and bean harvest can be brought in, prepared with the bean slicer and pea huller and frozen rapidly. The beans should not be tough and stringy and the peas should be young and succulent, and after preparation both should be blanched by dropping into a large quantity of boiling water. Runner beans should be boiled for 1 minute and peas for 1–2 minutes, then both should be drained and cooled quickly by holding under cold running water. The vegetables are then ready to pack in a container, either a plastic box, waxed carton or a plastic bag, and put in the deep freeze.

Potato Peeler

This machine can be used for carrots, turnips and other root vegetables as well as potatoes, and these can be put into the machine mixed together. Some water (the amount varies with different machines) is put in with the vegetables, and this helps to clean them and to wash away the pieces of peel. Some machines take longer than others to peel potatoes, but as the machine works unattended this is no problem. It is obvious the process must be stopped as soon as the potato is peeled, or the body of the potato itself will be worn away too. It is necessary to remove the eyes from the potato by hand afterwards. Best results are obtained by using potatoes of a uniform size and if they are very large they should be cut into medium-sized pieces. This machine particularly saves time when used with new potatoes whose thin skins rub off very quickly against the rough walls, but which are laborious to scrape by hand.

Coffee Grinder

Coffee should be freshly ground, so only prepare the amount you are going to use at any one time.

In several places it has been suggested that an attachment is used to its best advantage if it is permanently fitted up to the motor. Obviously it is not possible to have all the attachments like this, so one must decide which tool is used most often, and therefore where most is gained by having it always at hand.

THE BLENDER

As already explained, this can be either an attachment to a mixer or an entirely separate machine. In the following pages many specific uses for the blender have been explained but it is as well to remember that it works best of all when dealing with liquids, so for more efficiency it is best to add the liquid in a recipe to anything which needs chopping; for instance, the parsley chopped in the milk for parsley sauce, the mint in the vinegar for mint sauce etc. For many other sauces the flour is blended with the cold liquid and then cooked with the melted fat.

Drinks (see recipes pp. 254–63): The blender is superb for drinks, hot, cold or alcoholic. It can make an excellent substitute for a cocktail shaker, although this is not discussed further here as there are many other books about mixing cocktails. The blender is excellent for mixing dry powder smoothly into liquids and so can be used to mix hot milky drinks such as Ovaltine, Horlicks, and drinking chocolate. All the ingredients are put in the blender and mixed for a short while until the drink has a deep frothy top. This blending to give velvety smooth drinks from dry powders is especially useful for mixing dried milks, and particularly important to the mother of a young baby fed on powdered milk. The water should be measured into the blender first, then the powder put on top and the motor switched on at slow speed for a few seconds. Of course the blender must always be kept scrupulously clean and especially so when used for milk or baby food.

Cream: A recipe is given later (p. 244) for using the blender for half-price cream, but here we consider using it to whip real cream. Either double or a mixture of equal parts double and single cream, is put in the jar and switched on at slow speed. When it begins to thicken it must be watched very carefully as it can easily over-whip, so the blender should be switched on/off to avoid this. (It is probably preferable to use the mixer if both pieces of equipment are available, for it is obviously difficult to retrieve all the whipped cream from behind the blender blades.)

Sauces, Batters, Gravies and Soups: Apart from the wide variety of legitimate culinary uses of the blender for these foods, many examples of which are given in the recipe section, the blender can be used for extensive rescue operations if things go wrong. Probably the most common disaster with sauces and gravies is that they go lumpy. The lumps *can* be strained away, which leaves the sauce thinner than it should be, whereas if the whole sauce is blended at fast speed for a few seconds the lumps are broken down and the sauce becomes smooth and thicker. The same is true of soups. Some sauces can also curdle (e.g. egg custard sauce), and provided the blender is used as soon as the curdling is noticed, it may well be that a few moments' fast blending will restore the sauce.

Left-overs: In the recipe section the use of the blender for making excellent soups from left-overs is demonstrated; although End Blend (p. 84) tends to be rather indeterminate it is equally possible to make specific soups (e.g. carrot, leek, pea, celery, chicken) from remains, with left-over sauce, gravy, potato or other thickening and with stock.

As with soups, so other remains which have been stored in plastic boxes in the refrigerator can be blended into tasty dishes which bear no resemblance to the possibly unpromising ingredients. Many left-over sweet puddings can be blended to give a very good sweet mould, which goes down well, especially with children. For example rice pudding, custard, apricot juice and orange jelly with a little yellow colouring would make a very good 'orange cream' (see 'Today's Delight', p. 157). Milk puddings, blancmanges, jellies, mousses, custards and sweet sauces lend themselves to being blended together (at medium speed increasing to fast) and if the mixture is too stiff to blend it can always be moistened with evaporated milk or fruit juice. Left-over meat or poultry can be diced in the blender with onion and other flavourings, and made into a very good meat spread or pâté. Although recipes for these are given (p. 106) the blender owner will soon experiment and make up her own recipes. Fish can be used up in similar ways: it is very good blended to a paste with a savoury sauce (white sauce, cheese, egg, parsley etc.) or with mayonnaise, and seasoned with anchovy essence or a little lemon juice. Obviously in making any of these left-over dishes it is most important for cook to taste very carefully at each stage. It may be that more seasoning is needed or that the mixture is insipid and an extra ingredient, such as an onion, herbs, or a flavouring essence, would improve matters. A little sugar added to meat dishes and soups nearly always brings out the flavour.

At this point a word of warning must be given about using left-over food – great care should be taken to see that it is in no way 'going off'. Most foods should keep perfectly well for 2–3 days in the refrigerator provided they are put away immediately and covered, but the food must not be left in a warm kitchen, say overnight. A warm atmosphere will encourage the growth of bacteria, with consequent danger of food poisoning. If commonsense is used there should be no danger of food poisoning – the smell or taste of the food is often a good guide as to freshness.

Baby Food and Invalid Diets: During the transition period between living solely on milk and eating ordinary food, a baby requires a diet which is mixed, yet smooth and easily digested. It is this transitional food which a mother with a blender can provide so easily, instead of using tinned baby dinners.

When weaning first begins a baby is not accustomed to any flavour other than milk and usually dislikes the savoury foods, if not the sweet. Therefore very small amounts of food are given at first, only one or two spoonfuls, and it is quite all right to serve nothing but gravy and vegetables blended to a smooth purée. Once a baby has become used to the flavour, however, the puréed dinner becomes quite a large portion of his daily food and it is then most important to include a sizeable amount of protein in the form of meat, liver, fish, cheese or egg. A typical main course would consist of:

 1 oz. (25 g.) cooked meat
 1 tbs. mashed or boiled potato
 1 tbs. cabbage or other green vegetable
 2 tbs. gravy

Unless the meat is minced or very soft it is best chopped roughly across the grain and blended at fast speed with the gravy for a few seconds, before adding the vegetables. The whole dinner must then be blended at fast speed until quite smooth. The portion needed at once should be taken out and rewarmed if necessary, and the remainder stored in a clean covered container in the refrigerator. *Great care must be taken* to see that this remainder does not lie around in the warm kitchen, nor is kept for longer than 2 days in the refrigerator, where bacteria might multiply and give the baby a gastric upset. Although a few recipes for making into puréed baby dinners are given (p. 264) by far the best arrangement is to purée a portion of the meal the rest of the family is having, provided the food is suitable. This means that the baby will get used to the varied flavour of everyday meals, and also that the food is freshly cooked. Here a small blender has the advantage over a larger one, for it is not so wasteful when blending enough food for one day only. With a larger blender, more is wasted on the sides and it is better to blend three days' supply at once – *but not more*.

A word about liver, which is a food of exceptionally high nutritional value giving many of the vitamins and minerals a baby needs in large amounts. This can be bought from the butcher in quantities as small as 1–2 oz. (25–50 g.) and is therefore an excellent standby for the baby on the days when the family meal is not suitable. It can be fried or baked in the oven and blended at fast speed very easily with a little gravy or stock. As an alternative, a small fillet of fish can easily be bought, cooked and blended on its own, on another similar occasion.

A baby's pudding is a very simple matter for the mother with a blender, and again this can be made up to serve three days. Any milk pudding or custard can be put in the blender with fruit. Fruits with pips must be sieved first and of course stones removed before blending. Raw apple, peeled and cored, or ripe bananas are good standbys to blend with milk pudding or even evaporated milk, if no other fruit is available. Do remember, however, that the slight lumps of, say, rice pudding, are a good introduction to the uneven texture of adult food and should be given as soon as possible, for although this book is written to encourage the use of mixers and blenders, a word of warning must be given here. Much as the child enjoys the blended dinners, they should not be continued too long. Once he has got used to a variety of flavours, it is important to give a change of texture, and to encourage chewing. The gums are hard enough to chew on long before the back teeth are through and by about the time he is a year old the child should be having family meals when suitable, chopped up very small and served with lots of gravy. Children are very conservative, and also lazy about chewing and when given their own choice, one does find children of three and four years old still eating puréed dinners; so, much as they may be enjoying the blended food, it should be stopped as soon as they can digest normal meals. It is also so much easier for the mother when children of all ages have the same food.

In the same way as for babies, the blender can be used to purée food for those on medical diets. Many ordinary foods such as stews, roast meat, liver, casseroles, baked, grilled or steamed fish, etc., can be puréed with gravy or a sauce, but in the case of adults the vegetables are usually blended separately and potatoes mashed smooth. Very few ulcer patients are now wholly restricted to puréed foods, but they are necessary for anyone who has difficulty in swallowing or who needs a low residue diet, and in this case any pips or skins must be sieved out of the fruits or vegetables after blending. (See also p. 26 for low residue diets.) It is most important that the food used for blending for these invalids should not be too highly spiced or seasoned.

With any illnesses it is important to tempt the patient with attractive drinks, particularly those containing milk (which is so nourishing) and the fruit juices high in vitamin C (orange, blackcurrant, tomato), and the blender is superb for making these (see p. 53 and section on drinks, p. 261). Given in the recipe section are one or two ideas for blending drinks especially high in nourishment, but many others can be tried. Their ingredients depend very much on the taste of the invalid.

Chopping Solid Foods: The blender will chop a wide range of solid food, some examples of which follow:

Cooked Meat and Fish: if meat, bacon or fish are chopped they can be made into savoury spreads by blending with stock, sauce or melted butter. However, as many blenders find it difficult to chop the fibres of meat, it is best to cut it across the grain before putting it into the jar. If sauce or gravy is to be included in the recipe, this will also aid blending, and it should be put in the jar with the meat or fish. A blender cannot be considered as a substitute for a mincer for chopping meat because it will only deal with small quantities at a time, and in fact will not chop raw meat at all (p. 49).

Vegetables can be puréed when they are cooked, but they can also be chopped raw, and there are two ways of doing this. The prepared vegetables (e.g. carrots) can be dropped in chunks on to the blades of the blender revolving at fast speed, and are in this way chopped finely, although the result does not resemble that given by the slicer/shredder. The other way is to put the prepared vegetables into the blender and two-thirds fill with water. Switch on at fast speed for a few seconds until the vegetable is chopped as fine as necessary, then drain off the water. This is particularly good for leafy vegetables such as cabbage or leeks, but wherever possible save the water for use in soups or gravies, otherwise the vitamins and minerals which leached out of the cut cells of the vegetables are wasted.

Fruit can similarly be puréed, raw or stewed, with or without water, depending on the juiciness of the fruit. Blend for a few seconds and then pass through a strainer if there are any pips or skins remaining. It is astonishing how few there are, and more often than not it is quite unnecessary to strain (see also p. 25 for uses of the colander/sieve). Fools and fruit creams or whips can be made quickly by adding cream, custard or jelly to the purée in the blender.

Nuts can be chopped in the blender at slow speed. They should be dropped in a steady stream through the hole in the lid on to the revolving knives. For some purposes nuts need only rough chopping, which means blending for a very short while, or switching on/off several times. In other cases they need grinding to a flour (e.g. when grinding blanched whole almonds if ground almonds are required), so take much longer in the blender. By careful watching the blending can be stopped at any stage in between to obtain the size of pieces required.

Dried peas, beans or lentils can be chopped in the blender with blades revolving at fast speed; this cuts down their cooking time, but as they are very hard it is impossible to grind them to a flour without overstraining the blender.

Cheese can be chopped in the blender quite fine enough to use for sauces and other culinary purposes, but it does not give the wafer fineness of the slicer/shredder. The cheese must be cut into dice and dropped through the hole in the lid on to the blades revolving at slow speed, and it may be more satisfactory to switch on/off. The amount which can be chopped at any one time depends on the size of the blender, but if it becomes sticky, empty out and start a fresh batch.

Sugar can be ground down in the blender jar to turn granulated sugar into caster sugar in a few seconds, and then to icing sugar by grinding at medium speed for a little longer. This icing sugar is not quite as good a colour nor as smooth as the commercial variety, but it is excellent in an emergency and particularly decorative if it is coloured. Put only a small quantity of sugar in the blender at a time, probably about a quarter filling the jar.

Coffee: coffee beans can be ground in the blender; it is not a practice many manufacturers recommend for regular use (p. 27), but in an emergency the blender is a very useful coffee grinder. The beans should cover the knives, but not more than one-third fill the goblet, and be blended at slow speed with the lid on.

Blending should continue until the coffee is fine enough, and it may be necessary to stop and scrape down the sides several times during this time.

Fresh coconut is not often used in this country, but when available it can be chopped finely in the blender for use in many ways. It is especially good served with curry. The coconut is pierced, drained, and then cracked, and both the hard shell and the inner brown coating removed. Cut the white nut into small dice and place enough in the jar to cover the blender knives. Switch on at slow speed until the coconut is sufficiently fine, stopping when necessary to scrape down the sides. As it quickly deteriorates, the grated nut should be kept in a refrigerator, or better still a deep freeze.

Dates: these are tricky to chop dry and it can only be done in certain blenders. If block cooking dates are being used they must be divided into pieces of not more than a 1 in. (2½ cm.) cube in size before blending, and even this is not very satisfactory. It is much better to put the date pieces in the jar with any liquid to be used in the recipe and then chop them at fast speed.

Grated lemon rind: it is often necessary to have the finely grated yellow rind of a lemon (or orange) which is thinly pared off the outside of the fruit using a sharp knife or a potato peeler. This cannot be satisfactorily chopped in the blender dry as the pieces left are too large to be palatable, so in some recipes it is necessary to use a hand grater. However, if the lemon rind is to be used with liquid in the recipe, the two can be blended together at fast speed to reduce the rind to a fine sediment. This will take half to one minute, depending on the blender.

Breadcrumbs, cake or biscuit crumbs: one of the greatest assets of a blender, and one which will save the cook a great deal of time, is its ability to make crumbs very quickly. It is essential to have a removable cap in the lid of the blender and through this are dropped cubes of bread or cake, or pieces of biscuit, on to the knives revolving at fast speed. Allow the machine to finish crumbling one piece before adding another and stop and empty out when the jar is about one-third full and the crumbs have built up at the sides, thus preventing the knives from working efficiently. The great joy of the blender is that it will crumb fresh bread as well as stale, which would be impossible by hand. It will also form crisp bread raspings from stale bread which has been baked hard and pale gold at the bottom of a slow oven. This crisp bread is then dropped a piece at a time on to the blades revolving at fast speeds. The crumbs so made are used for many culinary purposes. Similarly to bread, stale cakes or biscuits can be made into crumbs. A box can be kept in the kitchen into which all ends of cake, crumbs from cake tins, broken or stale biscuits can be collected. When this has reached a sizeable amount they can all be made into crumbs and turned into such teatime delicacies as Rum Truffles (p. 194). Even iced and/or fruit cakes can be used in this way, provided they are ground up well, and very old cake and biscuit crumbs taste perfectly satisfactory when incorporated in appropriate recipes.

Crushing Ice: Very few blenders will break up large lumps of ice because they will damage the blades, so if ice is needed in drinks the lumps should be broken first. This is easily done by placing them between the folds of a tea towel and crushing them with a rolling pin. The crushed ice can then be put in the drink and blended as necessary. Just a few of the bigger blenders are robust enough to chop up large lumps of ice, and then the manufacturers' instructions should be followed.

When not to use the Blender

Having discussed the very wide range of jobs which can be done in the blender, here are just a few things for which it is not designed and which should not be attempted in it.

1. It should not be used to chop anything with very hard and large lumps, such as might be found in stale or very hard cheese (particularly Parmesan), or if extremely stale cake is being used to make crumbs. Large lumps can jam under the blender blades and because they cannot be moved, cause the motor to seize up

and even to burn out as a result of too much of this treatment. These hard substances can be successfully blended if they are cut up into smaller pieces with a knife first.

2. It will never beat egg whites sufficiently to aerate them as the mixer does.

3. It will not mash potatoes successfully; they turn to a sticky and waxy mess.

4. The blender knives are not designed to chop raw meat or bacon, and will not do this satisfactorily – a mincing attachment is the tool to use here.

BATCH COOKING WITH THE MIXER AND BLENDER

Obviously it does take time to fix up the mixer and to wash up afterwards, so the most advantageous use of the equipment is to cook a large batch of any one mixture and either to utilize it in different ways, or to store half for another day. Naturally a deep freeze is a perfect partner to a mixer and blender in this respect, for large batches of cooked food can be stored away for use in the months ahead, but even in a domestic refrigerator much food will keep for several days and can be served twice, and yet a variety of menu still be maintained. If, therefore, using a deep freeze, you always aim to cook two or three times what is needed and eat some while storing the rest, you will always have a reserve of meals ready to bring out when needed. Even without a freezer there are many basic recipes which can be made in double or treble qualities and then finished in different ways. Here are just a few examples of foods well worth processing in large quantities, but there are many others:

1. *Victoria Sandwich:* this basic cake mixture can be used to make large cakes, plain, flavoured or iced, small cakes such as cherry buns or Queen cakes and puddings such as Eve's pudding or upside-down pudding.

2. *Sponge Cake Mixture:* can also make a swiss roll or a sponge flan case to store away until needed.

3. *Genoese Sponge Cake:* this is a version of sponge cake incorporating fat and it therefore keeps better than sponge cake. It is ideal for making in a large batch and finishing in different ways: e.g. (a) sandwiched with jam or lemon curd. (b) sandwiched with butter cream, and iced. (c) flavoured and iced with such as coffee, lemon, etc. (d) slab approx. 1 in. (2–3 cm.) thick to cut into various shapes for iced fancies which can be decorated with a number of coloured icings and with cream. (e) a sponge flan case can be baked which will keep for several days and be filled with fruit when required.

4. *Rubbing in Fat:* rub fat into twice its weight of flour. This can be prepared in a large quantity and stored in a tight-fitting box in the refrigerator. It will keep as long as the fat alone would have done, at least several weeks. It can then be used as required for shortcrust pastry or, if prepared with butter or margarine, in a variety of ways, such as the following:

    a.   fruit crumble topping – add sugar
    b.   flan pastry – add sugar and bind with egg yolk
    c.   cheese pastry – add seasoning, cheese, and bind with egg yolk
    d.   sweet biscuits – add baking powder, egg and sugar

5. *Batters:* make up more than is needed for Yorkshire pudding and use the remainder for pancakes, or vice versa. (This only keeps successfully for a day or two.)

6. *Yeast Doughs:* make up a large quantity and finish in several different ways – e.g. white bread and rolls, teacakes and pizza. Risen bread dough can be knocked back, then stored in the icebox of a refrigerator for several days, to be brought out, thawed and baked when fresh bread or rolls are required.

7. *Icecream:* make up a large quantity and flavour the basic mix in a variety of ways.

8. *White Sauce:* a large quantity of basic white sauce can be made and flavoured with such as parsley, cheese, sweet vanilla, etc. These sauces can be kept in the refrigerator in covered containers, and should they go lumpy on being reheated, they can

easily be made smooth in the blender, or by using a hand-held mixer.

9. *Meringues:* these are easiest made in large quantities which can be successfully stored for some time in an *airtight* tin. Alternatively the mixture can be piped to make a flan case and served with fruit and cream or with icecream.

10. *Butter Cream:* as this keeps well for several weeks in a covered container in the refrigerator, it can be made up plain in a large quantity and then flavoured as and when required.

11. *Duchesse Potatoes:* can be made to cover a fish pie or a shepherd's pie and any extra potato piped on to a greased baking tray in individual whirls, to keep overnight in a cool place and bake the following day, or to freeze.

12. *Grated Cheese and Breadcrumbs:* they can be stored in large quantities. Both tend to go mouldy in a few days if left in the kitchen or in the refrigerator, but if stored in a plastic box with a tight lid or in a tightly closed plastic bag in the icebox of the refrigerator they will keep for several weeks, or much longer still in a deep freeze. It is clearly worth grating a pound of cheese, or making a large loaf into breadcrumbs, for storing away ready for immediate use when required.

13. *Bread Raspings* (p. 61): these can also be prepared in large quantities and stored for months in an airtight jar.

...A large table mixer
fitted up for whisking,
surrounded by its other
attachments.

A. Table mixer
B. Standard bowl
C. Motor housing
D. Wire whisk
E. Blender fits here
F. Other attachments fit here
G. Blender
H. Stainless steel bowl
I. Potato peeler
J. Slicer/shredder
K. Pusher
L. Slicing and shredding drums
M. Key for unlocking drums
N. Cream maker
O. Coffee grinder
P. Colander/sieve
Q. Centrifugal juicer with cup
R. Citrus juice extractor
S. Beater for heavy processes
T. Dough hook
U. Tin opener
V. Bean slicer/pea huller
W. Sausage filler and coarse min-
   cer screen
X. Mincer

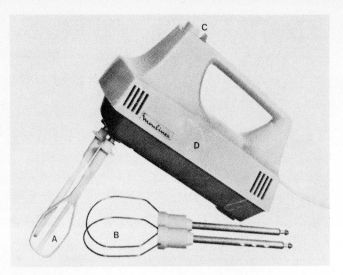

2. Hand-held mixer, showing two types of beater.

A. Robust beaters   C. Finger controls
B. Wire whisks   D. Motor housing

3. Hand-held mixer in use.

4. Independent blender with coffee grinding attachment. Note sharp knives which revolve in use.

5. Citrus juice extractor attachment with revolving cone, strainer to retain pulp and pips, and outer container to catch juice.

6. Colander/sieve attachment to table mixer, showing paddle, colander bowl and sieve.

7. Table mixer with central spindle, showing blender and potato peeler.

A. Central spindle with two revolving wire whisks
B. Potato peeler with carborundum lining (lid not shown)
C. Blender with cap funnel in lid

8. Centrifugal juice extractor, lid removed to show interior.

A. Motor housing
B. Dry waste chute
C. Revolving grating disc
D. Filter drum

E. Juice emerges here
F. Dry residue
G. Fruit fed here—lid with pusher in position

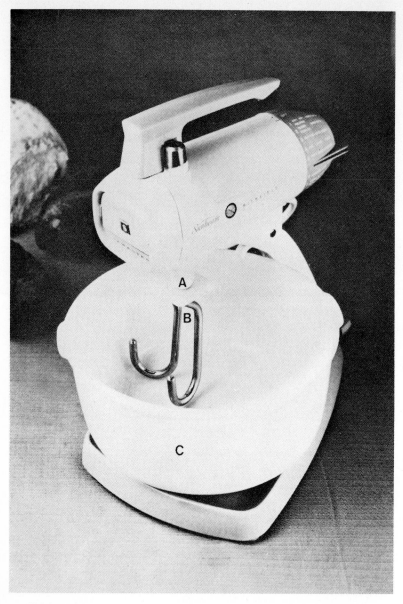

9. Table mixer, detachable from stand for use as hand-held mixer.

A. Attachments fit here
B. Dough hooks with plastic guard above
C. Bowl, on rotating plate

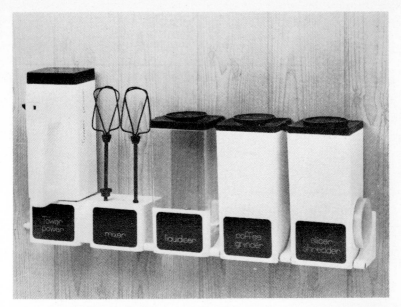

10. Power unit of a no-flex mixer fitted to the wall for recharging, together with its attachments.

11. The power unit of a no-flex mixer used to operate the slicer/shredder.

12. Mincer attachment.

A. Drive shaft turned by mixer motor   C. Pusher
B. Hopper   D. Large ring nut unscrews to change
                                           screens

13. The sausage-making attachment to mincer, showing sausage skin rucked back on adaptor.

PART II

3

Introduction to the Recipes

This does not attempt to be a comprehensive cookery book, but in the following section a wide range of recipes has been included to show the versatility of mixers and blenders. Recipes for everyday food have been included, but also more interesting and extravagant dishes for special occasions. Many readers will have recipes of their own which they will want to adapt for their machines, and often the method given here for a recipe can be employed with other ingredients.

POINTS TO NOTE

Equipment Required

After the title of each recipe is given the machine or attachment to be used, e.g. mixer, blender, mincer, etc. For some recipes either mixer or blender can be used equally well, and this is indicated. Occasionally a second machine can be used for a small part of the preparation, and this is then printed in brackets; if this second equipment is not available, it is usually quite easy to do that part of the preparation by hand.

Mixer Tools

Naturally such tools as beaters and whisks provided with the different mixers vary slightly from manufacturer to manufactuer, and the instruction book must be read carefully to decide which is to be used for the different cookery processes. Thus no attempt has been made to indicate which of these tools should be fixed to the mixer. Dough hooks are quite distinct and must be used only for the kneading of all dough mixtures.

Speed

This varies with each machine; some may have as many as twelve different speeds, others only one or two. Slow speed must be used with care, for if employed for a long time it often imposes undue strain on the motor: it is primarily needed for dry ingredients and for folding in, although in some machines slow speed is still too fast to fold in dry ingredients successfully, and this must then be done by hand. The instructions in this book have been confined to fast, medium and slow speeds; if your machine has more, use the intermediate ones with intelligence and in consultation with the manufacturer's instructions, although sometimes speeds recommended in the instruction booklets are *not* the most successful, and a little experiment is well worthwhile.

Timing

As with speed, it has been impossible to include an exact length of time for mixing and blending operations as so many factors affect this, although an approximate time is sometimes given. One must therefore watch the machine and the process carefully until experience teaches how long it is likely to take. Timing is often included in the manufacturer's instructions, but it is usually obvious to the cook when the time has come to switch off. Remember that machines work very fast, so watch carefully to avoid overmixing and spoiling the result.

Capacity of Mixers and Blenders

This again varies enormously from machine to machine and as this book endeavours to cover the whole range it may well be that the quantities given in the recipes are too large or too small for your machine. In this case they can be halved or doubled etc., or the process carried out in two or three batches. With a large machine it is probably easier to prepare very small quantities by hand.

Butter and Cream

The term 'butter' is used in the recipes but although real butter will give a better flavour, margarine can always be substituted most successfully and is nutritionally just as good, if not better (by being higher in vitamins) than butter. Its use is a very painless economy. There are just a few cases where the flavour is all-important, and where it is therefore worthwhile to use butter; such are shortbread, melting moments, plain biscuits, and brandy butter. Cakes made with butter do not get so dry and keep better than those made with margarine, so that for a rich cake, particularly such as a Christmas cake where the ingredients are expensive, it is sensible to spend a little extra on butter for its flavour and its keeping qualities. The flavour of butter can be used to enhance meals for special occasions. Similarly where *cream* has been used in these recipes it can very often be replaced by evaporated milk. This, again, is more nutritious than cream, but has its own distinctive flavour which is best masked by another stronger one. Hence it is probably a more useful ingredient in highly-flavoured savoury dishes such as soups or sauces or in dishes flavoured with strong coffee, chocolate, or well-flavoured fruits. Another, slightly more expensive substitute for cream is 'half-price cream' (p. 244) which is hardly distinguishable from dairy cream in most dishes.

Quantities

In the recipes these are generally given by weight as this is the most accurate method of measurement, producing the best results; when a teaspoonful or tablespoon is used, unless otherwise stated, a rounded spoonful is meant, that is having the same quantity heaped above the lip of the spoon as in the bowl. Thus a rounded spoonful contains twice as much as a level spoonful. An egg when mentioned in the recipes is generally taken to mean a standard 2 oz. (55 g.) egg. However, there are many recipes where it makes no difference whether a larger or smaller egg is used.

WEIGHTS AND MEASURES

As Britain is turning more to the use of the metric system of measurement, metric measurements have been included alongside the imperial weights in the following recipes. In connection with this there are several important points to remember, namely:

1. The recipes were originally worked out for use with imperial measures.
2. In altering to the metric system great care has been taken to see that the proportion of the different ingredients, especially of liquid to dry quantities, remains the same, and this is the most important consideration. For this reason IT IS ESSENTIAL TO USE EITHER ALL IMPERIAL MEASURES OR ALL METRIC MEASURES when cooking a particular dish.
3. Because of the difficult numbers involved in conversion (1 oz. actually = 28·35 g.) it is impossible to make a convenient conversion table suitable for all recipes, but 1 oz. = 25 g. has been generally, but not entirely, used. The finished product of some recipes may therefore be slightly smaller than would be expected using imperial measures. This is particularly true of recipes with a large number of ingredients, and it may be necessary to use slightly smaller baking dishes than for imperial measure.
4. Since this 1 oz. = 25 g. has generally been used, when using the metric system it is advisable to be more sparing when measuring unweighed ingredients. e.g. tablespoons – underfill level spoons, and heap up rounded spoons slightly less.

Eggs – do not use large eggs with metric measures.

CONVERSION OF OVEN THERMOSTAT MARKINGS TO CELSIUS SCALE OF MARKING

Approximate temperature in centre of oven in °Fahrenheit	Gas thermostat settings	Approximate temperature in centre of oven in °Celsius
225°F	$\frac{1}{4}$	110°C
250°F	$\frac{1}{2}$	120°C
275°F	1	140°C
300°F	2	150°C
325°F	3	160°C
350°F	4	180°C
375°F	5	190°C
400°F	6	200°C
425°F	7	220°C
450°F	8	230°C
475°F	9	240°C

IMPORTANT REMINDER LIST

1. Always keep the mixer or blender on the work-top, plugged in and ready to use.
2. Never allow a small child near a mixer or blender while it is switched on; small hands could so easily go into the blender or fingers be caught in the whisk. As the major pieces of equipment may be within their reach, be sure that the switches themselves are not.
3. When using the blender *never* put a tool or, worse still, the fingers into the blender while it is working. The knives revolve at extremely high speeds, and are very sharp, so they can do

immense damage very quickly, and the downward-pulling action can easily drag out of the hands a laxly held tool.

4. Follow carefully the manufacturer's recommendations for the maximum quantities which should be mixed or blended and the maximum times the machines should be run. (Over-running, especially with the blender, can cause motor wear, and with the mixer often spoils the finished result.)

5. Never immerse the motor of the machine in water; clean it by wiping the casing with a well-wrung-out cloth.

6. Never fill the jar of the blender more than two-thirds to three-quarters full, as the contents jump up when the motor starts. If necessary, blend the food in several batches. See that the lid is fixed on firmly, especially for hot liquids.

7. When creaming, the mixer bowl and beater should be warmed (p. 40) and the fat be soft but not oiled.

8. Egg whites will never whisk up stiff in the presence of the smallest amount of grease, so see that the bowl and beaters are scrupulously clean beforehand.

9. For some folding jobs, even the slow speed of the mixer is too vigorous, therefore use a tablespoon or spatula to fold in by hand (p. 44).

4

Soups

෨෩෨෩෨෩෨෩෨෩෨෩෨෩෨෩෨෩෨෩෨෩෨෩෨෩෨෩෨

The blender (or colander/sieve) is a tremendous asset to the cook during the preparation of soups, particularly cream or puréed soups, as it does away with the need for the laborious hair sieve. Occasionally it is necessary to strain the soup after putting it in the blender to take out unwanted skins or stringy pieces (such as are found in celery), but this is very quickly done through a nylon or metal strainer. It is this easy blending which should encourage more frequent soup-making, instead of the use of packets and tins. These, while admirable in an emergency, rarely compare favourably with a well flavoured home-made soup.

Cream of Celery Soup · Blender

Serves 7

1 *large head of celery*	*bouquet garni*
1 *medium onion (or 1 small*	1 *oz. (25 g.) flour*
onion and 1 small leek)	$\frac{1}{4}$ *pt. (125 ml.) milk*
1 *oz. (25 g.) butter*	4 *tbs. cream*
2 *pt. (1 l.) stock (or milk and*	*matchsticks of celery, diced*
stock mixed)	*bacon* or *croutons of fried*
salt and pepper	*bread to garnish*

1. Break stalks from the celery and wash thoroughly. Use nearly all the stalks and the leaves, but a small centre portion can be kept for salad use.

2. Prepare the onion and chop it roughly, and cut the celery into ½ in. (1–2 cm.) lengths.

3. Melt the butter in a large saucepan, and sauté the onion and celery in it until they are soft, but not browned – about 10 minutes.

4. Add the stock, seasoning and the bouquet garni and bring to the boil, then simmer until the vegetables are very soft – about ¾–1 hour. Remove the bouquet garni.

5. Transfer to the blender and blend at slow speed, increasing to medium, until the soup is completely smooth.

6. At this stage it may be necessary to pass the soup through a strainer to remove the stringy pieces of the celery, but this will not be necessary if the stalks were very tender.

7. Return the strained soup to the saucepan, reserving a little in the blender. To this add the flour and the milk and blend at medium speed until quite smooth. Reheat the soup, and stir vigorously as the flour mix is poured in from the blender.

8. Bring to the boil, stirring well, boil for 2 minutes and then draw off the heat before adding the cream. Taste for seasoning, and adjust if necessary.

9. Serve garnished with tiny matchsticks of celery, boiled in salted water, *or* tiny dice of bacon, grilled or fried, *or* croutons of fried bread.

Cream of Mushroom Soup · Blender

Serves 4

½ lb. (200 g.) mushrooms	1 egg yolk
1 small onion	2 teasp. lemon juice
1 oz. (25 g.) butter	salt and pepper to taste
1 oz. (25 g.) flour	2 tbs. cream or evaporated milk
¾ pt. (375 ml.) stock	croutons of fried bread to
½ pt. (250 ml.) milk	accompany

1. Wash the mushrooms and reserve 2–3 small ones to slice thinly for garnish.

2. Prepare the onion, cut in quarters and put in the blender with the mushrooms and the stock. Blend at fast speed for a few seconds,

just sufficient to chop the vegetables roughly. Turn into a pan and simmer for about ½ hour.

3. When the mushrooms are tender, pour the soup into the blender and starting at slow speed and increasing to fast speed, continue blending until the soup is quite smooth and the mushrooms are completely puréed.

4. Meanwhile make a roux by melting the butter in a pan and stirring in the flour. Cook for a few minutes until it resembles white breadcrumbs then gradually mix in the milk, stirring rapidly to keep it smooth.

5. Boil the sauce for 2 minutes, add it to the soup with the lemon juice, and blend at fast speed until smooth.

6. Reheat the soup to simmering point.

7. Mix the egg yolk with the cream, remove the soup from the heat and stir rapidly while adding the egg and cream mixture. Taste and adjust the seasoning.

8. Do not allow to reboil, but serve at once, garnishing each portion with the slices of mushroom, which have been fried or baked in the oven with fat. Serve with croutons of fried bread.

Quick Cream of Onion Soup · Blender

This recipe can be used to make cream soups with other vegetables, particularly left-overs. Either one variety or a mixture can be used, and as the soup contains such a large amount of milk it is particularly nourishing for children. Serves 3–4.

1 pt. (500 ml.) milk	1 oz. (25 g.) flour
¾ lb. (300 g.) onions, cooked (3 large onions)	1 level teasp. salt
	fresh ground black pepper
4 sprigs parsley or a few other fresh herbs	1 oz. (25 g.) butter

1. Prepare the onions and boil them. To save time they can be roughly sliced before boiling. Pour off the water.

2. Put all the ingredients into the blender and blend at fast speed until smooth.

3. Pour into a saucepan and bring to the boil while stirring. Simmer for 5 minutes. Taste for seasoning and serve.

Cream of Green Pea Soup · Blender

Serves 6

1 *medium onion*	*sprig of mint*
2 *oz.* (50 *g.*) *butter*	*salt and pepper*
1 *lb.* (500 *g.*) *frozen peas*	4 *tbs. whipped cream*
2 *oz.* (50 *g.*) *flour*	*croutons of fried bread to*
$\frac{3}{4}$ *pt.* (375 *ml.*) *milk*	*accompany*
$\frac{1}{2}$ *pt.* (250 *ml.*) *water*	

1. Melt the butter in a pan and sauté the roughly chopped onion in it until soft but not browned.
2. Add the frozen peas and continue to sauté slowly for about 10 minutes.
3. Stir in the flour, followed by the milk, adding the latter gradually while stirring well.
4. Add the water, mint and seasoning and bring to the boil slowly, stirring at intervals. Simmer for about $\frac{1}{2}$ hour.
5. Transfer to the blender and blend at fast speed. Pass the soup through a sieve if a completely smooth soup is preferred, but it is quite acceptable without straining.
6. Reheat the soup, adding more liquid if necessary and taste for seasoning.
7. Serve with a dollop of whipped cream on the top of each portion, and with croutons of fried bread.

Cream of Tomato Soup · Blender

Serves 6

1 *large onion*	2 *oz.* (50 *g.*) *flour*
$\frac{1}{2}$ *small leek*	2 *pt.* (1 *l.*) *pale stock (or water*
3 *oz.* (75 *g.*) *butter*	*with chicken stock cube)*

5 tbs. tomato purée, or
  2 lb. (1 kg.) tomatoes
bouquet garni or bay leaf,
  pinch of dried mixed herbs
  and a few stalks of parsley
2 teasp. sugar

seasoning
¼ pt. (125 ml.) cream (or
  evaporated milk)
croutons of fried bread or
  chopped parsley to garnish

1. Melt 2 oz. (50 g.) butter and stir in the flour. Allow it to cook gently without colouring until it resembles breadcrumbs.
2. Gradually add the stock and bring to the boil. It does not matter if it is a little lumpy at this stage, as it will blend smooth later.
3. Melt the remaining 1 oz. (25 g.) of butter and add to it the sliced onion and leek. Cook them gently without colouring for several minutes.
4. Add to the soup the leeks and onions, the tomatoes (purée or whole tomatoes cut in quarters), the bouquet garni, sugar and seasoning and simmer all together for about 45 minutes.
5. Blend at slow speed, increasing to fast for a few seconds, until the soup is completely puréed. If whole tomatoes have been used, the soup must at this stage be passed through a strainer to remove the pips and skins.
6. Reheat the soup, add the cream and bring almost to the boil. Taste for seasoning and add more sugar if necessary, also a few drops of red colouring to improve the appearance of the soup if desired.
7. Serve with croutons of fried bread or with a sprinkling of chopped parsley.

Crème Andalouse

Make the cream of tomato soup as above, and stir into it, just before serving, a garnish of:

  1 oz. (25 g.) boiled rice
  2 peeled tomatoes (remove the seeds and make small dice of the flesh)
  ½ oz. (15 g.) cooked (or tinned) red pimento, cut into fine strips

Cullen Skink (Smoked Haddock Soup) · Blender

Serves 6

1 lb. (500 g.) smoked haddock fillet (or whole Finnan haddock)
1 medium onion
1 lb. (500 g.) potatoes
1 oz. (25 g.) butter
1 pt. (500 ml.) milk

¼ level teasp. powdered mace
1 tbs. cream
pepper – salt if needed
croutons of fried bread or grated cheese to accompany

1. Peel the potatoes and onion and put them in a wide saucepan. Lay the smoked haddock on top, and add enough water just to cover the fish.
2. Bring slowly to the boil, then simmer until the fish is just cooked (6–10 minutes).
3. Lift the fish from the pan on to a plate, and remove the skin and bones. Put the flesh into a bowl.
4. Continue cooking the potatoes and onion until they are tender and add them to the fish. Save at least ½ pint (250 ml.) of the cooking liquor (more if a thinner soup is desired) and add it to the fish and vegetables, together with the butter, milk, mace and pepper.
5. Put the soup into the blender and blend at fast speed until quite smooth.
6. Return the soup to the saucepan, stir in the cream and taste for seasoning, adding more if necessary. This is now a very substantial soup, almost a meal, but if desired it can be thinned down with more of the fish cooking liquor and milk.
7. Reheat the soup and serve with either croutons of fried bread or grated cheese.

Kidney Soup · Blender

Serves 7

12 oz. (300 g.) ox kidney
2 carrots
1 small turnip

2 medium onions
2 oz. (50 g.) dripping
2 oz. (50 g.) flour

3 pt. (1½ l.) brown stock   gravy browning
bouquet garni   salt and pepper

1. Remove skin and fat from the kidney and cut into rough slices.

2. Prepare the vegetables and cut into rough pieces.

3. Melt the dripping and fry the kidney in it quickly for 3 minutes.

4. Remove the kidney from the fat, put in the vegetables and fry to brown them.

5. Sprinkle the flour round the vegetables and cook for a few more minutes, stirring occasionally.

6. Stir in the stock gradually, mixing well to prevent lumps developing, then add the kidney, bouquet garni and seasoning. Bring to the boil and simmer for 1 hour.

7. Remove the bouquet garni, pour the soup into the blender and blend at fast speed until the vegetables are puréed and the kidney finely chopped. (With this large quantity it will be necessary to refill the jar several times.)

8. Return the soup to the saucepan and reboil. Taste and add any further seasoning necessary, also a little gravy browning to give the soup a good brown colour.

Lentil Soup · Blender or Colander/Sieve

Serves 5–6

1 oz. (25 g.) dripping or butter   2 pt. (1 l.) ham stock or 2 pt. (1 l.)
8 oz. (200 g.) lentils   water and a ham bone or
1–2 carrots (4 oz., 100 g.)   2 pt. (1 l.) stock with bacon or
1–2 onions (4 oz., 100 g.)   ham rinds
2 sticks of celery or celery   salt and pepper
  trimmings   croutons of fried bread, or
bouquet garni   grated cheese or fried onions
¼ pt. (125 ml.) top of the milk or   to accompany
  milk with 2 tbs. evaporated milk

79

1. Wash the lentils and prepare and chop the vegetables.

2. Melt the dripping in a heavy saucepan and sauté the vegetables and lentils for 10–15 minutes.

3. Add all the other ingredients, except the creamy milk, and simmer slowly until all the vegetables are soft (2–2½ hours), stirring at regular intervals.

4. Remove any bones, rinds and the bouquet garni.

5. Pour the soup into the blender and purée at fast speed until quite smooth. Alternatively sieve through the colander/sieve.

6. If liked, pass the soup through a strainer to remove any brown lentil skins which remain.

7. Return the soup to the saucepan, reboil, and add the creamy milk and season to taste. Should it be too salty, a little sugar will improve matters.

8. Serve with fried croutons of bread, *or* grated cheese, *or* crisply fried onions.

Oat and Onion Soup · Blender

A cheap and easily made soup. Serves 6

1 *lb.* (400 *g.*) *onions*	½ *level teasp. paprika*
¼ *lb.* (100 *g.*) *porridge oats* (or *oatmeal*)	¼ *pt.* (125 *ml.*) *milk, or more salt to taste*
2 *pt.* (1 *l.*) *stock and/or water*	*chopped parsley to garnish*

1. Prepare the onions and roughly chop into largish pieces.

2. Put onions, oats, paprika and stock into a saucepan and bring to the boil, then simmer over a low heat until the onions and oats are very soft (¾–1 hour). Oatmeal will, of course, take longer to cook.

3. Put the soup into the blender, and blend at fast speed for a few seconds until it is quite smooth and creamy.

4. Reheat the soup adding salt to taste and thinning down with milk as desired. A ¼ pint (125 ml.) of milk will give a rather thick soup.

5. Serve with a sprinkling of chopped parsley on top.

Watercress and Potato Soup · Blender

Serves 6

6 oz. (150 g.) watercress (1 or 2
  bunches)
1 lb. (400 g.) potatoes
1 medium onion or piece of
  leek (3 oz. (75 g.))
2 pt. (1 l.) light stock or 2 pt.
  (1 l.) water with chicken stock
  cube

1 oz. (25 g.) butter
4 tbs. cream or evaporated
  milk
seasoning, including a pinch
  of nutmeg if desired

1. Wash the watercress thoroughly and remove any yellow leaves
or unpleasant stems. Save a few small sprigs for garnish, and sufficient
leaves to give 2 tablespoons when chopped.
2. Roughly chop the remaining leaves and the stalks.
3. Peel and slice the onion or leek.
4. Melt the butter in the saucepan and sauté the onions and
watercress over a gentle heat for 5 minutes without browning.
5. Peel and slice the potatoes and add them to the pan together with
the stock. Bring to the boil and simmer gently for 25 minutes until
the potatoes are soft.
6. Put the soup in the blender, and blend at fast speed until quite
smooth, then drop in 2 heaped tablespoons of watercress leaves and
run blender just sufficiently to chop these finely.
7. Reboil the soup. Taste and add seasoning and the cream, but do
not allow to reboil once this is added.
8. Serve garnished with sprigs of watercress.

Iced Cucumber Soup · Blender

Serves 8

2 large cucumbers
2 small onions or shallots
1 oz. (25 g.) butter
2 pt. (1 l.) chicken stock

1 pt. (½ l.) milk
1 tbs. arrowroot
¼ pt. (125 ml.) single cream or
  evaporated milk

> green colouring
> salt and pepper

> 2 stems mint and a handful
> of leaves to chop for garnish

1. Wash the cucumbers and reserve about a third of one to dice for garnish. Slice the remainder thickly.
2. Chop the onions roughly and cook them slowly in the butter, without colouring, until translucent.
3. Add the stock, milk, cucumber and the mint stems and cook till all the vegetables are tender. Remove the mint stems.
4. Put the soup into the blender and blend at fast speed until quite smooth.
5. Return the soup to the saucepan and mix in the arrowroot which has already been blended with a little milk. Stir while heating to reboil and thicken the arrowroot. Simmer for 1–2 minutes.
6. Take off the heat and stir in the cream. Taste for seasoning and colour with a very little green colouring, then cool, and store in the refrigerator until ready to serve – so that the soup is really cold.
7. Meanwhile prepare the garnish. Wash and chop the mint leaves. Peel the remaining cucumber third and cut into small $\frac{1}{4}$ in. (6 mm.) dice. Cook these in boiling, salted water for 10 minutes and drain.
8. Just before serving divide the diced cucumber between the serving bowls, pour on the chilled soup, and scatter a little chopped mint over the top of each.

Gazpacho · Blender

A tomato soup from Spain to serve ice-cold in high summer.
Serves 4

> 1 lb. ($\frac{1}{2}$ kg.) ripe tomatoes
> $\frac{1}{2}$ a small onion
> 1 clove garlic
> 1 teasp. lemon juice
> 2 tbs. olive oil

> 3 teasp. wine vinegar
> iced water – approx 6 tbs.
> salt and freshly ground black
>   pepper
> finely chopped parsley to garnish

Accompaniments
> $\frac{1}{2}$ large green pepper
> $\frac{1}{4}$ cucumber

> 2 tomatoes
> 2 slices of bread for croutons

1. Blend the peeled onion and the garlic with a little water at fast speed until they are partially chopped. Then drop in, through the hole in the lid, the washed halved tomatoes. Continue blending until all the tomatoes are completely puréed.

2. Pour the tomato mixture through a nylon strainer (to remove the skins and pips) into a bowl, stirring with a wooden spoon to ensure that only dry residue is left in the strainer.

3. Stir in the lemon juice, olive oil, vinegar and a little more water to thin down if necessary. The soup should be quite thin, and the amount of water needed depends on the juiciness of the tomatoes. Season to taste.

4. Chill in the refrigerator for at least an hour and meanwhile prepare the accompaniments:

Green pepper Remove stalk and seeds and make small dice of the flesh.

Cucumber Dice neatly, leaving the skin on.

Tomatoes Skin, and remove the pips, then dice the flesh carefully.

Bread Cut off the crusts, cut into $\frac{3}{8}$ in. (1 cm.) cubes and fry to a golden brown. Drain on paper.

5. When ready to serve, add a little crushed ice to each portion of soup and sprinkle with chopped parsley. Hand the accompaniments separately.

Salad Soup · Centrifugal juicer

Serves 5

1 lb. ($\frac{1}{2}$ kg.) ripe red tomatoes	$\frac{1}{4}$ teasp. salt
$\frac{1}{2}$ cucumber	pepper
$\frac{1}{2}$ small onion or 3–4 spring onions	2 tbs. sherry
	4 tbs. cream
1 teasp. sugar	chopped parsley to garnish

1. Peel the onion and wash the tomatoes and cucumber.

2. Put the vegetables through the centrifugal juicer, and mix the juices with the seasoning and sherry.

3. Chill in the refrigerator for at least an hour, then stir in the cream.

4. Serve really cold with chopped parsley sprinkled on top of each portion.

End Blend · Blender

One of the great benefits of a blender is the way it enables one to use and disguise left-overs and ingredients which would otherwise have been thrown away. If this soup were made regularly (perhaps at the same time as the refrigerator is turned out) the outlay on a blender would soon be recovered. What goes into the soup is completely a matter of taste, and considerable talent can be exercised in obtaining a good flavour from the ingredients available.

INGREDIENTS

Into a large heavy saucepan put a selection from any of the following.

1. *Bones – from the joint, stewed mutton or veal, a poultry carcase, ham bone, pig's trotter etc.*
2. *Left-over gravy, savoury sauces or stews*
3. *Cooked or raw vegetables including potatoes*
4. *Tomatoes, going soft and therefore unsuitable for salad*
5. *Remains of tinned spaghetti or beans in tomato sauce*
6. *Mince or left-over meat (chopped)*
7. *Green tops of leeks or celery – roughly chopped*
8. *Left-over porridge*
9. *Left-over pasta dishes e.g. macaroni cheese*
10. *Water in which vegetables have been cooked e.g. carrot water or leek water (especially good)*
11. *Liquor from tinned vegetables*

ADD

A bouquet garni (bay leaf, peppercorns, parsley, dried mixed herbs)

A chopped onion (or garlic clove, crushed) if there is no onion or leek among the left-overs

An appropriate amount of water

1. Bring the mixture to the boil and simmer for 2–3 hours.

2. Remove from the pan the bouquet garni, any bones and rinds.

3. Fill the blender two-thirds full with soup and blend at fast speed until a smooth purée is formed – probably about 30 seconds.

4. Strain if necessary and reheat. Refill the blender jar if there is any soup remaining.

5. Taste carefully, and if the addition of salt and pepper does not improve the flavour sufficiently other flavourings can be added, such as:

Worcester sauce

Ketchup

Concentrated tomato purée

A small quantity of wine or sherry

A little sugar always brings out the flavour and is especially useful if the soup is too salt.

6. If desired stir in a little cream or evaporated milk just before serving.

7. This soup may be served with a variety of accompaniments according to taste:

e.g. croutons of toasted or fried bread, grated cheese, diced flesh of tomatoes, chopped parsley or chervil or chives.

5

Sauces and Stuffings

৩০৫২৩০৫২৩০৫২৩০৫২৩০৫২৩০৫২৩০৫২৩০৫২৩০৫২৩০৫২৩০৫২

Vinaigrette or French Dressing · Blender

Makes $\frac{1}{3}$ pt. (175 ml.)

4 tbs. vinegar (can be either
malt, wine or tarragon
vinegar or lemon juice, or
indeed a mixture of any two
of these in proportions as
desired)
$\frac{1}{4}$ pt. (125 ml.) salad oil
small clove of garlic and/or
1 thin slice from medium-
sized onion

1 rounded teasp. sugar
1 rounded teasp. made
mustard
$\frac{1}{2}$ level teasp. salt
freshly ground black pepper
herbs such as parsley,
tarragon, chives, chervil,
thyme can be added if
desired

1. Put all the ingredients, including any herbs, in the blender and blend at fast speed for a few seconds until completely amalgamated and any herbs are chopped small.

French dressing made in the blender will keep much longer (at least 1–2 days) without separating than that made by hand, and should the ingredients separate out then the dressing can quickly be restored by reblending at fast speed for a few seconds.

Cooked Mayonnaise · Blender

Makes almost 1 pint ($\frac{1}{2}$ l.)

$1\frac{1}{2}$ oz. (40 g.) flour
1 level teasp. salt
2 level teasp. sugar
1 level teasp. dry mustard
6 oz. (150 ml.) water
($\frac{1}{4}$ pt. + 2 tbs.)

5 tbs. vinegar
4 egg yolks (or 2 whole eggs)
8 oz. (200 ml.) salad oil
($\frac{1}{4}$ pt. + 6 tbs.)

1. Put the flour, salt, sugar, mustard, water and vinegar into the blender and blend at medium speed until quite smooth.
2. Pour the mixture into a saucepan and bring to the boil, stirring all the time. Allow to boil for 1 minute only, stirring rapidly all the time.
3. Put the egg yolks into the blender, and blend at medium speed, adding the hot mixture a little at a time until all is blended smooth.
4. Now continue with the blender at medium speed, and pour in the oil through the hole in the lid, at a steady, but slow, pace until it is all incorporated. If it is rather thick, more vinegar, or hot water may be used to thin it.
5. Pour into a jar and store in a cool place.

This mayonnaise may be modified by using lemon juice instead of vinegar, and cream can also be stirred into it before serving.

Mayonnaise · Mixer or Blender

Although the mixer or blender will completely take the effort from making homemade mayonnaise, it still requires skill, and must never be made in a hurry. The flavour can be altered considerably by the use of different quantities of vinegar or lemon juice and seasonings, and this must depend on the taste of the cook. Olive oil is the best for flavour and for making an emulsion, but substitutes such as corn oil, sunflower oil and groundnut oil are very satisfactory.

Mayonnaise (cont.)
Makes approx $\frac{3}{4}$ pint (350 ml.)

2 *egg yolks*	1$\frac{1}{2}$ *level teasp. sugar*
$\frac{1}{2}$ *pt. (250 ml.) salad oil*	1 *level teasp. dry mustard*
2–3 *tbs. lemon juice or*	$\frac{1}{4}$ *level teasp. white pepper*
vinegar (or wine or tarragon	$\frac{1}{4}$ *level teasp. paprika*
vinegar)	*(optional)*
1–1$\frac{1}{2}$ *level teasp. salt*	

MIXER METHOD
1. Put the egg yolks in the mixer bowl. For large machines it may be easier to double the quantities in the recipe.
2. Add the seasonings and beat at medium speed.
3. Add the oil, the first tablespoon drop by drop, the second slightly quicker, and then in a *very slow* stream. Some mixers have an 'oil dripper' attachment which allows the oil to run in with the required slowness. On no account must the addition of the first oil be hurried or an emulsion will not be established. Should the mixture suddenly become thin, and appear curdled, stop the machine, scrape out the mixture, break another egg yolk into the bowl and start all over again, adding the previous mixture little by little to the new egg yolk until a thick emulsion is established. Towards the end the oil may be poured in more quickly, but all the time try to drop it into the centre of the mixture near the beaters. If the mayonnaise becomes very thick, add some of the lemon juice or vinegar to thin it down and prevent the mixer labouring.
4. Beat in the remaining vinegar or lemon juice, and a little hot water if the sauce is still too thick.

BLENDER METHOD
This is very quick but care must be taken not to overstrain the motor by running it for longer periods than recommended by the manufacturer. Check in the instruction book and rest the motor during the making of the mayonnaise if necessary. See that the mayonnaise does not become so thick that the blender cannot emulsify it. If not moving quickly, add a little vinegar or hot water.

1. Put the egg yolks in the jar with the seasonings, and blend at slow speed.

2. Add the oil through the hole in the lid, directly on to the blades, drop by drop to begin with, then more quickly (see 3 in Mixer Method). Stop and scrape down the sides if necessary, and thin with the vinegar or lemon juice if it becomes too thick.

3. Add the remaining vinegar when all the oil has been added, and a little hot water to thin the mayonnaise if necessary.

The two following recipes are variations on this basic mayonnaise.

Orange Mayonnaise · Blender or Mixer

For salads to be served with duck, pork or ham. Makes approx ¾ pint (350 ml.)

½ *level teasp. salt*
½ *level teasp. dry mustard*
good shaking of white pepper
2 *level teasp. caster sugar*
2 *egg yolks*

½ *pt. (250 ml.) salad oil*
1 *tbs. wine vinegar*
rind and juice of 1 *medium-sized orange*

1. Make as for mayonnaise, but finally blend in with the vinegar the finely grated rind and the juice of the orange.

Tartare Sauce · Mixer and/or Blender

Serve with hot or cold fish, especially fried fish, and shell fish. Serves 8

½ *pt. (250 ml.) mayonnaise (as above recipes)*
3 *good sprigs parsley*

1 *large (or* 2–3 *small) gherkins*
2 *teasp. drained capers*

1. Make the mayonnaise using either the mixer or the blender, then transfer to the blender.

2. Put the washed sprigs of parsley into the jar and blend at fast speed for a short time to chop them.

3. Drop in the capers and gherkins and blend at fast speed for a few seconds only, to chop them.

If only the mixer is available, the parsley, capers and gherkins must be chopped with a sharp knife.

Hollandaise Sauce · Blender

This normally tricky sauce is simple and foolproof when using a blender. It makes a perfect accompaniment to vegetables such as cauliflower, broccoli or asparagus, and to almost all types of fish. (See also p. 95 for Mock Hollandaise sauce.) Serves 4

4 oz. (100 g.) butter
3 egg yolks (or 2 whole eggs)
2 tbs. lemon juice

¼ level teasp. salt
pepper to taste

1. Put the butter in a small saucepan and heat to bubbling, but do not let it brown.
2. Put the remaining ingredients into the blender and blend at slow speed.
3. Immediately pour in the hot butter, through the hole in the lid, maintaining a steady stream until it is all added, then switch off.
4. Serve immediately, as it is difficult to keep hot. However if it must wait, put the sauce in an upright jug standing in a saucepan containing 2 in. (5 cm.) of simmering water.

Should the sauce require thinning add 1 tablespoon of hot water or more, and mix in well.

Cucumber Sauce · Blender

For serving with vegetables, any fish – but especially salmon, with chicken and with many savoury foods. Serves 4

yolks of 2 eggs, or 1 whole
  egg
1 tbs. tarragon vinegar
salt, pepper, cayenne pepper

3 oz. (75 g.) butter
about 1 in. (2½ cm.) cut from a
  cucumber (makes 2 tbs. of
  dice)

1. Boil the vinegar in a small pan until it is reduced by half and transfer it to the blender.
2. Put the butter into the same pan and heat it until bubbling, but do not let it brown.
3. Add the eggs and the seasoning to the vinegar in the blender, switch on at fast speed and pour on the hot butter in a slow, steady stream until it has all been added. Switch off immediately.
4. Peel the cucumber and cut into tiny dice, adding these to the sauce from the blender. Use hot or cold; if required to keep hot put the sauce in a jug in a saucepan of gently simmering water.

Avocado Sauce or Dip · Blender

Serve as a sauce with any boiled, baked or fried fish. Alternatively it makes an excellent dip for parties with cheese biscuits or crisps. Serves 4

1 *large avocado pear*	$\frac{1}{2}$ *teasp. sugar*
1 *tbs. vinegar*	$\frac{1}{2}$ *teasp. salt*
3 *tbs. salad oil*	$\frac{1}{4}$ *teasp. freshly ground black*
$\frac{1}{2}$ *tbs. lemon juice*	*pepper*

1. Peel and stone the avocado, and break the flesh into rough chunks.
2. Put the avocado, with all the other ingredients, into the blender and blend at slow speed until all is smooth. It will probably be necessary to scrape down several times during this process, but eventually the sauce will have the consistency of mayonnaise.

Barbeque Sauce · Blender

Serve hot with gammon, pork chops, sausages, steak, etc., or cold as a savoury relish. Serves 8

8 *oz.* (250 ml.) *tomato juice, tinned or fresh*	1 *level tbs. dry mustard*
4 *tbs. tomato ketchup*	1 *large onion*
	1 *clove garlic*

2 tbs. Worcester sauce
2 tbs. vinegar
½ level teasp. salt

2 rounded teasp. sugar
strip of yellow lemon rind
freshly ground black pepper

1. Peel and roughly chop the onion, and put it, with all the other ingredients, into the blender, and blend at fast speed until the sauce is quite smooth.
2. Pour into a pan, bring to the boil and simmer for 5 minutes.

Bread Sauce · Blender

Serves 8

1 pt. (500 ml.) milk
1 large onion
5 oz. (125 g.) crustless bread
1 oz. (25 g.) butter

4 cloves
¼ level teasp. powdered mace
salt
white pepper

1. Peel the onion and stick the cloves into it.
2. Put the milk and onion into a heavy-based pan, bring to the boil and simmer for 10–15 minutes, to cook the onion.
3. Remove the cloves from the onion and put it together with the milk, butter, salt, mace and a good shaking of pepper into the blender. Blend at fast speed until the onion is puréed.
4. Break the bread into rough pieces and put several in the blender. Switch on at fast speed, gradually adding more bread through the hole in the lid as the sauce becomes smooth. Switch off when all the bread is incorporated.
5. Return to the heavy-based pan or a double saucepan. Rewarm and keep hot until required.

This quickly made bread sauce comes out smoother than that made with breadcrumbs. However, if preferred, dry breadcrumbs can be used (p. 60) and the sauce made in the traditional manner. In this case only 4 oz. (100 g.) breadcrumbs are needed.

Oxford Sauce · Mixer or Blender

A sweet, spicy sauce to serve with salt beef or pork, brawns, galantines or cold beef loaf. Serves 6

2 *level tbs. soft, dark brown*
   sugar
2 *level teasp. strong, made,*
   yellow mustard
½ *level teasp. salt*

½ *level teasp. freshly ground*
   black pepper
6 *tbs. salad oil*
2 *tbs. wine vinegar*

1. Put all the ingredients except the oil and vinegar into the mixer bowl or blender.
2. Switch on at slow speed and start to dribble in the oil slowly through the hole in the lid.
3. Increase to medium speed while still adding the oil very gradually; if the mixture becomes too thick to mix or blend without labouring, add a little vinegar.
4. When all the oil is added, pour the vinegar in slowly while still blending at medium speed. The sauce should have the appearance and consistency of thick, dark honey.

Tomato Sauce · Blender

Serves 8–10. Makes 2 pints (1 l.) sauce

2 *tbs. salad oil*
1 *lb. (500 g.) tomatoes*
1 *medium onion*
1 *stick celery*
1 *medium carrot*
2 *oz. (50 g.) bacon and/or rinds*
2 *oz. (50 g.) flour*

1 *pt. (500 ml.) stock (the liquor*
   from boiled bacon is suitable)
bay leaf
¼ *teasp. mixed herbs*
1 *level teasp. paprika*
1 *level teasp. salt*
1 *rounded teasp. sugar*
red colouring if desired

1. Put the oil in a heavy-based pan and in it fry gently the peeled and sliced onion, the chopped, washed celery, and the scrubbed carrots cut into chunks.

2. Add the tomatoes, washed and cut in halves, and the chopped bacon, and fry a little longer, then stir in the flour.

3. Cook for 2–3 minutes more then stir in the stock, bay leaf, herbs and seasonings. Bring to the boil and simmer for 20–30 minutes.

4. Remove the bay leaf and any bacon rinds, and pour everything else into the blender, and blend at fast speed until smooth, then strain to remove the pieces of tomato skin and the pips.

5. Reheat; taste and then add more sugar or salt if necessary. Tomato purée can be added to improve the flavour or a few drops of red colouring to give a better colour.

White Sauce · Blender

This plain white sauce is the basis for so many sauces, both savoury and sweet. It is given here first plain, then followed by a number of variations. The sauce can be made in the conventional way by making a roux with fat and flour and blending this with the milk. However a quicker way, and just as satisfactory, is to blend the flour and milk and pour them into the melted fat, then bring to the boil, stirring. The sauce must be boiled for 2–3 minutes in order to cook the flour thoroughly. This method comes into its own when other ingredients (e.g. parsley) need chopping and this can be done, with the milk, in the blender. Serves 4

1 oz. (25 g.) butter	salt and pepper for a savoury
1 oz. (25 g.) flour	sauce
½ pt. (250 ml.) milk	

This makes a fairly thick sauce, of coating consistency. If a sauce of pouring consistency is wanted, add extra milk (up to ¼ pint) (125 ml.) when the sauce is boiling in the pan.

1. Melt the butter in a saucepan.

2. Put the milk into the blender, followed by the flour and seasoning, and blend at fast speed until quite smooth.

3. Pour the contents of the blender into the saucepan, and stir well while bringing to the boil. Boil for 2–3 minutes, stirring all the while.

VARIATIONS ON WHITE SAUCE

Anchovy Sauce

Very good with steamed or baked white fish.

Add approximately 6 anchovy fillets to the flour and milk and blend until smooth then proceed as for basic white sauce. Alternatively stir in 2 teaspoons of anchovy essence when the sauce is made.

This sauce will not need much added salt.

Cheese Sauce

This forms the basis of many cheese dishes such as cauliflower au gratin, macaroni cheese etc., and it is also served with vegetables, hard-boiled eggs and fish. Most dishes are improved if a little grated cheese is sprinkled on top of the sauce, and browned under the grill or in a hot oven.

Switch on the blender at fast speed, put in the white sauce, and drop in 2 oz. (50 g.) strongly flavoured cheese, cut roughly into cubes, through the hole in the lid. Add also ½ teaspoonful of made mustard. Blend until smooth. Alternatively the cheese can be grated on the slicer/shredder attachment or chopped in the blender, in which case it should be stirred into the sauce in the pan. The sauce should not be boiled once the cheese is added.

Hard-boiled Egg Sauce

This has many uses, but is especially good with fish or with boiled fowl.

When the white sauce has boiled, pour it into the warmed blender and add 2 hard-boiled eggs, shelled; blend at medium speed until the eggs are chopped but have not completely disappeared into the sauce.

Mock Hollandaise Sauce

Serves 8

½ pt. (250 ml.) *white sauce, as above*
½ pt. (250 ml.) *mayonnaise*
1 *tablespoon lemon juice*
salt and tabasco to taste

Make the white sauce as usual, then return to the blender and, while blending at fast speed, pour the mayonnaise and lemon juice through the hole in the lid. Season to taste.

Mustard Sauce

To serve with herrings, ham or tongue.

To ½ pint (250 ml.) of white sauce add:

Either	Or
1 *level tbs. French mustard with* 1 *teasp. vinegar*	2 *teasp. dry mustard with* 2 *teasp. vinegar*

Put in blender and blend well.

Soubise Sauce

For eggs, potato, artichokes, cauliflower, fish or mutton.

6 *oz.* (150 *g.) onions, peeled*	½ *pt.* (250 *ml.) white sauce*
2 *tbs. cream*	

Boil the onions in water until tender, then drain and put them in the blender with the milk and flour. Blend at fast speed until the onions are quite puréed. Cook the sauce as before, then draw off the heat and add the cream.

Parsley Sauce

For vegetables, fish, tongues, ham, chicken etc. The blender can be a real time-saver here, but more parsley than usual must be added to the sauce, as the parsley is cooked for longer than in conventional methods and so tends to lose its flavour a little.

Wash and pick enough parsley leaves to half-fill a teacup. Put these into the blender together with the milk and flour and blend at fast speed until the parsley is finely chopped. Do not overblend as the milk will tend to become coloured green. Cook the sauce as before, boiling for 2-3 minutes.

SWEET SAUCES FROM BASIC WHITE SAUCE

Omit the seasoning and add 1 oz. (25 g.) sugar, and whatever flavouring is required, e.g.:

Coffee Sauce

Stir into the sweet white sauce, when it has boiled, enough powdered instant coffee, or coffee essence to give the required flavour.

Or Make the sauce of ¼ pint (125 ml.) milk and ¼ pint (125 ml.) strong black coffee.

Vanilla Sauce

This goes with such a multitude of puddings, and is especially good with Christmas pudding, for children. It can always be used as a substitute for custard.

Make the sweet white sauce with vanilla sugar or add ¼ teaspoon vanilla essence.

Apple Sauce · Blender

Serves 6–8

> 1½ *lb.* (¾ *kg.*) *cooking apples*   2 *oz.* (50 *g.*) *sugar*
> 4 *tbs. water*   1 *oz.* (25 *g.*) *butter*

1. Peel, quarter and core the apples.
2. Put them in a saucepan, with the water and sugar, and simmer gently until they are tender.
3. Put them into the blender, with the butter, and blend at fast speed until the apples are quite smooth.
4. Put into a warm dish, or reheat gently in a saucepan if necessary.

Gooseberry Sauce · Blender

Serve cold with icecream, or hot as an unusual accompaniment to pork, gammon or mackerel. Serves 8

> 1 *lb.* (½ *kg.*) *gooseberries*   4 *tbs. water*
> 2 *oz.* (60 *g.*) *sugar*

1. Wash the gooseberries, but do not top and tail.
2. Put them in a saucepan with the sugar and water, bring to the boil, and simmer until the gooseberries are thoroughly cooked, about 10 minutes.
3. Pour everything into the blender, and switch on at fast speed for 30 seconds or so, until the fruit is completely puréed.
4. Pour through a nylon strainer to remove the pips. It may be necessary to turn it over with a spoon several times, to ensure that the fruit purée goes completely through the strainer.

5. The sauce is now ready for use:
a. with icecream – chill in the refrigerator.
b. hot – warm very gently to simmering point.

Mint Sauce · Blender

1 *teacupful of washed mint*
   leaves, loosely packed
8 *tbs. vinegar*

4 *tbs. water*
1 *oz. (25 g.) caster sugar (1 tbs.)*

1. Put all the ingredients in the blender and switch on for a short time until the mint leaves are sufficiently chopped. Leave to stand for at least an hour before serving, to develop its flavour.

(A recipe for bottled mint sauce is given on p. 274.)

Meat Sauce · Mincer and Blender

To serve with spaghetti, macaroni or other pasta. Serves 4–5

½ *lb. (200 g.) lean stewing steak*
1 *medium onion*
1 *carrot*
½ *stick celery*
2 *oz. (50 g.) mushrooms*
few sprigs parsley
3 *tbs. white or red wine or*
   sherry

2 *tbs. concentrated tomato*
   purée
½ *oz. (15 g.) dripping*
½ *pt. (250 ml.) stock*
1 *oz. (25 g.) flour*
1 *teasp. paprika*
salt, pepper

1. Using the fine screen on the mincer, mince the onion, and fry in a pan with the dripping until brown.
2. Mince the meat and the scrubbed carrot, and add to the pan to brown these.
3. Wash the mushrooms and celery and roughly chop.
4. Stir the flour into the pan and then add the stock, mushrooms, celery, parsley, wine, tomato purée and seasonings. Simmer for 30–40 minutes with the lid off.

5. Cool slightly then pour into the blender and blend at fast speed until smooth. If too thick add a little water.

6. Return to the saucepan to rewarm. Serve with pasta and sprinkle with finely grated Parmesan cheese.

Sage and Onion Stuffing · Blender

Serves 6

2 *large onions*
2 *level teasp. dried sage or*
  6 fresh sage leaves
$\frac{1}{2}$–1 *oz. (15–25 g.) butter*

3 *oz. (75 g.) white breadcrumbs*
  (p. 60)
1 *level teasp. salt*
generous shaking of pepper
suet or dripping

1. Peel the onions and boil them until they are tender.

2. If using fresh sage leaves, chop in blender at fast speed before adding the onions. Chop these finely, and quickly add the butter so it may be melted by the heat of the onions.

3. Empty the onions into the breadcrumbs and mix all the ingredients together, seasoning well and adding dried sage if used.

4. Bind together with a little milk or egg if this should prove necessary.

5. Use as a stuffing, or pack into a small, greased, ovenproof dish and dot the top with chopped suet or with pieces of dripping, and bake in a moderate oven until the top is browned, usually in the oven with the roast meat with which it is served.

Veal Forcemeat · Blender

This can be used to stuff veal, lamb, hearts or poultry. Alternatively it can be rolled in flour to form small balls which can then be fried or baked in the oven in fat.

4 *oz. (100 g.) white*
  breadcrumbs (p. 60)
2 *oz. (50 g.) suet chopped*

1–2 *oz. (25–50 g.) bacon or ham*
$\frac{1}{2}$ *cup parsley leaves, picked*
  and clean

rind of ½–1 lemon, grated   1 *egg*
½ *teasp. dried mixed herbs*   *salt and pepper*

1. With a few breadcrumbs in the blender, roughly cut the bacon rashers or ham into ½ in. (1 cm.) strips and drop these and the parsley into the blender to fall directly on to the rotating knives. Blend until the bacon is well chopped.
2. In a basin combine all the breadcrumbs, chopped suet, parsley, bacon, herbs and grated lemon rind.
3. Mix in the salt and pepper and bind with the egg, and a little milk if necessary to make a firm stuffing.

Butterscotch Sauce · Blender

Serve hot or cold with puddings or icecreams. Serves 6

6 *oz.* (150 *ml.*) *evaporated milk*   1 *oz.* (25 *g.*) *butter*
  (1 *small tin*)   1 *tbs. golden syrup*
¼ *pt.* (125 *ml.*) *water*   ½ *teasp. vanilla essence*
5 *oz.* (125 *g.*) *soft, light brown*   1 *oz.* (25 *g.*) *flour*
  sugar

1. Melt the butter in a saucepan.
2. Put all the other ingredients (except the vanilla) into the blender and blend at fast speed until they are completely smooth.
3. Pour the mixture on to the melted butter, and cook, stirring, until it has thickened and boiled for 1 minute.
4. Stir in the vanilla and use hot, or store in the refrigerator, covered, until required cold.

Chocolate Sauce · Blender

Serves 4

1½ *oz.* (40 *g.*) *cocoa*   1½–2 *oz.* (40–50 *g.*) *sugar*
¼ *oz.* (5 *g.*) *arrowroot or cornflour*   ½ *pt.* (250 *ml.*) *water* (or *milk*)
  (1 *teasp.*)   *few drops of vanilla essence*

1. Put all the ingredients (except the vanilla) into the blender and switch on at fast speed, blending till quite smooth.
2. Pour into a saucepan and bring to the boil, then boil for 1 minute, stirring all the time.
3. Stir in the vanilla and serve.

Fruit Sauce · Blender

This is excellent served hot or cold with moulds, mousses, icecreams, or milk puddings. If needed for a party it can be made several days beforehand and stored in a covered container in the refrigerator. Serves 6–10.

1 lb. (½ kg.) fruit	2 teasp. arrowroot
sugar as necessary	1 teasp. lemon juice (optional)
water	

1. Wash, pick over, stone (if necessary) and stew the fruit, using just sufficient water to prevent it sticking.
2. If the fruit will need sieving (e.g. fruits with pips) put it in the blender at this stage and blend at fast speed until it is completely puréed – then pass through a nylon strainer to remove the pips.
3. Put the arrowroot into the blender together with the lemon juice and 2 tablespoons water and switch on for just a moment to blend them.
4. Add the fruit and blend again until the fruit is quite puréed. Add sugar during blending until the sauce is sufficiently sweet.
5. Turn into a heavy-based pan, bring slowly to the boil, stirring all the time, and boil for 2 minutes. Turn into a sauceboat and cover to prevent a skin forming.

Hard Sauce (Brandy Butter) · Mixer

Makes 15 oz.

8 oz. (200 g.) butter	1 oz. (25 g.) ground almonds
4 oz. (100 g.) caster sugar	4 tbs. (3 tbs.) brandy

1. Warm the mixer bowl and the beaters and soften the butter.
2. With the mixer running at medium speed cream the butter and sugar until they are white and fluffy.
3. Add the ground almonds and continue beating until they are incorporated.
4. Gradually beat in the brandy, a teaspoonful at a time.
5. Press the sauce into jars, cover and store in a cool place until required.

Sabayon Sauce – Hot or Cold · Hand-held Mixer

Serves 8

HOT SABAYON SAUCE
(for steamed or baked sponge or fruit puddings)

   4 oz. (100 g.) sugar   4 egg yolks
   $\frac{1}{4}$ pt. (125 ml.) sherry or marsala
    or white wine

COLD SABAYON SAUCE
(for fruit jellies or moulds, sugared fruit or icecream with or without meringue)

   2 oz. (50 g.) sugar   4 egg yolks
   $\frac{1}{4}$ pt. (125 g.) sherry or marsala

Method for both
1. Bring about 1 in. ($2\frac{1}{2}$ cm.) of water nearly to the boil in a saucepan, and over it fit a $1\frac{1}{2}$ pint (750 ml.) basin (approx. size).
2. Put all the ingredients into the basin and whisk with the hand-held mixer working at medium speed until the mixture thickens. As this may well take 10–15 minutes (depending on the bowl and the mixer) it may be left without beating for 1–2 minutes several times while the mixture is warming up, provided the water underneath does not boil. It should be heated just enough to keep it very hot.

As the mixture thickens the mixer may be turned up to fast speed.

3. Once the mixture is so thick that the whisk leaves a trail for a moment when lifted out, the bowl should be taken out of the sauce-pan. If the sauce is to be used *warm* it should be put in a warm sauce-boat and served immediately. If the sauce is to be used cold it should be continually whisked at fast speed until it is cold, then put into a bowl and chilled in the refrigerator. Thus chilled it may be kept overnight before use, but it is better used the same day.

6

Meat and Fish

¤¤¤¤¤¤¤¤¤¤¤¤¤¤¤¤¤¤¤¤¤¤¤¤¤¤¤¤¤¤¤

Salmon Mousse · Blender

Just right for serving in hot weather as a starter for a dinner or a cold buffet table. It can be made in individual moulds, or in a large one. Serves 5

$7\frac{1}{2}$ oz. (210 g.) tin salmon (the cheaper pink variety can be used most successfully if more colouring is used)	2 tbs. boiling water
	2 tbs. french dressing
	1 tbs. mayonnaise
	salt and pepper
$\frac{1}{2}$ cucumber	a few drops of red colouring
$\frac{1}{2}$ oz. (15 g.) gelatine	lettuce leaves, tomato and
$\frac{1}{4}$ pt. (125 ml.) evaporated milk or cream	lemon slices to garnish

1. Halve the $\frac{1}{2}$ cucumber. Dice one portion and put to steep in the french dressing. Peel the remaining portion and cut into thick slices. Boil these for 5 minutes in salted water and drain well.
2. Dissolve the gelatine in the boiling water, stirring thoroughly.
3. Put fish (including liquor and bones, but not any very dark skin), the boiled cucumber, mayonnaise, dissolved gelatine, evaporated milk and a little salt and pepper in the blender and blend at fast speed until quite smooth.
4. Stop the blender and taste for seasoning, add more if necessary and also a few drops of red colouring if desired. Blend again. Stop

blender, drop in the diced cucumber and stir over with the plastic spatula.

5. Wet the mould, then pour in the salmon mixture.

6. Put in a cool place until set, then turn out on to a dish and garnish with lettuce leaves, tomato and slices of lemon.

Grapefruit and Tuna Pâté · Blender

A delicious and unusual pâté to start a meal, or to serve at high tea. Serves 4–6

2 *grapefruit*	3 *oz. (75 g.) fresh white*
1 *can (7 oz. (200 g.)) tuna fish*	*breadcrumbs (p. 60)*
½ *small onion*	*salt and pepper*
1 *large egg*	*lettuce and tomato to garnish*

1. Wash and dry grapefruit. Grate the peel of one very finely.

2. Put the roughly chopped onion in the blender with the juice squeezed from the peeled grapefruit.

3. Add the tuna with its oil, the grated rind, the egg and sufficient salt and pepper to season well. Blend until the mixture is completely smooth, starting at medium, and increasing to fast speed.

4. Put the breadcrumbs in a bowl, pour on the tuna mixture and stir together with a spoon. Taste for seasoning.

5. Grease well a 1 lb. (500 g.) loaf tin (or tin of smaller base), pour in the pâté mixture and smooth down.

6. Bake at 350°F (180°C, Gas No. 4) until firm all over, about 40 minutes. Cool in the tin.

7. *To serve:* turn the pâté out of the tin on to a board and slice downwards; arrange the sliced pâté on a few lettuce leaves on a plate. Slice the remaining grapefruit thinly, slash each slice to the centre, and arrange in attractive twists beside the pâté. Serve with sliced skinned tomatoes.

Chicken Liver Pâté · Blender

Serves 6–8

12 oz. (300 g.) *chicken livers*
7 oz. (175 g.) *butter*
1 *medium onion*
1 *level teasp. dried mixed herbs (or chopped fresh herbs)*

½ *clove garlic*
1 *tbs. brandy or sherry*
salt and pepper
lettuce, tomato and cucumber to garnish

1. Peel and roughly chop the onion and garlic and sauté very gently in some of the butter in a heavy-based pan, without browning, until transparent.
2. Add the chicken livers and the herbs and continue sautéing very slowly for 10–15 minutes.
3. Transfer to the blender, together with the remaining butter and blend at slow speed. It will probably be necessary to stop and scrape down the sides of the jar with the spatula once or twice.
4. Add the brandy or sherry, then blend until the pâté is a smooth cream. Season to taste.
5. Pour into a dish and leave, covered, in a cool place to set.
6. Serve, when quite firm, with toast, butter and a garnish of lettuce and thin slices of tomato and cucumber.

Economy Pâté · Blender

This is an excellent way to make a party dish from left-overs, and the recipe can be varied according to what is in the larder. As the pâté must be fairly fatty it is always a good idea to include some bacon. This is just an indication of the quantities which might be used. Makes approx. 1 lb. (500 g.) pâté.

½ *lb. (250 g.) end of a joint of bacon or ham (if this is not fatty add some butter)*
giblets (heart, liver, gizzard) of one chicken

4 oz. (125 g.) *ox or pig's liver*
1 *small onion*
pinch of dried marjoram or a very few leaves of fresh marjoram

salt and pepper   1 tbs. wine (can be stale) or
1 tbs. vinegar   cooking sherry
bread raspings

1. All the meats must be cooked and if the liver or giblets need this the liver can be fried and the giblets and bacon boiled. Then cut all the meats into rough chunks.

2. Blend the vinegar, wine, marjoram and onion at slow speed for a few seconds to chop the onion.

3. Continue at slow speed and drop the chunks of meat one by one on to the knives through the hole in the lid. If the knives stop rotating, switch off and scrape the mixture down the sides with a rubber spatula. If it is obvious that the blender is labouring and becoming too full, then empty it out into a basin and continue chopping the remaining meat in the blender.

4. Turn all the mixture into a basin and mix well together, seasoning to taste.

5. Add sufficient bread raspings (probably about 1 tablespoon) to make a firm pâté, then turn into a dish and leave in a cool place to set before use.

Mixed Meat Pâté · Mincer (and Mixer)

This recipe for a pâté of excellent flavour and varied texture is given for a large quantity because it is more convenient to buy the meats like this. It is exciting served on a cold buffet table at a party, or as a family standby to cut at a holiday week-end. However, it is just as successful if the quantities are halved. Serves 12–14

8 oz. (200 g.) belly of pork	½ pt. (250 ml.) top of milk (or ¼ pt.
8 oz. (200 g.) stewing beef	(125 ml.) milk + ¼ pt. (125 ml.)
8 oz. (200 g.) pig's liver	evaporated milk)
8 oz. (200 g.) sausage meat	1 large onion
2 meat stock cubes	1 clove of garlic
5 eggs (3 of them hard boiled)	pinch mixed herbs
4 oz. (100 g.) mushrooms	1 tbs. chopped parsley

freshly ground black pepper
  and salt
½ teasp. mixed spice
2 rounded tbs. plain flour

12 rashers streaky bacon
  with rinds removed
lettuce or watercress, tomato,
  radish or cucumber to
  garnish

1. Cut the liver, beef and pork into 1 in. (2½ cm.) strips and mince them all together with the peeled onion. Finish off with a small piece of stale bread to clean the mincer.

2. Warm the milk sufficiently to melt the stock cubes in it.

3. Wash and slice the mushrooms downwards.

4. Mix all the ingredients well together (except the bacon rashers and hard-boiled eggs). This can be done in the mixer bowl at slowest speed.

5. Grease a convenient-sized loaf tin, or ovenproof dish, and line with the streaky rashers.

6. Fill the dish with half the mixture, then lay the hard-boiled eggs end to end down the centre, and cover them with the remaining mixture.

7. Cover with foil or buttered paper, stand the dish in a tin of hot water, and bake in the oven at 325°F (160°C, Gas No. 3) for 1½ hours, until the pâté shrinks away from the tin.

8. Turn out when completely cold and serve sliced, garnished with lettuce or watercress, tomato, radish or cucumber.

Beefburgers · Mincer (and Mixer)

Makes 8–12 beefburgers.

1 lb. (½ kg.) stewing steak
1 large onion
1 large potato
1 heaped teasp. chopped
  parsley

½ teasp. mixed herbs
1 teasp. Worcester sauce
salt and pepper
baps or soft bread rolls for
  serving, if desired

1. Peel the onion and potato, and cut them into suitably sized sticks for putting down the mincer shaft.

2. Cut the meat into strips, removing any gristle.

3. Mince the onion, potato and meat, using the fine screen on the mincer, into the mixer bowl.

4. Add all the other ingredients, and mix together well, using the beater at slowest speed. Season to taste.

5. On a floured board form the mixture into very flat cakes, flouring both sides.

6. Melt a little dripping or lard in a large meat tin and bake at 400°F (200°C, Gas No. 6) for 25–30 minutes. Alternatively fry for about 10 minutes turning once.

7. Serve between sliced rolls, or as a supper dish, with mashed potatoes or noodles and tomatoes or tomato sauce.

Hamburgers

Use the recipe above, but substitute for the stewing steak 1 lb. ($\frac{1}{2}$ kg.) raw bacon (rashers or piece from joint or cheap bacon pieces) not too fatty, *or* 1 lb. ($\frac{1}{2}$ kg.) cooked bacon or ham.

Galantine of Beef · Mincer (and Mixer)

Serves 6

1 lb. ($\frac{1}{2}$ kg.) lean stewing steak
8 oz. (250 g.) bacon (rashers, pieces, or piece of boiling bacon)
6 oz. (200 g.) breadcrumbs (p. 60)
1 egg

6 tbs. (approx.) stock
$\frac{1}{2}$ teasp. dried mixed herbs
1 medium onion
$\frac{1}{2}$ teasp. salt
pepper

1. Peel and quarter the onion, and cut the meat into chunky strips. Remove any rind from the bacon.

2. Mince the onion, meat and bacon, using the fine screen of the mincer, into the bowl of the mixer. Finish with a small piece of stale bread to clean the mincer.

3. Put all the other ingredients into the mixer bowl, and either by hand, or by using the mixer at slow speed, mix them well together.

4. Press the mixture well into a greased 2 pint (1 l.) pudding basin and cover tightly with greased paper and with foil. Steam for 3–4

hours, or stand in a saucepan of boiling water reaching halfway up the basin, for the same time. The galantine can also be pressure cooked most successfully, for approx. 30 minutes at 15 lb. (7 kg.) pressure.

5. Turn out and serve hot with tomato sauce or brown gravy, or cold with salad. Oxford Sauce (p. 93) is also excellent with this galantine.

Moussaka · Mincer, Blender and Slicer/Shredder

This interesting dish from Eastern Europe is particularly useful to the cook/hostess, as it can be fully prepared some hours or even the day before, then stored in a refrigerator, put in the oven 1½ hours before the meal and served without further attention. Serves 6–7

3 oz. (75 g.) butter	FOR THE SAUCE
2 large onions	1 oz. (25 g.) butter
1½ lb. (750 g.) potatoes	1 oz. (25 g.) flour
2 large aubergines	½ pt. (250 ml.) milk
1 lb. (500 g.) stewing steak	1 egg
(or mince)	2 oz. (50 g.) well-flavoured cheese
3 tomatoes	salt and pepper

parsley to garnish

1. Slice the aubergines in slices about ¼ in. (½ cm.) thick and leave on a plate sprinkled lightly with salt for 20–30 minutes, then pour off the moisture which collects. This removes the bitter taste.
2. Peel the onions and slice, using the coarsest cutter of the slicer/shredder, then fry them in the butter until they are just soft.
3. Peel the potatoes and use the slicer/shredder to slice them.
4. Drain the onions from the pan and toss the sliced potatoes and aubergines in the remaining fat.
5. Use the mincer attachment with the fine screen to mince the meat if necessary.
6. Make the cheese sauce as follows:
a. Melt the butter in a small pan.
b. Put the milk, seasonings, flour and the cheese roughly cut into

cubes into the blender and blend at medium speed until all is smooth.

c. Pour the contents of the blender slowly on to the melted butter and stir well, heating until it boils. Then draw off the heat, and when a little cooled beat in the egg.

7. Grease a deep oven dish or casserole and fill it with layers in the following order:

a. Sliced potatoes

b. Sliced aubergines

c. Minced meat   Season well

d. Fried onions

e. Tomato – skinned and sliced

f. Layer of cheese sauce

Continue until the dish is full, finishing with a layer of potatoes and aubergines.

8. Place in the middle of the oven and cook at 325°F (160°C, Gas No. 3) until the aubergines and potatoes are quite soft (test with a skewer). The dish can be cooked with the lid on the casserole, or alternatively with no lid and then the top can be sprinkled with grated cheese.

9. Serve sprinkled with chopped parsley.

Pork Sausages · Mincer and Sausage Filler

1½ lb. (750 g.) fatty pork (e.g. belly of pork)	large pinch powdered cinnamon
1 level teasp. salt	1 teasp. chopped sage or thyme (fresh or dried)
½ level teasp. ground pepper	2–4 oz. (50–100 g.) breadcrumbs (p. 60)
large pinch ground nutmeg	
large pinch ground cloves	sausage skins

1. Soak the sausage skins in water overnight to soften. Next day wash thoroughly by fixing one end on the tap and running the water through.

2. Cut the meat into 1 in. (2–3 cm.) strips, removing any rind, and feed through the mincer fitted with the coarsest screen. Put the meat into a bowl and mix well together with all the other ingredients.

3. Screw the sausage filler on to the front of the mincing attachment and push the softened skins back on to it, rucking the skin back until the required length is on the filler and the end of the skin just protrudes over the end of the filler.

4. Put the sausage mixture through the mincer, fitted with the coarsest screen, and as it extrudes through the end of the sausage filler gently pull the skin over it. Fill the skin in one long sausage and later squeeze and twist into small sausages of the required size. Fry, grill or bake as desired.

Skinless Sausages

If no skins are available, most successful skinless sausages can be made by catching the extruded sausage meat on a flat, floured tray, so that it does not fall and break. This long sausage can then be cut into suitable lengths and the individual sausages each rolled in flour and fried.

Stuffed Marrow · Mincer (and Mixer)

Marrow can be equally well stuffed with fresh raw meat, minced, or with left-overs of cooked meat. This recipe uses cooked meat as it is such a tasty way of using up the tag-ends of a joint. Serves 5

> ½ lb. (250 g.) cold roast mutton and ½ lb. (250 g.) cold boiled bacon or other combinations of of meats or poultry
> 1 medium onion
> 2 oz. (50 g.) breadcrumbs (p. 60)
>
> 2 tbs. brown gravy or stock
> 1–2 teasp. Worcester sauce
> salt and pepper
> 1 medium marrow
> dripping

1. Peel the marrow and either cut into two lengthways or cut into individual sized boat-shaped pieces. In either case scrape out the seeds.

2. Blanch the marrow by dropping into boiling, salted water and boiling for 1 minute. Then drain well.

3. Peel and quarter the onion, and using the fine screen on the

mincer, mince it into the mixer bowl, followed by the cold meats. Clean through the mincer by feeding in a small piece of stale bread.
4. Add the breadcrumbs, gravy and seasonings and mix well together, either by hand or by using the mixer at slow speed.
5. Pack the stuffing into the marrow cavities.
6. Melt the dripping in a baking tin in the oven at 400°F (200°C, Gas No. 6) and then put the pieces of stuffed marrow in. Baste well and bake until the marrow is tender. Baste again and cover with greaseproof paper if it is getting too dry.

Toad in the Hole · Mixer or Blender

Serves 6

1 *lb.* (500 *g.*) *sausages or*	2 *eggs*
chipolatas	$\frac{1}{2}$ *level teasp. salt*
1 *pt.* (500 *ml.*) *milk*	*pepper*
8 *oz.* (200 *g.*) *plain flour*	*chopped herbs if desired*

1. Prick the sausages and put to cook in a baking tin, with the oven at 425°F (220°C, Gas No. 7) until the fat runs.
2. In the meantime mix the batter in one of two ways:
a. Put the flour, seasoning, herbs (if desired) and eggs in the mixer bowl, add half the milk and beat well at medium, increasing to fast speed, for at least 30 seconds until the batter is completely smooth. Then turn the speed to medium again and add the remaining milk.
or
b. Put the milk and eggs in the blender and add the seasoning, herbs and flour. Switch on at medium, then increase to maximum speed for at least 30 seconds, until a smooth and aerated batter has been made. If the capacity of the blender is too small, only half the quantity of milk need be added to make the batter, then the remainder can be stirred in afterwards.
3. When the sausages are ready, pour the batter quickly into the hot fat and over the sausages. Return to the oven and cook until the batter is well risen and well browned – about 40 minutes.
4. Serve, cut in squares, with gravy or tomato sauce if desired.

Tuesday Quickie · Blender

Of course there are many other ways of using up the tag ends of the Sunday joint, but this is one of the quickest. Serves 3

cold meat from the joint
(approx. 8 oz. (250 g.)) with a
little fat
cold gravy (left over from
Sunday) approx. ¼ pt. (125 ml.)

1 small onion
½ level teasp. paprika
few drops Worcester sauce
salt to season

1. Prepare and halve the onion, and chop it in the blender at fast speed. When the onion is chopped pour in the gravy and blend the two together thoroughly.
2. Put the onion and gravy in a saucepan and simmer gently for 5–10 minutes. Thin with a little vegetable water or stock if necessary.
3. Meanwhile, cut the meat into rough chunks, removing any gristle and large lumps of fat.
4. Start the blender at fast speed, and with the lid on drop the chunks of meat one at a time through the hole in the lid. If the jar becomes too full to chop efficiently, empty it out into the saucepan and continue chopping the rest of the meat.
5. Stir all the meat into the hot gravy, add the paprika, Worcester sauce and salt to taste, and gently heat but do not boil.
6. Serve with cooked, green vegetables, carrots or baked tomatoes and boiled rice, or noodles or mashed potato.

Steak and Kidney Pudding

See p. 180.

7

Vegetables and Salads

Cheese Potato · Mixer

These are delicious for supper or at a fireworks party served with watercress and/or grilled tomatoes. Serves 5

5 large potatoes
3 oz. (75 g.) butter
8 oz. (200 g.) strongly flavoured
  Cheddar cheese, grated

6 tbs. milk
1 teasp. made mustard
salt and freshly ground black
  pepper

1. Scrub the potatoes and score them right round, lengthways, with a knife.
2. Place on a baking tin in a hot oven 425°F (220°C, Gas No. 7) for about 45 minutes (or longer in a cooler oven), until the potatoes are cooked right through (test with a skewer).
3. Break the potatoes open where scored, and use a spoon to scoop out the centre into the mixer bowl.
4. Add the butter, milk, seasoning and two-thirds of the cheese to the potatoes.
5. Beat at medium speed until the mixture is quite smooth and creamy. Taste for seasoning.
6. Pile the potatoes back into the empty half skins and sprinkle the remaining cheese on top of each one.
7. Return potatoes to the oven and bake until the cheese is golden brown, about 15 minutes.

Duchesse Potato · Mixer

Serves 5–6

> 2 lb. (1 kg.) potatoes   salt and pepper
> 2 oz. (60 g.) butter   yolks of 2 eggs
> ¼ pt. (125 ml.) milk

If a hand-held mixer is used the mixture can be made in the saucepan in which the potatoes were cooked.

1. Prepare the potatoes either by peeling and boiling until tender, or by steaming in their skins until cooked and then peeling off the skins by hand. The latter is the preferable method, as it is important to have the potatoes as dry as possible. Drain them well if boiled.

2. Put the potatoes in the mixer bowl, together with the seasoning, the milk and butter, and beat at medium speed as the egg yolks are dropped in one at a time. Continue beating until the potato is mashed completely smooth.

3. Pipe through a large star pipe into cones or whirls on to a well-greased baking tray, and bake at 425°F (220°C, Gas No. 7) until attractively browned – 10–15 minutes.

Mashed Potato · Mixer

Serves 6

> 2 lb. (1 kg.) potatoes   5 tbs. hot milk
> 1–2 oz. (25–50 g.) butter   salt and pepper

One of the most important things about mixer mashed potatoes is that they should still be really hot when they reach the table. Hence a hand-held mixer which can be used in the saucepan is ideal, but it is necessary to warm the bowl and beaters very well first if using a mixer on a stand. Mash for the minimum time, quickly turn into a hot vegetable dish, and keep warm. A blender is not suitable for mashing potatoes as it forms a waxy purée rather than a fluffy mash.

1. Boil the potatoes in salted water until cooked.

2. Warm the milk and the butter together and pour on to the

potatoes in the saucepan or the mixer bowl, then beat at medium speed until they are light and fluffy. Season with pepper and extra salt if necessary.

3. Turn quickly into a warmed vegetable dish and serve.

Potato Crisps · Slicer/Shredder

potatoes   *salt*
deep fat for frying

1. Peel as many potatoes as needed, selecting those medium-sized ones which will have a neat oval cross-section, using the potato-peeling attachment to the mixer if available.

2. With the fine slicing disc or drum fitted into the slicer/shredder, slice the potatoes, taking care to arrange them in the chute and hold them with the pusher so as to slice them with the best cross-section. Catch the slices in a bowl of cold water.

3. Rinse the slices to remove the surface starch, soak for at least $\frac{1}{2}$ hour and rinse again. Drain off the water and dry well in a towel or absorbent paper.

4. Place the slices in a frying basket (in batches if necessary) and lower gently into deep fat which is very faintly smoking at 360°F (185°C). Cook for a few minutes (2–4 minutes) until crisp and golden – turning them about to ensure even colouring.

5. Lift out, sprinkle with salt and turn on to absorbent paper to drain. When cool they can be stored in an airtight tin.

Creamed or Puréed Spinach · Blender

Serves 3

1 *lb.* ($\frac{1}{2}$ *kg.*) *spinach*   2 *dsp. cream or spinach water*
$\frac{1}{2}$ *oz.* (15 *g.*) *butter*

1. Wash the spinach very thoroughly and chop roughly into about 1 in. pieces. Most stalks can be included, but any very rough ones must be discarded.

2. Cook the spinach in a minimum (less than $\frac{1}{2}$ in. (1 cm.)) of fiercely boiling salted water. Boil rapidly for 5–7 minutes.

3. Drain well, and put half into the blender, together with 1 dessertspoon of the cream, or spinach water. (A very powerful blender will take the whole quantity at once.) Blend at a fast speed, until the purée is quite smooth. With the less powerful blenders it may be necessary to stop and start several times, scraping down the sides with a plastic spatula each time. Alternatively, more liquid can be added, but this results in a rather sloppy purée.

4. Turn the purée into a small saucepan, and gently rewarm with the butter and the seasoning, meanwhile blending the remaining spinach.

Sweet and Sour Red Cabbage · Slicer/Shredder or Blender

Very good with goose, pork or any fatty meat. Serves 4

1 *small red cabbage*	1 *oz. (25 g.) demerara sugar*
1 *medium onion*	6 *tbs. vinegar*
1 *cooking apple*	*salt and pepper*
1 *oz. (25 g.) butter*	

1. Cut off the outside leaves of the cabbage and cut into four down the centre, so that the wedges of stalk can be removed.

2. Either slice the cabbage using the slicer/shredder with a plain slicing disc, or chop in the blender. In the latter case some of the cabbage is put in the jar, covered with water and the blender switched on at fast speed. The water is then drained off the chopped cabbage.

3. Peel the apples, core them and slice fairly thickly with a knife. Peel the onions and slice finely using the slicer/shredder.

4. Melt the butter in a heavy saucepan or casserole and put in a layer of cabbage, then apple and onion. Sprinkle with brown sugar, salt and pepper.

5. Repeat the layers until all the ingredients are used up, then pour the vinegar over.

6. Shut the lid tightly, using paper if necessary. Simmer over a low heat or cook in a moderate oven 350°F (180°C, Gas No. 4) until tender ($\frac{3}{4}$–1 hour).

Vichy Carrots · Slicer/Shredder

Serves 4

1 lb. ($\frac{1}{2}$ kg.) carrots   salt and pepper
1 oz. (25 g.) butter   chopped parsley for garnish
4 tbs. water

1. Wash and scrape the carrots.
2. With the thin slicing disc or drum fitted into the slicer/shredder, stand the carrots in the chute so that a neat round cross-section is cut. Slice at the slowest speed, pushing through firmly with the pusher.
3. Put the carrots in a saucepan or casserole together with the butter, water, and seasoning and shut the lid over a piece of paper to ensure it is very tight fitting.
4. Cook on a very low heat or in a moderate oven (around 375°F, 190°C, Gas No. 5) until tender ($\frac{3}{4}$–1 hour) stirring occasionally. By this time the water should have evaporated, but if not, cook with the lid off for a few minutes, until the liquor has disappeared.
5. Serve sprinkled with chopped parsley.

Coleslaw · Slicer/Shredder or Blender

This is primarily a salad mainly based on finely sliced cabbage, and to this can be added a number of other ingredients, according to taste. All the ingredients are bound together with mayonnaise or other dressing.

heart of a cabbage, preferably the white variety
1 teasp. salt
dressing

grated carrot (slicer/shredder)
chopped celery
1 oz. (25 g.) sultanas
1 oz. (25 g.) chopped nuts (blender)
chopped green pepper
parsley or chives, chopped (blender)
1 dessert apple, chopped but with the skin left on
chopped spring onion

optional

1. It is essential that the cabbage be crisp, so wash it and if it is at all limp put it in the refrigerator in the crisper tray, or in a plastic bag, for at least 2 hours. Drain well.

2. Cut the cabbage heart into four and slice the stalk from each section.

3. Slice the cabbage quarters into thin slices with the slicer/shredder, or if this is not available another method, though not so good, is to use the blender. Put the quarters one at a time into the blender and cover with cold water: switch to fast speed just long enough to chop the cabbage (about 10–20 seconds) and then strain, and drain till dry.

4. Mix the cabbage in a bowl with the selected salad additions; it is better not to include more than two or three at any one time. Sprinkle with salt.

5. Mix the Coleslaw with dressing according to taste. Coleslaw can be dressed with any salad dressing or mayonnaise (p. 87), or vinaigrette (p. 86), or the following dressing which is very pleasant with the cabbage. Mix well together.

4 tbs. mayonnaise
4 tbs. sour cream
2 teasp. chopped chives
A good sprinkling of black pepper

Stuffed Marrow

See p. 112.

8

Soufflés, Omelettes and Batters

Cheese Soufflé · Mixer (Hand-held Mixer best)

Serves 4

4 eggs (separated)
1½ oz. (40 g.) butter
1½ oz. (40 g.) plain flour
½ pt. (250 ml.) milk

4 oz. (100 g.) grated cheese
½ level teasp. salt, and pepper
1 level teasp. made mustard

1. Tie a greaseproof paper collar round a 2 pint (1 l.) china soufflé dish to stand 3 in. (8 cm.) above the rim and grease the dish and the collar well.
2. Light the oven at 400°F (200°C, Gas No. 6). Melt the butter in a saucepan, and stir in the flour. Continue cooking gently until the roux resembles white breadcrumbs.
3. Gradually add the milk, stirring vigorously with a wooden spoon, or beat with a hand-held mixer at medium speed, to ensure that the mixture is completely smooth. Bring to the boil and cook for a minute.
4. Remove from the heat, cool slightly, transfer to the mixer bowl if necessary, and add the cheese and seasonings. Then beat in the egg yolks, one at a time. Use medium speed and beat for 15 seconds between the addition of each egg yolk, to ensure that the mixture is smooth.
5. Whisk the egg whites at fast speed, to the soft peak stage.
6. Fold the egg whites into the cheese mixture very gently with a metal tablespoon and quickly turn into the prepared soufflé dish.
7. Bake at 400°F (200°C, Gas No. 6) for 25–30 minutes.

8. When well risen, set and brown, cut away the paper collar and serve immediately.

Smoked Haddock Soufflé · Mixer (Hand-held Mixer best)

Serves 5

½ lb. (200 g.) fillet of smoked haddock (or a little more if with bones)
½ pt. (250 ml.) milk
2 oz. (50 g.) butter

2 oz. (50 g.) plain flour
4 eggs (separated)
1 extra egg white if possible
pepper and salt if necessary

1. Well grease a 3 pint (1½ l.) soufflé dish and light the oven at 375°F (190°C, Gas No. 5).
2. Put the milk in a shallow pan, bring to the boil and put in the fish. Poach gently until tender (about 10 minutes).
3. Drain the milk from the fish, reserving it for the sauce, then remove all the skin and bones and flake the fish.
4. Melt the butter in a saucepan and stir in the flour, cooking the roux gently until it resembles fine breadcrumbs. Then slowly mix in the milk which has been used in cooking the haddock. This is best done with a hand-held mixer, but if this is not available a wooden spoon must be used.
5. Continue cooking until thick, then take off the heat and cool a little.
6. Add the egg yolks one at a time to the sauce, beating thoroughly at medium speed between each addition. Using a hand-held mixer this can be done in the saucepan, but otherwise the mixture must be transferred to the mixer bowl. Finally give the mixture at least ½ minute's beating.
7. Mix in the flaked fish using the mixer at its lowest speed, add pepper and salt if needed.
8. Whisk the egg whites at fast speed to soft peak stage.
9. Very gently fold the whites into the fish mixture, using a metal tablespoon, and transfer to the prepared soufflé dish.
10. Bake for 40 minutes until well risen and golden brown. Serve immediately.

Hot Chocolate Soufflé · Mixer (Hand-held Mixer best)

Serves 6–7

2 oz. (50 g.) *plain flour*	4 oz. (100 g.) *plain block chocolate*
2 oz. (50 g.) *butter*	2 oz. (50 g.) *caster sugar*
½ pt. (250 ml.) *milk*	6 eggs (*separated*)

1. Prepare a 2 pint (1 l.) soufflé dish by buttering well and dusting with caster sugar. Light the oven at 425°F (220°C, Gas No. 7).
2. Warm the milk in a saucepan or double boiler with the sugar, break the chocolate in and stir until it is dissolved.
3. Melt the butter in another pan, and stir in the flour, cooking gently until it resembles breadcrumbs.
4. Beat in the chocolate-milk using a wooden spoon (or a hand-held mixer can be used at medium speed) until the mixture is quite smooth and thick and leaves the side of the pan.
5. Pour into the mixer bowl, thus cooling slightly, and with the mixer at medium speed, beat in the egg yolks one at a time until a very smooth mixture results.
6. Whisk the egg whites at fast speed to soft peak stage.
7. Gently fold the egg whites into the chocolate mixture using a metal tablespoon, until the mixture is homogeneous.
8. Pour into the prepared soufflé dish and bake for 40 minutes.
9. Serve immediately, dusted with sugar and with chocolate sauce (p. 100).

Cold Chocolate Soufflé · Mixer (Hand-held Mixer best)

Serves 6

3 eggs (*separated*)	¼–½ pt. (125–250 ml.) *cream*
2 oz. (50 g.) *cocoa*	(*double or whipping*)
¼ pt. (125 ml.) *milk*	*few drops vanilla essence*
3 oz. (75 g.) *caster sugar*	*decoration: piped whipped*
4 level teasp. *gelatine*	*cream, chocolate vermicelli*
4 tbs. *white wine (or 2 tbs.*	*or grated plain chocolate*
water and 2 tbs. sherry)	

1. Prepare a $1\frac{1}{2}$ pint (750 ml.) soufflé dish by tying a greaseproof paper collar round it to stand 2 in. (5 cm.) above the top.

2. Put the egg yolks with the cocoa, sugar and the milk in a basin over a pan of boiling water.

3. Whisk the mixture well, using a hand-held mixer if available or a hand-operated whisk, until the mixture is quite thick. Be careful to scrape down the sides of the basin at intervals during this whisking, or the chocolate will stick. Remove from the heat when thick.

4. Put the gelatine with the wine into a small basin or cup and warm over hot water. Stir rapidly until the gelatine is all dissolved, and then add to the chocolate mixture while whisking.

5. Whip the cream in the mixer bowl at fast speed until light and frothy but not stiff (half-whipped stage).

6. When the chocolate mixture is cool, but not set, use the mixer at the slowest speed to fold it into the half-whipped cream and the vanilla.

7. Whisk the egg whites at fast speed to soft peak stage.

8. Switch off the mixer and fold the chocolate mixture into the egg whites with a metal tablespoon.

9. Pour into the prepared soufflé dish, and leave in a cool place to set.

10. When ready to serve, carefully remove the paper collar and decorate the soufflé with piped whipped cream and chocolate vermicelli or grated chocolate.

Lemon Soufflé Delight (Cold) · Mixer

Serves 8

3 (*medium sized*) *lemons*
8 *oz.* (200 *g.*) *caster sugar*
5 *eggs* (*separated*)
2 *oz.* (50 *g.*) *cornflour*
$1\frac{1}{2}$ *pt.* (750 *ml.*) *milk*
1 *oz.* (25 *g.*) *gelatine*
4 *tbs. double cream*

FOR DECORATION
$\frac{1}{4}$ *pt.* (125 *ml.*) *double cream*
$1\frac{1}{2}$ *oz.* (40 *g.*) *chopped pistachio nuts or almonds*
sugared violet petals or small pieces of glacé cherry

1. Prepare a 2 pint (1 l.) soufflé dish by tying a greaseproof paper collar round it, to stand 3 in. (8 cm.) above the top.

2. Grate the lemon rinds finely into the mixer bowl, and add the egg yolks, sugar, cornflour and sufficient of the milk to make a creamy paste. Mix at medium speed until the paste is quite smooth. The lemon rind can be chopped in the blender with the milk (p. 60).

3. Bring the remaining milk to the boil and pour it boiling into the mixer bowl while the beaters are working at medium speed.

4. Return the mixture to the pan, stir over a gentle heat until it boils and simmer for two minutes. Leave to cool.

5. Squeeze the juice from the lemons and measure. Make up to ¼ pint if necessary with bottled pure lemon juice (or water).

6. Melt the gelatine in some of the lemon juice in a basin over a pan of boiling water, stirring until all is dissolved.

7. When the gelatine is cool (but not setting) stir into the lemon mixture, together with all the lemon juice, and the double cream, half-whipped.

8. Whisk the egg whites at fast speed to soft peak stage. Then fold them lightly into the lemon mixture, using a metal tablespoon.

9. Pour the mixture into the prepared soufflé dish and leave to set.

10. Using the mixer whip the ¼ pint (125 ml.) double cream, at fast speed, until stiff, and ready for decoration.

11. When ready to serve, peel off the paper collar and spread some of the cream thinly round the upstanding edge of the soufflé. Cover the cream with chopped nuts.

12. Use the remaining cream to pipe rosettes round the top of the soufflé and decorate these with violet petals or tiny pieces of glacé cherry.

Orange Soufflé (Cold) · Mixer

Serves 4–5

3 *small eggs (separated)*	2 *tbs. boiling water*
2 *oz.* (50 g.) *caster sugar*	¼ *pt.* (125 ml.) *cream (preferably*
3 *oz.* (75 ml.) *frozen concentrated*	½ *double and* ½ *single cream)*
orange juice (undiluted)	or *whipped evaporated milk*

1 *or* 2 *tbs Cointreau*
1 *teasp. lemon juice*

3 *rounded teasp. gelatine*
($\frac{3}{8}$ *oz.* (10 *g.*))

1. Prepare a 5 in. (12 cm.) soufflé dish by tying a greaseproof paper collar round it to stand 2 in. (5 cm.) above the top.
2. Stir the gelatine in the boiling water until it is completely dissolved.
3. Put the egg yolks and the sugar into the mixer bowl and whisk at fast speed until they are thick, pale and creamy.
4. Continue whisking at fast speed and gradually add the thawed orange juice, the lemon juice and the Cointreau, a teaspoonful at a time.
5. Whisk the cream in a small bowl until it is at the half-whipped stage, then turn it into the orange mixture and fold in for the minimum time with the mixer running at its slowest.
6. Next fold in the dissolved gelatine by pouring in while the mixer is whisking very slowly.
7. Whisk the egg whites at fast speed to soft peak stage.
8. Using a metal tablespoon gently fold the egg whites into the orange mixture, then turn the mixture into the prepared soufflé dish, or into sundae bowls, and leave in a cool place to set.
9. Just before serving carefully remove the paper collar by easing with a knife dipped in warm water, and decorate as follows:
Cover the sides which rise above the top of the dish with chopped walnuts. Decorate the top with either mandarin orange segments or piped cream and cherry with angelica.

Orange and Wine Soufflé (Cold) · Mixer

Serves 8

$\frac{3}{4}$ *pt.* (375 *ml.*) *orange juice (tinned or reconstituted frozen juice can be used)*
$\frac{1}{4}$ *pt.* (125 *ml.*) *sweet white wine, or sherry*
4 *oz.* (100 *g.*) *sugar*

2 *tbs. lemon juice*
8 *oz.* (200 *ml.*) *double cream (or use* $\frac{1}{2}$ *evaporated milk)*
1 *oz.* (25 *g.*) *gelatine*
$\frac{1}{4}$ *pt.* (125 *ml.*) *boiling water*

1. Prepare a 2 pint (1 l.) soufflé dish by tying a greaseproof paper collar around to stand 2 in. (5 cm.) above the rim. Brush the inside of the dish and the collar lightly with oil.

2. Melt the gelatine in boiling water, stirring until it is completely dissolved.

3. Put the sugar, orange juice, lemon juice and wine in the large mixer bowl and whisking at medium speed gradually add the dissolved gelatine.

4. Stand the bowl in a cold place and leave until the jelly is on the point of setting – it then has the consistency of egg white.

5. Put the cream into another bowl and whisk at medium speed until half-whipped (that is aerated but not yet too stiff to fold in easily). Alternatively, whip by hand.

6. Whisk the jelly again, with the mixer running at fast speed, until it is very light and frothy. The whisk should leave a trail for a short while if lifted out.

7. Add the cream to the orange mixture, and fold in by running the mixer at its slowest speed for the minimum time necessary to fold the cream in completely.

8. Turn into the prepared soufflé dish and leave in a cool place to set – about 2 hours.

9. Just before serving decorate the top with chocolate vermicelli in a band around the edge, or with whipped cream and mandarin orange segments. Peel off the paper collar carefully, by easing with a warm knife.

Strawberry Soufflé (Cold) · Mixer (and Blender)

Serves 8

1 lb. (500 g.) hulled strawberries (reserve a few for decorating)	½ oz. (15 g.) gelatine
	2 tbs. boiling water
4 eggs (separated)	½ pt. (250 ml.) double cream
4 oz. (100 g.) caster sugar	red colouring

1. Prepare a 7 in. (17 cm.) soufflé dish by tying a greaseproof paper collar round it to stand 2½ in. (6 cm.) above the rim.

2. Blend the strawberries on slow speed until the fruit is completely puréed.

3. Put the egg yolks and sugar into the mixer bowl and whisk at fast speed until the mixture is pale, very thick and fluffy and a trail made by the whisk remains for a moment.

4. Melt the gelatine in the boiling water, stirring until it is completely dissolved.

5. Continue whisking while adding the fruit purée and also the dissolved gelatine. Leave until it is *beginning* to thicken as the gelatine sets.

6. Whisk the egg whites at fast speed to soft peak stage.

7. Half-whip the cream until it is thick, but not stiff.

8. When the strawberry mixture is on the point of setting fold in the cream with a metal tablespoon and then fold in the egg whites.

9. Pour into the soufflé dish and leave to set in a cool place.

10. When ready to serve, carefully remove the paper and decorate the soufflé with the few strawberries saved, cut in half if they are large. Whipped cream can also be used to decorate.

Omelettes · Blender (or Mixer)

The mixer or the blender can be used most successfully for beating up eggs to make omelettes, but the blender is superb if chopped ingredients are needed with the eggs. The traditional French dish often has the flavouring laid as a stuffing down the centre and the omelette folded over this. The blender-made omelette containing chopped ingredients does not achieve this, but the flavour can be excellent and the method is so quick and easy.

Plain Savoury Omelette

Serves 1

2 *eggs*	*salt and pepper*
1 *tbs. water*	$\frac{1}{2}$ *oz.* (15 *g.*) *butter*

1. Put all the ingredients into the blender and switch on at fast speed for a few seconds to break up the eggs. Alternatively, whisk in the mixer bowl at fast speed.
2. Heat the butter in an omelette pan until it just begins to smoke, then pour in the mixture.
3. Stir quickly with a fork until lightly set, then fold, allow to brown on the bottom and invert on to a hot serving dish.

Cheese Omelette

To the basic plain omelette mixture in the blender, add 1 oz. (25 g.) well-flavoured cheese, cut in rough chunks, and blend at fast speed until the cheese is chopped small. Cook as before.

Omelette Fines Herbes

Add to the basic plain omelette mixture in the blender some or all of these:

few sprigs of parsley

$\frac{1}{2}$ teasp. thyme leaves

6–7 marjoram leaves

few leaves of tarragon

few sprigs of chervil

Blend at fast speed until the herbs are just chopped. If blended too long the mixture will turn green in colour, but still be delicious. Cook as before.

Bacon Omelette

Fry one thin rasher of bacon until it is very crisp. Then put in the blender together with the other ingredients and blend at fast speed until the bacon is chopped small, but not too small. Cook as before.

Mushroom Omelette

Wash and fry 1–1$\frac{1}{2}$ oz. (25–40 g.) mushrooms in butter, then drop into the blender after the eggs have been broken up, as for a plain omelette. Blend for only a short time, just sufficient to cut the mushrooms roughly. Cook as before.

Sweet Soufflé Omelette · Mixer

Serves 2

4 eggs (*separated*)
1 oz. (25 g.) *caster sugar*
1 oz. (25 g.) *butter*

2 tbs. jam or other filling,
  e.g. stewed fruit with a
  minimum of juice, fruit purée,
  mashed strawberries or
  raspberries

1. Turn on the grill to heat.
2. Put the egg yolks and the sugar into the mixer bowl and whisk at fast speed until they are very pale and thick. The whisk should leave a trail over the mixture when lifted out.
3. Whisk the egg whites at fast speed to soft peak stage.
4. Using a metal tablespoon gently fold the stiff egg whites into the whisked yolks, until the two are completely amalgamated.
5. Meanwhile heat ½ oz. (15 g.) butter in an omelette pan and then pour in half the prepared mixture. Cook slowly and evenly until slightly browned underneath, half-cooked through and well risen.
6. Put under a hot grill and cook until lightly browned on top.
7. Turn the omelette on to sugared paper, press a line down the centre and fold in two along this line. Then reopen, spread with warm jam or warm fruit and refold.
8. Meanwhile heat the remaining butter in the pan and cook the second omelette.
9. Serve immediately, sprinkled with caster or icing sugar.

Surprise Soufflé Omelette

The mixture used in the above Sweet Soufflé Omelette can be utilised as in Baked Alaska (p. 165) to insulate icecream from the heat of the oven. Pile well-frozen icecream on a sponge cake or sponge flan and cover completely with the omelette mixture. Bake in a very hot oven 450°–475°F (230–240°C, Gas No. 9) for 3–4 minutes only, until lightly set and browned. Serve immediately.

Batters for Pancakes, Yorkshire Pudding and Fritters
Blender or Mixer

A basic batter makes all these dishes, and it is then cooked in a variety of ways. A mixer or blender is equally useful.

4 oz. (100 g.) plain flour
1 egg
½ pt. (250 ml.) milk (or milk and
  water) – use ¼ pt. (125 ml.)
  for fritters

¼ teasp. salt
(pepper for savoury dishes)

Blender Method
1. Put first the milk, and then the egg, the flour and the salt in the blender.
2. Blend at fast speed until the batter is quite smooth and has bubbles on top. Take care that all the flour becomes incorporated by scraping down the sides with a plastic spatula.

Mixer Method
1. Put the flour, salt and egg into the mixer bowl.
2. Add ¼ pint (125 ml.) of liquid and mix with the beaters running at medium speed until the batter is completely smooth (1–2 minutes) – then turn down to slow speed and mix in the remainder of the milk.

By either method the batter is now ready for use.

Pancakes
Makes 6–8 pancakes
1. Mix the batter as above and heat a knob of lard in a frying pan or omelette pan, until it is smoking and covers the base of the pan. Run a thin layer of the batter over the bottom of the pan, cook until browned underneath, then turn by tossing the pancake or turn with a palette knife. Cook until the second side is browned, then turn out.
a. *Sweet Pancakes.* Turn out on to sugared paper, sprinkle with lemon juice and caster sugar, roll up and serve with wedges of lemon. These are best eaten immediately.
b. *Savoury Pancakes.* Turn out on to plain paper, fill down the

centre with some savoury filling and roll the pancake round it. Serve with a savoury sauce such as tomato (p. 93). These can be kept hot much more successfully, or they can be filled, allowed to cool, and then rewarmed in a low oven, covered with foil or greaseproof paper.

Yorkshire Pudding

Serves 6

1. Heat about ½ oz. (15 g.) of lard or dripping in a large roasting tin, 8 in. × 10 in. (20 cm. × 25 cm.), in an oven at 400–425°F (200–220°C, Gas No. 6–7), until smoking hot. Alternatively a set of small tins can be used to make individual portions, putting a little fat in each.
2. Make the batter by one of the methods above, and pour into the roasting tin when the fat is hot. Return to the oven and cook until well browned, set and puffed-up – this will take 40–45 minutes for a large pudding and 20 minutes for the small ones.
3. Remove from the tins and serve immediately.

Fritters

Here the batter is used to coat other food, then it is fried in deep fat, and it must therefore be made thicker, only ¼ pint (125 ml.) of milk being used instead of ½ pint (250 ml.). Make in the mixer or blender exactly as before.

Dip the food to be fried in the batter, coating every part of it, and fry in deep fat which is just smoking, 360°F (185°C), until well-browned and the food is cooked through.

Food which is suitable for fritters includes: firm fruits such as apples, tinned pineapple, and bananas, already cooked meat such as corned beef, and luncheon meat, and fish. Fritters quickly spoil, losing their crispness, so serve immediately. Dust sweet fritters with sugar.

9

Hot Puddings

≈≈≈≈≈≈≈≈≈≈≈≈≈≈≈≈≈≈≈≈≈≈≈≈≈≈≈≈≈≈

(For other hot puddings see sections on soufflés, omelettes and batters, and on pastry)

Apple Soufflé · Mixer and Blender

Serves 4

1½ lb. (¾ kg.) cooking apples (makes 1 pt. (500 ml.) purée)	good pinch of ground cinnamon
3 oz. (75–100 g.) caster sugar	2 large eggs (separated)
rind and juice of ½ lemon	cherry and angelica for decoration

1. Light the oven at 350°F (180°C, Gas No. 4).
2. Peel and core the apples, stew them with a minimum of water until soft, then transfer to the blender, and blend at slow speed until quite smooth.
3. While still blending at slow speed add the egg yolks, sugar, cinnamon, and the juice and finely grated rind of half a lemon.
4. Whisk the egg whites at fastest speed to soft peak stage.
5. Gently pour the apple mixture from the blender down the side of the mixer bowl and, with a metal tablespoon, very carefully fold the apple and egg white together.
6. Pour into a well-greased 1½ pint (1 l.) pie dish or soufflé dish and bake in centre of oven for 30–40 minutes until golden and firm to the touch.
7. Decorate with cherry and angelica if desired and serve immediately with cream or pouring custard sauce.

Eve's Pudding · Mixer

Serves 7

Although traditionally made with apples this pudding is equally good with other fruit (rhubarb, blackcurrants, apricots etc.) in their place. More sugar may then be needed.

1½ *lb.* (¾ *kg.*) *cooking apples*	CAKE MIXTURE (see note
2 *oz.* (50 *g.*) *sugar*	below)
grated rind of ½ *lemon*	4 *oz.* (100 *g.*) *butter*
	4 *oz.* (100 *g.*) *caster sugar*
	2 *eggs*
	4 *oz.* (100 *g.*) *self-raising flour*

1. Light the oven at 375°F (190°C, Gas No. 5).
2. Peel the apples, slice them and put in a greased 3 pint (1½ l.) pie dish adding the sugar and grated lemon rind when half the apples are in the dish.
3. Make the cake topping as for Victoria Sandwich (p. 200) and spread over the top of the apples.
4. Bake until risen, brown and resilient to the touch, about one hour.
5. Dredge with caster sugar and serve with custard or cream.

Note: This recipe deliberately uses the Victoria Sandwich mixture as the cake topping, so that the pudding can be made at the same time as a sandwich cake, using a double batch of mixture. If however, only a pudding is required, 6 oz. (150 g.) of flour can be used instead of 4 oz. (100 g.), to give a slightly plainer mixture.

Fruit Crumble · Mixer

This family standby is so easily made with a mixer, but the maximum time is saved if two or three times the required amount of crumble topping is mixed and the extra stored in a covered container in the refrigerator. This will keep as long as the fat of which it is made would keep, several weeks at least, and can be hurried out to spread over fruit and produce a hot pudding at a moment's notice. Serves 4

1 *lb.* ($\frac{1}{2}$ *kg.) fruit – raw, stewed or tinned*	CRUMBLE MIXTURE
sugar as necessary	4 *oz.* (100 *g.) plain flour*
	3 *oz.* (75 *g.) butter*
	2 *oz.* (50 *g.) sugar*

1. Light the oven at 375°F (190°C, Gas No. 5).
2. Prepare the fruit if raw (peel and slice apples, stone plums, etc.).
3. Put the fruit in an ovenproof dish, adding sufficient sugar to sweeten it. Drain tinned fruit.
4. Put the flour, butter and sugar in the mixer bowl and mix at slow speed until the fat is rubbed in. Do not continue so long that the ingredients amalgamate and become sticky.
5. Spread the crumble mixture over the fruit and bake in the oven for 35–45 minutes until the fruit is cooked and the crumble golden brown. This is a very good-tempered pudding which does not seem to come to much harm if put in with other food at higher temperature.
6. Serve with custard or cream.

Great Grandmother's Christmas Pudding · Blender and Mixer

This Victorian recipe is the English Christmas pudding at its best, and it is one that improves with keeping, even from one year to the next. Makes 3 puddings, e.g. 1 of 3 lb. (1500 g.), 1 of 2½ lb. (1250 g.), 1 of 1½ lb. (750 g.) (Metric measures give smaller puddings.)

1¼ *lb.* (500 *g.) raisins*	6 *oz.* (150 *g.) cooking apples*
1 *lb.* (400 *g.) sultanas*	*rind of half a lemon, grated*
1 *lb.* (400 *g.) currants*	*rind of half an orange, grated*
¼ *lb.* (100 *g.) moist brown sugar*	¼ *pt.* (125 *ml.) brandy (optional)*
¼ *lb.* (100 *g.) sweet almonds*	6 *oz.* (150 *g.) self-raising flour*
¼ *lb.* (100 *g.) chopped mixed peel*	10 *oz.* (250 *g.) breadcrumbs*
½ *nutmeg (or 1 rounded*	(p. 60)
teasp. grated nutmeg)	6 *eggs*
1½ *medium carrots*	1 *lb.* (400 *g.) suet, chopped*

1. Peel the carrots, cut roughly into 1 in. (2 cm.) lengths and chop finely in the blender at fast speed by dropping through the hole in the lid. Put into the mixer bowl.

2. Peel and core the apples and drop the quarters through the hole in the lid and blend at fast speed. Add the almonds and chop for a few seconds, so that the pieces are still quite large. Transfer the apples and nuts to the mixer bowl.

3. Add all the other dry ingredients to the mixer bowl, including the nutmeg, grated finely, and the suet, chopped. If packet suet is used this is ready prepared, but suet from the butcher must have all the stringy portions removed and the fat chopped. Because of the high proportion of suet in this recipe, it is impossible to chop it all in the blender with the flour and the breadcrumbs. However, some of the suet can be dropped on to the fast revolving blades, alternately with the bread and the flour, so that only a small part is left to be chopped with a sharp knife on a board.

4. Break up the eggs and mix with the brandy. Mix them into the dry ingredients at slow speed.

5. Turn the mixture into greased pudding basins; it is often an advantage to make puddings of differing sizes to serve on varying occasions. Cover tightly with greased foil or greaseproof paper and steam for 6 hours.

6. Steam a further 2 hours on the day of serving.

7. Turn out and sprinkle with caster sugar or flame with brandy. Serve with brandy or rum butter (p. 101) or vanilla sauce (p. 97).

Norwegian Apple Cake · Mixer (and Slicer/Shredder)

A versatile recipe which makes either a pudding or a teatime cake. Bake, and serve hot with cream for lunch, then cut what is left over into squares, sprinkle fresh with caster sugar and serve for tea. Serves 12 as pudding or makes 18 square cakes.

2 eggs	¼ pt. (125 ml.) creamy milk or
9 oz. (225 g.) caster sugar	top of the milk or evaporated
4 oz. (100 g.) butter	milk
	6½ oz. (170 g.) plain flour

136

| 2 rounded teasp. baking | 4 large cooking apples |
| powder | (about 1½ lb. 700 g.) |

1. Light the oven at 400°F (200°C, Gas No. 6).
2. Peel, core and quarter the apples, then slice either by hand with a sharp knife, or use the coarsest slicer on the slicer/shredder attachment at medium speed. It is possible to obtain neater and slightly thicker slices by hand, which can be arranged in neat rows over the cake, but the fine apple slices obtained from the machine are perfectly acceptable, and much quicker to prepare.
3. Put the eggs and 8 oz. (200 g.) sugar into the mixer bowl, and whisk at fastest speed until they are very thick and pale and the whisk leaves a trail if it is lifted out.
4. Melt the butter in a pan with the milk and bring to the boil. Pour it boiling on to the eggs and sugar in the mixing bowl, gradually adding it whilst whisking at medium speed.
5. Sift the flour and baking powder together, then fold into the batter with the mixer running at the slowest speed, just until all the pockets of flour are mixed in, then switch off immediately.
6. Butter and flour a roasting tin, and pour the mixture in.
7. Arrange the sliced apples all over the surface of the mixture and sprinkle with 1 oz. (25 g.) caster sugar.
8. Bake for 20–25 minutes until it is risen, golden brown and firm to the touch in the centre.
9. Serve hot, or cool before cutting into slices for tea.

VARIATIONS

The apple in this recipe can be replaced with many suitable fruits drained of juice:
    Rhubarb
    Cooked dried or fresh apricots
    Plums – cut in half and stoned
    Tinned pineapple, peaches or apricots
All these, however, are 'wetter' than apple and give a soggier cake which is more suitable as a pudding than at teatime.

Queen of Pineapple Puddings · Mixer and Blender

Serves 8

1 *large tin of pineapple pieces*	3 *eggs (separated)*
6 *sponge cakes or a jam swiss roll*	3 *oz. (75 g.) butter*
	$\frac{1}{2}$ *pt. (250 ml.) milk*
1 *oz. (25 g.) cornflour*	4 *oz. (100 g.) caster sugar*

1. Light the oven at 275°F (140°C, Gas No. 1).
2. Break the sponge cakes in pieces or slice the swiss roll, and place in a shallow ovenproof dish, or a pie dish.
3. Cover with a layer of pineapple, together with a little juice. Reserve $\frac{1}{2}$ pint (250 ml.) of the remaining juice to make the custard.
4. Put the egg yolks in the blender with the cornflour and the milk and blend at fast speed for a few seconds. Continue at fast speed while gradually pouring in the $\frac{1}{2}$ pint (250 ml.) of pineapple juice through the hole in the lid.
5. Melt the butter in a saucepan and pour in the blended mixture; stir thoroughly while cooking until thickened, but do not boil. Pour over the pineapple and sponge in the dish.
6. Whisk egg whites at fast speed to soft peak stage. Continue whisking while adding rapidly 3 oz. (75 g.) caster sugar, a teaspoonful at a time.
7. Pile the meringue over the pineapple custard, taking care to come right to the edge of the dish. Sift the remaining ounce (25 g.) of sugar over the meringue.
8. Bake in the oven for about 1 hour until the meringue is golden brown.

Spicy Apple Pudding · Mixer

Serves 6

4 *oz. (100 g.) butter (softened)*	2 *medium or 1 very large apple*
4 *oz. (100 g.) caster sugar*	
6 *oz. (150 g.) self-raising flour*	4 *tbs. mincemeat*
2 *eggs*	

1. Half-fill the bottom of the steamer with water and heat up to boiling. Grease a $2\frac{1}{2}$–3 pint ($1\frac{1}{2}$ l.) pudding basin.
2. Prepare the apple and chop it fairly coarsely.
3. Put the butter and the sugar in the mixer bowl and cream at medium speed until the mixture is very light and fluffy.
4. Add the eggs one at a time, and continue beating until they are completely incorporated.
5. Sift in the flour, add the apple and mincemeat and fold all together with the mixer at very slow speed.
6. Turn into the prepared basin, cover with greased paper or foil and place in the steamer to cook for 2–$2\frac{1}{2}$ hours.
7. Turn out, sift with caster sugar and serve with pouring custard or cream.

Steamed Cake Puddings · Mixer

For these puddings a basic plain cake mixture is usually flavoured or has various dried fruits added. This is then steamed and served with a sauce to suit the pudding. Custard or vanilla sauce (p. 97) or sabayon sauce (p. 102) go well with any pudding of this kind. Serves 5

BASIC PLAIN MIXTURE
6 oz. (150 g.) self-raising flour
3 oz. (75 g.) butter
2–3 oz. (50–75 g.) sugar
grated rind of $\frac{1}{2}$ lemon
1 egg
5 tbs. ($5\frac{1}{2}$ tbs.) milk

AND FOR MIXED FRUIT
PUDDING
$1\frac{1}{2}$ oz. (40 g.) currants
$1\frac{1}{2}$ oz. (40 g.) sultanas
1 oz. (25 g.) chopped mixed peel

FOR CURRANT PUDDING
3 oz. (75 g.) currants
FOR SULTANA PUDDING
3 oz. (75 g.) sultanas
FOR DATE PUDDING
3 oz. (75 g.) chopped dates
FOR COCONUT PUDDING
3 oz. (75 g.) desiccated coconut
FOR LEMON or ORANGE
PUDDING (serve with lemon
or orange sauce)
grated rind of 1 lemon or
  orange

FOR JAM PUDDING
3 tbs. jam, put in the bottom
of the pudding basin then

*covered with the basic plain
mixture as above (serve
with jam sauce)*

1. Half-fill the bottom of the steamer with water and heat up to boiling. Grease a 1½ pint (750 ml.) pudding basin.
2. Put the flour, sugar and butter into the mixer bowl and, with the mixer at slow speed, rub the fat into the flour until the mixture resembles breadcrumbs.
3. Add the lemon rind and any fruit, etc.
4. Mix the egg with the milk, and add to the pudding mixture, using the mixer at its slowest speed. The mixture should be of medium to soft dropping consistency, and if it does not seem soft enough add a little more milk.
5. Turn into the prepared basin, cover well with greased grease-proof paper or foil, and steam for 2½–3 hours.
6. Turn out, sprinkle with sugar and serve with an appropriate sauce.

Steamed Sponge Pudding · Mixer

Serves 6

8 oz. (200 g.) *self-raising flour*
pinch of salt
4 oz. (100 g.) *butter (softened)*
3 oz. (75 g.) *sugar*

1 *egg*
6–7 tbs. (6–6½ tbs.) *of milk,*
sufficient to give a medium
dropping consistency

1. Half-fill the bottom of the steamer with water and heat to boiling. Grease a 2 pint (1 l.) pudding basin.
2. Put the flour, salt and butter, cut into rough lumps, into the mixer bowl and mix at slow speed to rub the fat into the flour, until the whole resembles breadcrumbs.
3. Add the sugar, and any fruit or flavourings, and the egg and milk and mix at the slowest speed until everything is incorporated.
4. Turn into the basin, cover with foil or greaseproof paper and steam 2½–3 hours. Serve with jam sauce or custard.

The above recipe is the basic plain pudding, but usually additions are made to give a more interesting pudding. Here are a few suggestions.

Steamed Jam or Syrup Sponge
Put a little jam or syrup at the bottom of the basin before putting in the sponge mixture. When turned out the pudding has a jammy or syrupy top. Serve with jam or syrup sauce.

Steamed Mixed Fruit Pudding
Add to the basic mixture:

2 oz. (50 g.) currants	1 oz. (25 g.) chopped mixed peel
2 oz. (50 g.) sultanas	grated rind of ½ lemon

Serve with custard or vanilla sauce (p. 97).

Steamed Currant Pudding
Add to the basic mixture:

4 oz. (100 g.) currants	grated rind of ½ lemon

Serve with custard.

Steamed Sultana Pudding
Add 4 oz. (100 g.) sultanas to the basic mixture. Serve with custard.

Steamed Date Pudding
Add 5 oz. (125 g.) chopped dates to the basic mixture. If stoned cooking dates are used these may be chopped in the blender. Put 2 oz. (50 g.) of the weighed flour into the jar, switch on at medium speed, and drop the pieces of date in through the hole in the lid. 2 oz. (50 g.) less flour must then be used for rubbing with the fat.

Serve with vanilla sauce (p. 97) to which a teaspoonful of grated nutmeg may be stirred in.

Swiss Apple Pudding · Blender

The nutmeg in this recipe gives an unusual and delicious nutty flavour. The pudding can be prepared overnight and put in the oven next day. Serves 6

2 lb. (1 kg.) cooking apples
4 oz. (100 g.) suet (grated or piece of butcher's suet)
about 2 oz. (50 g.) sugar

10 oz. (250 g.) crustless white bread (or breadcrumbs p. 60)
3 oz. (75 g.) demerara sugar
grated nutmeg

1. Light oven 325°F (160°C, Gas No. 3). Grease a 2 pint pie dish.
2. Peel, core, slice and stew the apples until tender with a little water and sufficient sugar to sweeten them. If they are rather tasteless a little thinly peeled lemon rind can be stewed with them to give more flavour.
3. Switch blender on at fast speed and through the hole in the lid drop alternately pieces of bread (approx. 1 in. (3 cm.) cubes) and pieces of suet (if butcher's suet is being used). Care must be taken to prevent the suet from becoming sticky, so it must be chopped with sufficient bread. Pour all the breadcrumbs and suet into a bowl and mix well together. In most blenders this must be done in several batches. If packet suet is being used, mix it with the breadcrumbs at this stage.
4. Put a layer of breadcrumbs and suet in the bottom of the pie dish, sprinkle with demerara and shake grated nutmeg over *very liberally*. Cover with a layer of stewed apple.
5. Repeat the layers of: breadcrumbs and suet, demerara sugar, grated nutmeg, stewed apple as many times as necessary, finishing with a thicker layer of breadcrumbs, suet and nutmeg (no sugar).
6. Bake for about 1–1¼ hours until the top is crisp and golden brown.
7. Serve with cream.

Upside-down Pudding · Mixer

This is a popular sweet, which can be made quickly for the family, but if more care is taken in the appearance of the fruit, it is very good for a festive occasion.

A toffee layer is run into the bottom of a cake tin, fruit is set in this, and a cake layer baked on top. When served the tin is turned upside-down on to a dish: the fruit decorates the top and the toffee forms a sauce. Serves 6–8

TOFFEE MIXTURE
2 oz. (50 g.) butter

4 oz. (100 g.) brown sugar
2 tbs. fruit juice

FRUIT
Approx. 1 lb. (400 g.) tinned or fresh fruit, stewed, e.g. apricots, peaches, pineapple, pears. Tinned or glacé cherries can be used with the other fruit to give a colourful pattern. More homely fruits such as lightly stewed apples or rhubarb are equally successful, although they do not look quite so attractive.

CAKE MIXTURE – or Victoria
Sandwich mixture (p. 200)
can be used
4 oz. (100 g.) butter (softened)

4 oz. (100 g.) caster sugar
2 eggs
6 oz. (150 g.) self-raising flour
1 tbs. milk

1. Grease a 7 in. or 8 in. (18 cm.) round or square cake tin. Light oven at 375°F (190°C, Gas No. 5).
2. Make the toffee by melting the butter in a small saucepan and stirring in the fruit juice and the sugar. Boil for a few minutes until a good brown colour, but do not allow it to darken to the point of burning.
3. Pour the toffee into the cake tin, and then arrange the well-drained fruit in it, in an attractive pattern.
4. Cream the butter and sugar at medium speed until light and fluffy.
5. Add the eggs, one at a time, while continuing to beat at medium speed.
6. Turn the mixer to slow speed just long enough to fold in the sifted flour and the milk.
7. Turn into the cake tin on top of the fruit and bake for about 35–40 minutes until well risen, firm and resilient to the touch.

8. Loosen the sides with a knife and immediately turn upside-down on to a warm dish. Serve with a fruit sauce, perhaps made with the remaining juice from the fruit, thickened with arrowroot or cornflour.

Easy Upside-down Pudding · Mixer

Serves 5

1 oz. (25 g.) *butter (softened)*	2 *eggs*
1 oz. (25 g.) *soft, light brown*	3 oz. (75 g.) *caster sugar*
sugar	3 oz. (75 g.) *plain flour*
fruit, tinned, fresh or stewed	

1. Light oven at 350°F (180°C, Gas No. 4).
2. Mix the butter and brown sugar together in a small basin and spread round a 2 pint (1 l.) ovenproof dish. (A soufflé dish, cake tin or casserole.)
3. Arrange the fruit either over the bottom or the bottom and sides of the dish. Tinned fruit such as apricot halves, peach slices, pineapple rings with glacé cherries look very good, or sliced apples, drained stewed blackcurrants or stewed or tinned pears with glacé cherries, but be imaginative and try other combinations.
4. Whisk the eggs and caster sugar at fast speed until they are very thick and creamy. The whisk should leave a trail for a moment when lifted out.
5. Sift the flour over the surface of the mixture and fold in very gently with a metal tablespoon.
6. Pour the sponge mixture over the top of the fruit and bake until well risen, golden brown and resilient to the touch. About 40–50 minutes. Loosen the sides with a knife.
7. Carry to the table on a dish and turn the pudding upside-down on to it. Serve with cream.

10

Cold Sweets

෨෬෨෬෨෬෨෬෨෬෨෬෨෬෨෬෨෬෨෬෨෬෨෬෨෬෨෬෨෬

(For other cold puddings see sections on icecream and water ices, pastry and dishes using pastry and soufflés, omelettes and batters)

Apple Snow · Blender and Mixer

Serves 5

1½ *lb.* (¾ *kg.) cooking apples*	*rind and juice of* ½–1 *lemon*
¼ *pt.* (125 *ml.) water*	*glacé cherries and angelica*
2 *oz.* (50 *g.) sugar*	*for decoration*
2 *egg whites*	

1. Peel and core the apples and stew gently with the water and sugar until they are soft.
2. Put the apples, lemon juice and grated lemon rind into the blender and blend at medium speed, until the apples are completely smooth, with the consistency of double cream.
3. Whisk the egg whites at fast speed to soft peak stage.
4. Fold the apple purée into the egg white either by pouring on to the whisk as it runs at the *slowest* speed, or by using a metal tablespoon.
5. Serve in individual sundae dishes, decorated with glacé cherries and angelica.

More Substantial Alternative
Slice sponge cakes into a dish, soak them with egg custard, and then top with the apple snow mixture.

145

Blackberry and Apple Snow · Blender or Colander/Sieve and Mixer

Serves 5

1 lb. (500 g.) cooking apples
½ lb. (250 g.) blackberries
¼ pt. (125 ml.) water

2 oz. (50 g.) sugar
2 egg whites

Proceed as for the apple snow recipe, but the blackberries and apple must be passed through a nylon strainer to remove the pips after blending, or a colander/sieve attachment could be used instead of a blender. Then the sugar should be stirred in and the blackberry purée folded into the stiffly beaten egg whites as in apple snow.

Banana Snow · Blender and Mixer

Serves 6

6 bananas
2 tbs. caster sugar
2 teasp. lemon juice
½ pt. (250 ml.) plain yoghourt
(2 cartons)

¼ pt. (125 ml.) double cream
3 egg whites
chopped roasted almonds for
  decoration

1. Skin and halve the bananas and put in the blender, together with the lemon juice, sugar, yoghourt and cream, and blend at medium speed for a few seconds until the bananas are quite puréed.
2. Whisk the egg whites at fast speed to soft peak stage.
3. Pour the banana mixture carefully down the side of the bowl and fold gently into the egg whites, using a metal tablespoon.
4. Pour into individual sundae dishes and serve sprinkled with chopped, roasted almonds.

Caledonian Cream · Mixer

Serves 4

A simple sweet, rich and delicious.

½ pt. (250 ml.) double cream
2 teasp. sugar
2 teasp. lemon juice
2 tbs. dark marmalade with
  plenty of peel

1½ tbs. whisky
chopped walnuts or mimosa
  balls and angelica for
  decoration

1. Put the cream, sugar and lemon juice into the mixer bowl and whisk at fast speed until the mixture is stiff, taking care not to over-mix and make the cream 'buttery'.
2. When stiff, turn the mixer to the slowest speed and fold in the whisky and the marmalade.
3. Serve in individual sundae glasses, decorate with chopped walnuts, or mimosa balls and angelica. As the cream is very rich, it goes well with sponge finger biscuits or Cats' Tongues (p. 128).

Coffee Mousse · Blender and Mixer

Serves 6

2 rounded teasp. instant
  coffee power
¾ pt. (375 ml.) boiling water
¼ pt. (125 ml.) milk
3 eggs (separated)

2 oz. (50 g.) sugar
½ oz. (15 g.) gelatine (1 level tbs)
cream and chopped walnuts
  to decorate

1. Blend the coffee, milk, egg yolks and sugar at medium speed until mixed thoroughly.
2. Continue blending, and pour the ¾ pint (375 ml.) of boiling water through the hole in the lid.
3. Turn into a saucepan and cook gently until it thickens and coats the back of the spoon. If overcooked and the mixture curdles, then

return to the blender and blend at maximum speed while adding the gelatine.

4. Dissolve the gelatine in a further 2 tablespoons of boiling water, and when the coffee mixture is a little cooled stir the two together.

5. Allow the liquid to become cold and on the point of setting, then whisk the egg whites at fast speed to soft peak stage. Pour the coffee mixture down the side of the bowl and fold into the egg whites with a metal spoon until they are fully mixed.

6. Pour into a bowl or individual dishes and leave in a cool place to set.

7. Serve either with pouring cream, or with double cream whipped stiff and piped on to the mousse. Decorate with chopped walnuts.

Fruit Creams · Blender or Colander/Sieve (and Mixer)

Serves 5–6

This luxury sweet can be made from any well-flavoured fruit, stewed, tinned or frozen. If stewed very little water must be used in the cooking, and if tinned, some of the syrup must be discarded to ensure making a good, thick purée. The berry fruits are particularly good, but they must be sieved to remove the pips, and for this reason it is better to use a colander/sieve to purée them, rather than a blender.

½ pt. (250 ml.) fruit purée *colouring if necessary*
sugar as necessary to sweeten *pieces of fruit – kept back*
½ pt. (250 ml.) whipping or *when making the purée,*
  double cream *angelica and whipped cream*
½ oz. (15 g.) gelatine *for decoration*
2 tbs. fruit juice or water

1. Stew the fruit, if necessary using a little water.
2. Make the fruit purée either by using the colander/sieve attachment to the mixer or by blending the fruit (with any stones removed), at fast speed until quite smooth. Any sugar necessary to

sweeten may be added at this stage. Berry fruits which have been blended must now be passed through a strainer to remove the pips.

3. Meanwhile dissolve the gelatine in 2 tablespoons fruit juice or water by standing it in a cup in a saucepan of boiling water.

4. Half-whip the cream so that it is aerated but not stiff. This can be done using the mixer at fast speed.

5. Rapidly stir the dissolved gelatine into the fruit purée – in the blender jar if this has been used. Add colouring if necessary.

6. Pour the fruit mixture over the whipped cream and fold the two together, either with a metal tablespoon or by using the mixer at slowest speed.

7. Pour into one large, or several small moulds, or into a glass dish, and leave in a cool place to set.

8. Turn out and decorate with pieces of fruit, angelica and whipped cream.

Fruit Fool · Blender (and Mixer)

1–1½ lb. (½–¾ kg.) fruit	1 rounded tbs. custard powder
2–3 tbs. water	¼ pt. (125 ml.) double or single
sugar to sweeten	cream
½ pt. (250 ml.) milk	few drops colouring

1. If using fresh fruit, prepare it, wash it, and stew till soft with a minimum of water, and enough sugar to sweeten it. Remove any stones after cooking. If using tinned fruit, drain off any syrup.

2. Put the fruit in the blender, and run at medium speed, until the purée is quite smooth. If the fruit being used has pips (e.g. blackberries, gooseberries, raspberries) it must be passed through a nylon strainer at this stage, to remove the pieces of pip which always remain after blending. Leave fruit purée in the blender to cool.

3. Make a thick custard with ½ pint (250 ml.) milk and 1 rounded tablespoon of custard powder.

4. When the custard and the fruit are cool, add the custard to the

blender, and run at medium speed for a short while, until the mixture is homogeneous. At this stage taste for sweetness and add more sugar if necessary. Add a little appropriate colouring if necessary.
5. Finally add the cream and blend in at medium speed for a short while. If liked, double cream can be whipped stiffly in the mixer bowl, and the fruit and custard mixture can be gently folded in, using a metal tablespoon.

Lemon Flummery · Blender and Mixer

This sweet is very popular and the quantities could easily be doubled or trebled to serve at a party. Serves 5

½ pt. (250 ml.) water
¾ oz. (20 g.) butter
1 large lemon
1 oz. (25 g.) plain flour
4 oz. (100 g.) caster sugar

2 eggs (separated)
4 digestive biscuits (optional)
cherries and angelica for
 decoration

1. Thinly slice the yellow rind from the lemon and put in the blender with the water, and blend at fast speed until the lemon is as finely chopped as it would be from a fine grater. Bring the water to the boil with the lemon rind and the butter.
2. Put the flour and sugar into the blender and, with the blender at medium speed, pour on the hot liquid through the hole in the lid.
3. When this mixture is quite smooth, add the egg yolks one at a time and blend at fast speed for a few seconds.
4. Return to the saucepan and bring the mixture slowly to the boil, stirring well. Simmer gently for 10 minutes. Add the lemon juice.
5. Whisk egg whites at fast speed to soft peak stage.
6. Fold the lemon mixture very gently into the egg whites with a metal tablespoon and chill the mixture.
7. Just before serving, fold in the crushed biscuits and decorate with cherries and angelica.

Lemon Syllabub · Mixer

This mixture will stay stiff for two days, although it is best eaten on the day of making. Serves 6–10

1 *lemon*	3 *oz. (75 g.) caster sugar*
4–6 *oz.* (100–150 *ml.*) *white wine*	½ *pt.* (250 *ml.*) *double cream*

1. Grate the lemon rind very finely and squeeze the juice.
2. Soak the rind in the juice and the wine overnight (or for several hours).
3. Add the sugar and the cream and place all in the mixer bowl.
4. Whisk at fast speed, until the mixture will stand in peaks (usually 2–4 minutes).
5. Turn into a glass serving dish – or preferably into individual serving dishes and serve chilled from the refrigerator.

Mandarin Whip · Mixer (and Blender)

Serves 6

1 *tin of mandarin oranges* (11 *oz.* (320 *g.*) *size*)	1 *small tin of evaporated milk* (¼ *pt.* (125 *ml.*))
1 *packet orange jelly, sufficient to make* 1 *pt.* (500 *ml.*)	*boiling water – about* ¼ *pt.* (125 *ml.*)

1. Add about ¼ pint (125 ml.) of boiling water to the jelly (sufficient to bring the volume to ½ pint (250 ml.)). Stir until dissolved. For quickness this can be done in the blender at fast speed.
2. Mix in ¼ pint (125 ml.) of syrup from the tinned fruit, and put in a cool place (refrigerator) until almost at setting point. The jelly then has the consistency of egg whites.
3. Put in the mixer bowl, start whisking at fast speed and while doing so pour on the chilled evaporated milk in a slow stream. Continue whisking until the mixture is thick and creamy, and the whisk leaves a trail when lifted out. This may well take 10 minutes.
4. Add the mandarins reserving a few for decoration. These can be

whisked in during the last few minutes of whisking the jelly, in which case they are partially broken up, or they can be cut in half and folded in with a metal tablespoon if they are preferred in large pieces, in which case they will tend to sink to the bottom of the bowl.

5. Pour into a large bowl or individual dishes, and when set decorate with the reserved mandarins.

VARIATIONS ON MANDARIN WHIP

This recipe can be varied in a number of ways which are all very popular, especially with children.

Fresh Orange Whip
Cut the peel and pith from two fresh oranges, and cut them into small segments then substitute them for the mandarins in the above recipe. Extra water must be used in place of the mandarin syrup.

Pineapple Whip
Substitute a small tin of pineapple pieces and a pineapple jelly.

Raspberry Whip
Substitute a raspberry jelly and a tin of raspberries, drain the raspberries well and do not use more than $\frac{1}{4}$ pint (125 ml.) of juice.

Strawberry Whip
As raspberry whip but use a small tin of strawberries and a strawberry jelly.

Banana and Lemon Whip
Use a lemon jelly and water to make up to $\frac{3}{4}$ pint (375 ml.). Whip in $\frac{1}{4}$ pint (125 ml.) of evaporated milk, and when light and frothy, fold in with a metal spoon 2–3 sliced bananas.

Pavlova · Mixer

A meringue flan case which can be filled in a great variety of delicious
ways and make a very festive sweet. Serves 6–8.

MERINGUE CASE
4 *egg whites*
8 *oz. (250 g.) caster sugar*
1 *teasp. good quality vinegar*
½ *teasp. vanilla essence*
3 *level teasp. cornflour*

FILLING
¼ *pt. (125 ml.) double cream*
¼ *pt. (125 ml.) single cream*
fruit as desired, fresh or
   tinned or stewed, drained

1. Light the oven at 225°F (110°C, Gas No. ¼).
2. Cover a baking sheet with greaseproof paper, and make a 7 in.
(17 cm.) circle on it by drawing round a cake tin or plate with a
pencil. Brush thoroughly, but lightly, with oil. Alternatively use
silicone-treated baking paper.
3. Whisk the egg whites at the fastest speed to soft peak stage, then,
while the machine is continuously working, beat in the sugar,
adding it rapidly, a teaspoonful at a time.
4. When all the sugar is added and the meringue mixture is stiff
and glossy, quickly fold in the vinegar, vanilla and sifted cornflour.
5. Use some of the meringue mixture to cover the circle drawn on
the baking sheet, making a floor to the case about ½ in. (1 cm.) thick.
6. Put the remaining meringue in a large nylon piping bag fitted
with a large star pipe, and use it to pipe an edge to the meringue
ring. Pipe another ring of stars on top of the first to build up a wall
to the flan.
7. Put the Pavlova case in the oven and cook for about 1½ hours until
the meringue is crisp on the outside and like a marshmallow inside.
8. Cool in the oven with the door open, then very carefully remove
the paper and place on the flat serving dish.
9. Fill with almost any fruit, provided it is well drained. Fresh or
frozen strawberries or raspberries are very good and these can be
mixed with the whipped cream. Alternatively a layer of well-drained
tinned fruit (peaches, apricots, strawberries, mandarins, pineapple)

can cover the meringue floor and then the whipped cream is piled on top. In each case a little fruit should be reserved to decorate on top of the cream.

Stewed fruit such as dried apricots, rhubarb or apple can be used in a similar way and equally well. The tart fruits go especially well with the sweetness of the meringue.

Prune Mould · Blender or Colander/Sieve

Serves 5

	to make	peeled rind of ½ lemon
¾ lb. (375 g.) prunes	1 pt.	4 level teasp. gelatine
½ pt. (250 ml.) water	(500 ml.)	2 tbs. boiling water
2 oz. (50 g.) sugar	of prune purée	cream to decorate

1. Soak the prunes overnight in the water.
2. Add the sugar and the lemon rind and stew gently until the prunes are quite tender.
3. Allow to cool, and then stone the prunes if the blender is to be used.
4. Make the prune purée either by rubbing through the sieve attachment to the mixer, or by putting pitted prunes and juice into the blender jar and blending at fast speed.
5. Meanwhile dissolve the gelatine in the boiling water, and stir into the sieved purée or add to the blender while it is switched on at fast speed.
6. Pour into individual moulds, a large mould or a glass dish, and leave in a cool place to set.
7. Turn out if necessary, and decorate with whipped cream. Alternatively serve with pouring cream.

Apricot Mould (using dried apricots)
Follow exactly the recipe for prune mould, using dried apricots instead of prunes, and checking that 1 pint (500 ml.) of purée is made.

Sponge Fruit Flan · Mixer

The sponge mixture in this recipe lends itself to being made in double quantities, the second portion being used to make a sponge cake (using a 7 in. (17 cm.) cake tin) or a swiss roll (p. 195). Serves 6

SPONGE FLAN CASE

2 eggs

2 oz. (50 g.) caster sugar

2 oz. (50 g.) plain flour – or slightly less

FRUIT FILLING

¾ lb. (375 g.) fresh fruit or 1 lb. (500 g.) tin of fruit

¼ pt. (125 ml.) fruit juice cream, whipped or pouring, for serving

1½ level teasp. gelatine or 1 rounded teasp. arrowroot (the arrowroot glaze is quicker and easier to do, but probably not quite so attractive)

1. Light the oven at 375°F (190°C, Gas No. 5). Prepare a 9 in (23 cm) sponge flan tin by lining only the centre with paper, and greasing thoroughly, and then flouring the whole tin.
2. Put the eggs and sugar into the mixer bowl and whisk at fast speed until the mixture is pale, fluffy and thick and the whisk leaves a trail on the surface for a short time if lifted out.
3. Sift the flour over the surface of the mixture, and fold in very gently with a metal tablespoon.
4. Turn into the prepared flan tin and bake for 20–25 minutes until golden brown, firm and resilient to the touch. Turn out and cool.
5. Prepare the fruit. If fresh fruit is to be used it must be prepared and stewed till tender with a little water and sugar to sweeten. A mixture of fruits may be used to give a decorative appearance to the flan, e.g. tinned mandarin oranges and sliced bananas, stewed or tinned pears with cherries, peaches with black grapes, a mixture of fruit including perhaps green and black grapes, cherries or strawberries, pears, peaches or mandarins.
6. Drain the fruit and arrange in the baked flan case, then store in the refrigerator until chilled.
7. Measure ¼ pint (125 ml.) of the juice to make the glaze.

a. *Gelatine glaze:* Put the juice in a small basin, add the gelatine and stand over boiling water, stirring until the gelatine completely dissolves. Then keep in a cool place until on the point of setting. Spoon over the fruit flan, cold from the refrigerator, and it will set almost immediately. If no fruit juice is available, a glaze can be made using a piece of packet jelly made up with half the quantity of water – but this is not so delicious as real fruit juice.

b. *Arrowroot glaze:* Mix the arrowroot with about 1 tablespoon of juice in a cup and blend it smooth. Boil the remaining juice in a small pan then mix some of it with the arrowroot in the cup. Return all to the pan and gently bring back to the boil, stirring all the time. When it boils it will thicken and clear, and at this point it must be spooned carefully over the fruit. It cools and sets almost immediately.

8. Serve the flan with whipped cream piped to decorate it, or with pouring cream.

Walnut Gateau · Mixer (and Blender)

Serves 7–8

40 *sponge finger biscuits*	1 *oz. (25 g.) flour*
½ *pt. (250 ml.) milk (approx., see recipe)*	2 *rounded teasp. instant coffee powder*
7 *oz. (175 g.) butter (softened)*	¼ *pt. (125 ml.) double cream*
6 *oz. (150 g.) caster sugar*	*walnuts, cherries and angelica*
1 *egg*	*for decoration*
4 *oz. (100 g.) walnuts*	

1. Line a 6 in. (15 cm.) cake tin with greaseproof paper (a cake tin with a loose bottom is an advantage).

2. Cream 6 oz. (150 g.) butter and the sugar in the mixer bowl until they are light and fluffy, then break in the egg and beat again.

3. Chop the nuts with the blender at slow speed. Chop only for a very short time, about 5 seconds, so that there are some large pieces of nut remaining.

4. Melt the remaining 1 oz. (25 g.) of butter and at high speed blend the flour and half the milk. Pour the mixture into the melted butter and heat slowly, stirring well, until the mixture thickens and boils

Cook for a further 2 minutes, then stir in the coffee. Cool, beating occasionally to prevent a skin forming.

5. With the mixer at medium speed, beat the coffee sauce into the creamed mixture, a teaspoonful at a time. Turn the mixer to slow speed and mix in the chopped nuts.

6. Line the cake tin (sides and bottom) with sponge fingers which have been dipped in the remaining $\frac{1}{4}$ pint (125 ml.) of milk.

7. Fill the centre of the tin with the creamed walnut mixture and the remaining biscuits, in alternate layers.

8. Put in the refrigerator to set firm and then turn out just before serving.

9. Whip the double cream in the mixer bowl at fast speed until stiff but not buttery, and cover the top of the gateau. Some can be piped with a star pipe round the edges and the gateau decorated with walnuts, cherries and angelica.

Today's Delight · Blender

Just as the savoury left-overs in the larder can, as in 'End Blend', be used up to make a delicious soup, so left-over puddings can be combined in the blender to make interesting sweets. Almost any combination of jellies, milk puddings, mousses, sweet sauces, fruit dishes, etc., can be put in the blender at medium to fast speed, and blended until homogeneous. If the mixture is too stiff to be blended easily, it can be thinned down with a little fruit juice, cream or evaporated milk. Taste the mixture when blended and add more sugar, flavouring or colouring if necessary. Lemon juice, jam or bananas (2 per pint (500 ml.) of mixture) are good additions if the whip is uninteresting. There is also great scope for decoration to make these sweets look more exciting. Here are the quantities for a typical mixture, but it is only one example of an infinite number of variations.

$\frac{1}{2}$ pt. (250 ml.) jelly (red gives an attractive colour)

$\frac{1}{4}$ pt. (125 ml.) custard, or fruit fool, or stewed or tinned fruit

$\frac{1}{2}$ pt. (250 ml.) blancmange, sweet white sauce or milk pudding (rice, tapioca etc.)

whipped cream, cherries etc., to decorate

1. Blend all the ingredients at medium speed, increasing to fast, until the whole is homogeneous.
2. Pour into individual glass dishes and decorate with whipped cream and cherries, chopped nuts or hundreds and thousands.

II

Icecream and Water Ices

❧❧❧❧❧❧❧❧❧❧❧❧❧❧❧❧❧❧❧❧❧❧❧❧❧

Icecream and Water Ices

The greatest problem of making icecream domestically is the difficulty of achieving, as nearly as possible, the smooth texture obtained by commercial firms. The gritty feel of homemade ice-cream is caused by the large crystals of ice which form in it. This can be avoided if the mixture is frozen *quickly* in the ice-making compartment (with the refrigerator set at its coldest setting) and beaten vigorously when half-frozen. This beating serves to break down the large ice crystals and to aerate the mixture. It is very hard work by hand, but the mixer is an ideal tool and the cook who owns one can produce large quantities of unusual and delicious icecream with a minimum of effort. This is a particular advantage if there are children in the family, for not only is icecream very popular but the homemade variety is usually cheaper and more nutritious than the commercial product. If made with evaporated milk, or eggs, icecream is high in protein for body-building, and if fresh fruits are included it is a valuable source of Vitamin C. In some icecream recipes it is a great advantage to have more than one mixer bowl and for this reason a hand-held mixer is also very useful, provided it is powerful enough to beat the quantities being made.

Points to remember when making icecreams
1. When using cream in icecream, never over-whip it, as the cream becomes rather solid and buttery, and makes the icecream heavy. If whipping at fast speed in the mixer, stand over it ready to stop the

minute the cream is fairly stiff; that is when the whisk leaves marks on the cream as it rotates.

2. Evaporated milk is often used as a cream substitute in icecreams. It gives the desired high fat content and is more economical and nutritious, and provided its flavour is masked by another pronounced flavour, it gives a pleasant and light icecream. The texture is improved if the evaporated milk is whisked first to make it light and fluffy. This can be done in two ways:

a. Boil the unopened can in water for 15 minutes. Cool and leave overnight in the refrigerator. (Several cans may be prepared at once and stored in the refrigerator for weeks – to be opened as needed.) Open the can and whisk the milk in the mixer bowl at fast speed until very light and fluffy.

b. To an opened 12 oz. (350 ml.) can of evaporated milk add 2 teaspoonfuls of lemon juice. Whisk in mixer bowl at fast speed until very light and fluffy.

3. When eating iced foods one's sense of taste is not so acute, so when tasted before freezing the mixture should seem oversweet and overflavoured. The finished icecream will then taste just right.

4. The mixture (apart from water ices or sorbets) must freeze as quickly as possible, therefore the refrigerator must be set to its coldest setting 30 minutes before putting the icecream into the ice-making compartment. Likewise all bowls and utensils, including the mixer bowl and whisks, must be cold when used, preferably from out of the refrigerator.

5. The time taken for the icecream to freeze depends largely on the refrigerator used and the quantity of icecream to be frozen. Usually after about 1 hour the mixture is sufficiently frozen to be removed and whipped. By then it should be fairly firm for an inch in from the edge of the dish, and it should be beaten at fast speed in the cooled mixer bowl for about 2 minutes. Once the mixture is returned to the ice-making compartment of the refrigerator it will probably need at least 2 hours to freeze it firm, after which the refrigerator can be turned back to the normal setting. Icecream is more pleasant and flavoursome to eat if it is not too cold when served.

6. Icecream can, of course, be frozen in a deep freeze cabinet. The

method is exactly the same as when using the icebox of the refrigerator, but as the temperature is lower the mixture should freeze faster. Once frozen solid it is very hard, and should be brought out and stored in the icebox of the domestic refrigerator 6–8 hours before it is to be served.

7. Once a bowl of icecream is ready in the refrigerator it can be used in a large variety of fancy puddings and sundaes, by combining it with various sauces, fruits, nuts, sponge cakes and jellies. As these do not usually require the further use of the mixer, recipes are not included in this book, but can be found elsewhere. The imaginative cook will enjoy inventing her own iced sweets.

Here then are a few of the many recipes for icecreams:

Vanilla Icecream I · Mixer

This is a basic icecream which can be flavoured in many ways. Serves 5–6.

$\frac{3}{4}$ pt. (375 ml.) milk
2 egg yolks
2 oz. (50 g.) sugar (if using a deep freeze use vanilla sugar and omit the vanilla essence)

$\frac{1}{3}$ pt. (200 ml.) double cream or evaporated milk (thickened and whipped as described on p. 60)
$\frac{1}{2}$ teasp. vanilla essence

1. Turn the refrigerator to the coldest setting.
2. Stir the egg yolks and sugar together in a double saucepan and beat for a moment with a wooden spoon.
3. Bring the milk to the boil, and pour immediately on to the yolks, stirring well.
4. Continue cooking in the double saucepan, stirring frequently, until the custard thickens and coats the back of the spoon.
5. Allow the mixture to cool completely, then add the vanilla.
6. Put the cream in the mixer bowl and whip to the 'half-whipped' stage using the whisk at fast speed.
7. Fold the cream into the custard, and turn into a freezing tray. Put the mixer bowl into the refrigerator.

8. With the refrigerator at its cold setting freeze the mixture until it is firm about $\frac{1}{2}$ in. ($1\frac{1}{2}$ cm.) from the edge.

9. Scrape the icecream into the cold mixer bowl, then beat at medium speed, until the ice crystals are broken down well and the mixture homogeneous (probably about 2 minutes).

10. Return to the freezing tray, and freeze again until firm 1 in.– $1\frac{1}{2}$ in. (3–4 cm.) from the edge, then again beat as above. Return to the tray and finally freeze until solid.

11. Once the icecream is quite hard, turn the refrigerator back to its normal setting, to store.

This icecream can be flavoured in a variety of ways, by omitting the vanilla and adding another flavour at the same point in the recipe. Here are a few examples:

Burnt Almond Icecream
Blanch and brown in the oven 3 oz. (75 g.) of almonds. Chop only very roughly then add to the icecream and freeze as before.

Chocolate Icecream
Dissolve 2 oz. (50 g.) cocoa or 3 oz. (75 g.) drinking chocolate in 2 tablespoons of warm milk and add to the mixture.

Coffee Icecream
Dissolve 3 teaspoons instant coffee powder in 1 tablespoon hot water and add to the icecream mixture.

Strawberry or Raspberry Icecream
Put 1 lb. (500 g.) strawberries or raspberries in the blender jar and purée them at medium speed. Pass the purée through a strainer to remove the pips (not strictly necessary in the case of strawberries). Add the fruit purée to the icecream mixture.

The texture of strawberry icecream will be improved if 1 teaspoon of gelatine is dissolved in 2 tablespoons of boiling water and added with the purée.

Vanilla Icecream II · Mixer

Serves 5–6. Freezing time 5–6 hours

4 *egg whites*	*a deep freeze, use 3 oz. (75 g.)*
¼ *pt. (125 ml.) double cream*	*vanilla sugar and omit the*
¼ *pt. (125 ml.) single cream*	*vanilla essence)*
3 *oz. (75 g.) icing sugar (if using*	1½ *teasp. vanilla essence*

1. Whisk the egg whites at the fastest speed to soft peak stage.
2. Add the sifted icing sugar in dessertspoonfuls while continuing to whisk at fastest speed.
3. In another bowl whisk the double cream at fastest speed – this can be done with a hand-held mixer or with a hand whisk or using the mixer, if it has two bowls. When it is thick but not stiff, pour in the single cream, while still continuing to whisk so that the whole mixture finishes up at 'half-whipped' stage.
4. Fold half the cream into the egg whites, using the mixer at its slowest speed, and turn into the freezing tray of the refrigerator set at its coldest setting. Put the mixer bowl into the refrigerator.
5. When the mixture is frozen an inch (2½ cm.) in from the sides, turn it into the cold mixer bowl and whisk at fast speed for a short time (about 15 seconds).
6. Fold in the remaining cream and the vanilla, using the mixer at its slowest speed.
7. Return to the freezing tray and continue freezing until quite solid.
8. Then turn the refrigerator back to its normal setting to store.

This recipe lends itself to variations in flavouring, which can be added instead of the vanilla at the end of the making process. This quantity may be divided into two and flavoured in different ways.

Chocolate Cream Ice
Mix 2½ oz. (60 g.) drinking chocolate powder with 1 tablespoon of hot milk and when cool whisk into second half of cream instead of vanilla.

Coffee Cream Ice

Mix 4 rounded teaspoons instant coffee powder with 1 tablespoon hot milk and when cool whisk into second half of cream instead of vanilla.

Almond Cream Ice

Stir in 2 teaspoons almond essence and 3 oz. (75 g.) browned, chopped almonds instead of vanilla.

Peppermint Cream Ice

Add a few drops of oil of peppermint or peppermint essence to taste, instead of vanilla and colour pale green. Grate chocolate over the top when serving.

Liqueur Cream Ice

A luxury icecream can be made by substituting 2 good tablespoons of any sweet liqueur for the vanilla in the above recipe. Kirsch, apricot brandy or cherry brandy are particularly good.

Icecream (using evaporated milk) · Mixer

Serves 10–12. Freezing time 3–4 hours

1 *large* 12 *oz.* (300 g.) *tin of evaporated milk (boiled and cooled as in 2a on p. 160)*	1 *tbs. boiling water*
	2–3 *oz.* (50–75 g.) *caster or icing sugar*
1 *level teasp. gelatine*	*flavouring (see below)*

1. Open the can of milk which has been at least 12 hours in the refrigerator. Empty into the mixer bowl and whisk at fast speed until very light and fluffy, with the whisk leaving a trail.
2. Dissolve the gelatine in the boiling water and pour slowly into the evaporated milk while continuing to whisk it. Whisk in the sugar.
3. Pour into the freezing tray and freeze for about 45 minutes until half-frozen. Put the mixer bowl into the refrigerator.

4. Return mixture to the cold mixer bowl and whisk at fast speed until very light and fluffy and the ice crystals are broken down.

5. Whisk in the flavouring. At this stage the mixture may be divided into two and different flavourings added to give two varieties of icecream, if desired.

6. Return to the freezing compartment and freeze until solid. Turn refrigerator back to its normal setting to store.

FLAVOURINGS FOR THIS QUANTITY OF BASIC ICECREAM

Vanilla. Add 1½ teaspoons vanilla essence. If using a deep freeze, omit this essence and sweeten with vanilla sugar.

Coffee. Dissolve 4 teaspoons instant coffee powder in 1 tablespoon boiling water, cool and add.

Chocolate. Dissolve 1½ oz. (40 g.) cocoa or 2 oz. (50 g.) drinking chocolate powder in 3 tablespoons hot milk. When fully dissolved, cool and add to the icecream, together with 1 teaspoon vanilla essence.

Fruit. Make a thick purée by using a variety of fresh or stewed fruits, and puréeing them in the blender jar at fast speed. Sieve if necessary to remove pips and skins, and add when cool to the icecream mixture which may need a little further sweetening.

Suitable fruits – strawberries, raspberries, blackcurrants, blackberries, prunes, gooseberries, apricots, dried, tinned or stewed.

Mocha. Dissolve 1½ oz. (40 g.) drinking chocolate powder and 2 teaspoons instant coffee in 1 tablespoon hot milk. Cool and add.

Baked Alaska · Mixer

This is a sweet which is very easy to prepare with a mixer, but the combination of icecream inside hot meringue makes it seem rather 'special'. It is most successful when served at a children's party – perhaps instead of the traditional birthday cake.

1 *block icecream, bought or homemade (pp. 161–172)*
1 *sponge cake about 1 in. (2½ cm.) thick and the same size as*
the icecream. See sponge cake recipe (p. 194) or genoese sponge cake (p. 196).
fruit (optional, see recipe)

4 *egg whites*
4 *oz. (100 g.) caster sugar (up to*
  8 *oz. (200 g.) of sugar can be*

used but it makes a very sweet
pudding)

1. Choose an ovenproof dish in which the alaska may be baked and
served. Light the oven at 450–475°F (230–240°C, Gas No. 9).
2. Place the sponge on the dish, soaking it with a little fruit syrup if
desired. If liked cover with the drained fruit, preferably cold from
the refrigerator, but this can be omitted.
3. Turn the icecream on to the sponge and fruit. It should be very
firm, ideally having been stored in the icebox of the refrigerator, set
at its coldest, or in a deep freeze, for some time before use. If home-
made icecream is used this can have been frozen in a suitably shaped
container (e.g. a pudding basin to match a round sponge cake).
Two coloured icecreams can be used.
4. Whisk the egg whites at fast speed to soft peak stage.
5. Continue whisking, gradually adding the caster sugar a teaspoonful at a time until it is all beaten in.
6. Pile or pipe (using a large nozzle on a piping bag) this meringue
mixture on to cover the icecream, fruit, and sponge cake completely. It is most important that they should all be covered as the
air bubbles in the meringue act as insulation and prevent the icecream melting in the hot oven.
7. Place in the oven for 3–4 minutes only, until the meringue is
lightly browned. Serve immediately.

This can be prepared comfortably by a hostess at a dinner party,
if the fruit is on the sponge, the icecream ready to turn out, and the
egg whites in the mixer bowl, with the oven preheated, all before the
meal begins. The meringue is so quickly prepared in the mixer and
the baking takes so short a time that all can be finished while the
dishes are being cleared from the main course.

VARIATIONS ON BAKED ALASKA

These are legion, depending on the taste and ingenuity of the cook,
but here are a few suggestions for altering the basic recipe.

Apple Alaska
Stewed apple, well drained, with vanilla or lemon icecream. A lemon-flavoured sponge could be used.

Blackcurrant or Blackberry Alaska
Stewed or canned blackcurrants or blackberries (well drained) or fresh ripe blackberries, crushed with sugar, with vanilla icecream.

Cherry Alaska
Drained canned or stewed cherries, or cherry pie filling, with vanilla or neapolitan icecream.

Decorate the meringue before baking with a few cherries from the filling or with glacé cherries.

Chocolate Alaska
Moisten the spongecake with orange juice or with a little sherry.

Use chocolate icecream.

Serve the alaska with hot or cold chocolate sauce.

Pear Alaska
Sliced, drained tinned or stewed pears, with coffee icecream.

Raspberry or Strawberry Alaska
Frozen or fresh strawberries or raspberries, mashed with sugar or drained canned strawberries or raspberries, with strawberry or raspberry icecream. Leave the fruit to stand on the cake for a while so that the juice may soak in.

Reserve a few of the whole fruits to decorate the meringue after baking.

Blackberry Icecream · Colander/Sieve and/or Blender and Mixer

Serves 6–8

1 lb. (½ kg.) blackberries
1 tbs. lemon juice
4 oz. (100 g.) sugar
1 oz. (25 g.) cornflour

2 tbs. water
½ pt. (250 ml.) single cream
2 eggs (separated)

167

1. Turn the refrigerator to the coldest setting.
2. Wash the blackberries and put in a pan with the sugar, gently bring to the boil and cook until soft.
3. Pour into the blender and blend at medium speed until the fruit is quite puréed, then pass the purée through a nylon strainer to remove the pips, alternatively put it through the colander/sieve attachment to the mixer.
4. Put the cornflour in the blender with the water and blend for a few seconds, then add the blackberry purée and lemon juice and blend for a further few seconds to mix all together.
5. Return the blackberries to the pan and bring to the boil, stirring, then cook gently for 5 minutes.
6. Remove from the heat and return to the blender. While the machine is switched on at fast speed pour in the cream and the egg yolks.
7. Pour into freezing trays and partially freeze until solid 1 in. (2–3 cm.) in from the edge. Put the mixer bowl into the refrigerator.
8. Whisk the egg whites at fastest speed to soft peak stage.
9. Turn the blackberry mixture into the cold mixer bowl and beat at medium speed until the ice crystals are broken down and it is smooth, but not liquid.
10. Turn the egg white into the blackberries and fold the two together with a metal tablespoon.
11. Return to the freezing tray and freeze till firm and solid, then turn the refrigerator back to normal setting for storage.

Honey Icecream · Mixer

Serves 6. Freezing time 4–5 hours

Because it is rather sweet this unusual icecream is delicious served with fruit, or with a sharp sauce such as orange or apricot and lemon.

3 *tbs. honey*	½ *pt.* (250 *ml.*) *cream or*
2 *eggs* (*separated*)	*evaporated milk*
1 *teasp. vanilla essence*	1 *level teasp. gelatine*
	1 *tbs. boiling water*

1. Whisk either the cream or the evaporated milk at fast speed as follows:

(a) cream to half-whipped stage or (b) evaporated milk should have been pretreated as in point 2 in the introduction to this section (p. 160) then whisk until light and fluffy.

2. Dissolve the gelatine in the boiling water, stirring it carefully until it is quite smooth.

3. Pour the gelatine slowly on to the cream mixture while still whisking it at fast speed, then gradually pour in the vanilla, the egg yolks and the honey (which should be slightly warmed if it is very stiff).

4. Pour into a freezing tray and freeze the mixture on the coldest refrigerator setting until half-frozen. Put the mixer bowl into the refrigerator.

5. Just before getting out the icecream, whisk the 2 egg whites at fast speed to soft peak stage.

6. Scrape the icecream into the cold mixer bowl and whisk at medium speed, increasing to fast speed, for about 30 seconds to break up the ice crystals.

7. Remove from the mixer and using a metal tablespoon gently fold the egg whites into the icecream.

8. Turn back into the freezing tray and freeze on the coldest refrigerator setting until solid, then turn back to a normal setting to store.

VARIATIONS

Honey Walnut Icecream or Honey Peanut Icecream
Add 2–3 oz. (50–75 g.) walnuts or 4 oz. (100 g.) peanuts (chopped for a few seconds in blender jar at slow speed). These should be folded in with the egg whites.

Honey Macaroon Icecream
Use ½ teaspoon almond essence instead of vanilla essence.

Break up small 2 macaroon biscuits or 10 small ratafia biscuits and fold these in with egg whites.

Orange Icecream · Mixer (and Citrus Juice Extractor)

Serves 10. Freezing time 6–8 hours

2 eggs (separated)
2–4 oz. (75–100 g.) icing sugar
3 large oranges (rind and
 juice)
1 small lemon (rind and
 juice)

½ pt. (250 ml.) double cream or
½ pt. (250 ml.) evaporated milk
(thickened and whipped as
described on p. 160)

1. Put the egg yolks and the sugar into the mixer bowl (small if possible). Whisk at fast speed until they are thick and creamy.
2. Grate the orange and lemon rind very finely, taking care not to include any pith.
3. Squeeze the juice from the fruit using the citrus juice extractor if available.
4. Half-whip the cream or whisk the evaporated milk at fast speed until light and fluffy.
5. Using the mixer at slow speed stir in the rinds and juices to the egg yolk mixture, and add the mixture to half the quantity of whipped cream.
6. Pour into a freezing tray or bowl and freeze at the coldest setting until the mixture is firm about 1 in. (2–3 cm.) from the edge of the dish. Put the mixer bowl into the refrigerator.
7. Just before it is ready, whisk the 2 egg whites at fast speed to soft peak stage.
8. Turn the half-frozen mixture into the cold mixer bowl and whisk at fast speed until the ice crystals are broken up and the mixture seems smooth (about 2 minutes).
9. Fold in the egg whites and the remaining whipped cream by hand using a metal spoon.
10. Return to the freezing compartment and freeze until solid (3–4 hours approx.), then turn the refrigerator to its normal setting to store.
11. To serve, decorate with mandarin orange segments and angelica *or* serve with a chocolate or orange sauce.

Chocolate Orange Icecream

Make orange icecream as in the previous recipe, but fold in 3 oz. (75 g.) plain or milk chocolate (coarsely grated, or chopped, or as polka dots) at the same time as folding in the egg whites.

Lemon Icecream

Use the recipe for orange icecream, but substitute 4 lemons for the 3 oranges and 1 lemon.

1 oz. (25 g.) extra sugar is needed to sweeten it sufficiently.

Prune Icecream · Mixer and Blender

Serves 6–8. Freezing time 3–4 hours

8 oz. (250 g.) *dried prunes*	¼ *pt.* (125 *ml.*) *single cream*
1 *dsp. lemon juice*	(*or evaporated milk*
2 oz. (50 g.) *caster sugar*	*can be substituted, p.* 160)
¼ *pt.* (125 *ml.*) *double cream and*	

1. Soak the prunes in water for several hours (overnight).
2. Simmer the prunes gently until tender, then drain off the liquor. Reserve 2 tablespoons juice and put in the blender.
3. Stone the prunes (using the fingers is probably the easiest way) and put the flesh into the blender, together with the lemon juice, sugar and single cream. Blend at slow speed for a few seconds and then at fast until the mixture is quite smooth. It may be necessary to stop the motor and scrape down the sides of the blender once or twice.
4. Pour into the freezing tray of the refrigerator, and freeze on the coldest setting for 2–3 hours until the mixture is half-frozen. Put mixer bowl into the refrigerator.
5. Scrape into the cold mixer bowl, and whisk at medium speed for about 30 seconds until the mixture is smooth and the ice crystals are broken down.

6. Have ready the double cream, previously half-whipped either by machine or by hand, and fold into the prune mixture using the whisk at slowest speed.

7. Return to the freezing tray and freeze on the coldest setting till solid, then turn the refrigerator back to the normal setting to store.

Strawberry Custard Ice · Blender and Mixer

Serves 6. Freezing time 4–5 hours

1 *lb.* (½ *kg.*) *strawberries*	2 *oz.* (50 *g.*) *caster sugar*
½ *pt.* (250 *ml.*) *custard made with :*	½ *pt.* (250 *ml.*) *double cream*
½ *pt.* (250 *ml.*) *milk*	
½ *oz.* (15 *g.*) *custard powder*	
1 *oz.* (25 *g.*) *sugar*	

1. Set the refrigerator to the coldest setting.

2. Hull the strawberries and put them in the blender together with the sugar. Blend until the strawberries are puréed, starting on slow speed, then increasing to fast.

3. While still blending fast pour the custard through the centre hole in the lid (if this is not possible stop the blender, pour in the custard, then put on the lid and blend at fast speed again). Blend until the mixture is homogeneous, scraping down the sides of the jar if necessary.

4. With the mixer at fast speed, whip the cream to the half-whipped stage, and then gradually fold in the strawberry mixture, using the mixer at very slow speed.

5. Pour into a freezing tray and freeze rapidly until the mixture is solid for an inch (2–3 cm.) in from the edge. Put mixer bowl into the refrigerator.

6. At this stage turn the strawberry ice back into the cold mixer bowl and use the mixer at medium speed to break up the ice crystals and beat until smooth but not melted.

7. Turn back into the freezing tray and freeze at coldest setting until solid, then store at the normal refrigerator setting.

Instead of strawberries use:
1 lb. (½ kg.) raspberries
or 4 bananas with 1 tbs. lemon juice
or ½ pt. (250 ml.) of thick purée of some other fruit.

WATER ICES

These contain no milk or cream but sweetened fruit juice or fruit purée. Wines or liqueurs are sometimes used to flavour them, and water ices are most refreshing and very easy to make. The main problem is to avoid the sharp ice crystals usually formed when fruit juices are frozen, and this is done by vigorously beating (with the mixer) or by including egg white in the recipe as in sherbets and some sorbets. The mixture freezes well at the normal domestic refrigerator setting, although deep freezers can be used most success-fully, provided the ice is stored in the domestic refrigerator for some hours before serving.

Only a small selection of the variations possible is given here, but sufficient to show the value of the mixer in the rather heavy work of whisking the half-frozen ice, particularly if a large quantity is made.

Because they feel very cold in the mouth and have such a pungent flavour of fresh fruit, it is best to serve small portions. Hence it is very feasible to prepare more than is required at one time and store the remainder either in the icebox of the domestic refrigerator, or in a deep freeze. Water ices will keep safely in the domestic refrigerator much longer than icecreams.

Blackcurrant Water Ice · Mixer

For a large mixer it is probably best to make a double quantity. Serves 6–7

8 tbs. Ribena or other similar blackcurrant syrup	11 oz. (275 ml.) water to make up to ¾ pt. (375 ml.)
	1 egg white

1. Dilute the blackcurrant syrup with the water to make $\frac{3}{4}$ pint (375 ml.) in all.

2. Whisk the egg white at fast speed to soft peak stage.

3. Pour in the blackcurrant juice and fold together with the egg white, using a metal tablespoon.

4. Pour into the freezing tray and put in the icebox of the refrigerator set at its normal setting.

5. When partially frozen, after about 45 minutes, turn over lightly with a fork, then leave until frozen quite firm.

6. Serve piled into chilled sundae glasses, with cream if desired.

Green Gooseberry Sorbet · Blender and Mixer

Serves 8. Freezing time 4–6 hours

1 lb. ($\frac{1}{2}$ kg.) green gooseberries
6–8 oz. (200–250 g.) sugar
juice of 2 lemons
$\frac{3}{4}$ pt. (375 ml.) water

4 tbs. brandy (optional)
green colouring
glacé cherries and blanched
  almonds to decorate ·

1. Prepare the gooseberries, wash and stew with the sugar and some of the water. Only add 6 oz. (200 g.) sugar to begin with then taste when the mixture is ready to freeze and add a further 2 oz. (50 g.) if necessary.

2. When the gooseberries are soft, put them in the blender and blend for a few seconds at fast speed until they are completely puréed. Then sieve the purée through a nylon strainer to remove any remaining pips, rinsing through with the remaining water from the $\frac{3}{4}$ pint (375 ml.).

3. Mix in the juice of the lemons and taste for sweetness.

4. Pour into the freezing tray and freeze in the freezing compartment, set at the normal refrigerator setting, until the mixture is slushy. About 2–3 hours. Put the mixer bowl into the refrigerator.

5. Scrape into the cold mixer bowl and whisk at medium speed for 1–2 minutes until the mixture is smooth, but not melted, has become opaque and increased slightly in volume.

6. Stir in the brandy if to be used, and a few drops of green colouring to give an attractive colour.

7. Return to the freezing tray, freeze once again until slushy and then whisk once more in a cold bowl.

8. Refreeze until solid, then store until required, spooning into individual glass dishes to serve.

Decorate with glacé cherries and blanched almonds.

Orange and Lemon Sorbet · Mixer and Blender (and Citrus Juice Extractor)

Serves 6

2 *oranges*	3 *oz.* (75 *g.*) *sugar*
2 *lemons*	*water*
2 *eggs* (*separated*)	

1. Peel the oranges and the lemons thinly, leaving behind all the white pith.

2. Put the peel with some water in a saucepan and simmer for 10 minutes, then stand until cold.

3. Strain the liquid from the peel, and make up to $\frac{1}{2}$ pint (250 ml.) with water.

4. Squeeze the oranges and lemons (with a citrus juice extractor attachment to the mixer, if available) and strain.

5. Put the egg yolks in the blender together with the sugar. Run at medium speed for a few seconds, then add the liquids (juice and peel-flavoured water) and run at fast speed for another 30 seconds.

6. Put into a freezing tray and freeze at normal refrigerator setting until the mixture is almost solid. Put mixer bowl into the refrigerator.

7. Turn into the cold mixer bowl and whip for approximately 30 seconds to break down the ice crystals.

8. Refreeze until the mixture is almost solid again.

9. Whisk the egg whites at fast speed to soft peak stage.

10. Roughly break up the frozen orange mixture with a fork, add to the egg whites and fold in with the mixer running at the slowest speed for the minimum time to ensure that the mixture is homogeneous.

11. Return to the freezing tray and freeze at normal refrigerator setting until it is solid.

12. To serve – break up with a fork and pile into individual sundae glasses.

Strawberry Jam Water Ice or Icecream · Blender and Mixer

Serves 6. Freezing time 4 hours approx.

1 lb. (500 g.) strawberry jam
juice of 2 lemons

½ pt. (250 ml.) water or ¼ pt.
(125 ml.) water and ¼ pt.
(125 ml.) double cream

1. If using cream, turn the refrigerator to its coldest setting.
2. Put all the ingredients into the blender jar and blend at fast speed until any whole fruit is completely puréed.
3. Turn into a freezing tray and freeze until solid about 1 in. (2–3 cm.) in from the edge. Put the mixer bowl into the refrigerator.
4. Put the strawberry mixture into the mixer bowl and beat at medium or fast speed for 1–2 minutes, to break down the ice crystals. Do not let it become completely liquid, however.
5. Return to the freezing tray and freeze until solid. Store at the normal refrigerator setting.

Strawberry Water Ice or Sorbet · Blender and Mixer

Serves 6–8. Freezing time 6 hours approx.

1 lb. (½ kg.) strawberries –
fresh or frozen
6 oz. (175 g.) sugar

¼ pt (125 ml.) water
2 tbs. lemon juice
2 tbs. orange juice

1. Put the mixer bowl into the refrigerator to chill.
2. Put the water with the sugar in a pan. Warm and stir until the sugar is dissolved, then cool.
3. Hull the strawberries and put in the blender together with the cool syrup and blend at fast speed until quite puréed. At this point the strawberry purée can be passed through a nylon strainer to remove the pips, if desired, but it is not necessary.

4. Add the fruit juices, mix, and pour into the freezing tray. Freeze at the normal refrigerator setting until the mixture is slushy.

5. Turn the slushy mixture into the chilled mixer bowl and whisk at medium speed for 1–2 minutes until the mixture is smooth (but not melted), has become opaque and increased slightly in volume.

6. Return the strawberry mixture to the refrigerator and freeze for a further 2 hours or until it is half-frozen, then repeat the whisking in the chilled mixer bowl.

7. Return finally to the refrigerator and freeze till solid.

8. Serve straight from the refrigerator by spooning into individual glass dishes.

Rhubarb Sherbet · Mixer and Blender

Serves 6

¾ lb. (375 g.) rhubarb	2 egg whites
3 oz. (75 g.) sugar	chopped pistachio nuts for
3 tbs. water	decoration
¼ pt. (125 ml.) single cream or	
evaporated milk	

1. Wash the rhubarb, cut into short lengths and stew with water and 3 oz. (75 g.) sugar. A little lemon rind, thinly peeled, gives additional flavour if desired. Add more sugar after cooking if the fruit does not taste sweet enough.

2. Pour into the blender and blend at medium speed till the fruit is completely smooth.

3. Add the cream (or evaporated milk) to the blender, and blend at fast speed until the mixture is homogeneous.

4. Turn into a freezing tray and freeze at the normal refrigerator setting for about ¾ hour until the mixture is partly frozen and slushy.

5. Turn the mixture into the mixer bowl and whisk at fast speed for 30 seconds.

6. Meanwhile whisk the egg whites to soft peak stage.

7. Turn the egg whites into the mixer bowl and with the mixer

running at the slowest speed fold the egg whites into the rhubarb mixture. Only continue for the shortest time necessary for the mixture to become homogeneous.

8. Return the mixture to the freezing tray and freeze until firm – at a normal refrigerator setting.

9. To serve: scoop into individual sundae dishes and decorate with chopped pistachio nuts, or with cherries and angelica.

VARIATIONS USING OTHER FRUIT

Gooseberry or Blackcurrant or Redcurrant Sherbet

In the above recipe replace the rhubarb with ¾ lb. (375 g.) of prepared gooseberries, blackcurrants or redcurrants. After they are blended it will be necessary to pass them through a nylon strainer to remove the pips, but apart from this proceed as for rhubarb sherbet. Alternatively a colander/sieve attachment to the mixer can be used to make the fruit purée.

Strawberry or Raspberry or Blackberry Sherbet

These fruits do not need cooking, so prepare and weigh ¾ lb. (375 g.) of the fruit and put it straight into the blender jar together with 2 tablespoons of water. Blend at medium speed until completely smooth then pass through a nylon strainer to remove the pips or use a colander/sieve attachment to the mixer instead of the blender. Add 2 oz. (50 g.) caster sugar with the cream (blackberries need 2 oz. (50 g.) lemon juice as well) and then proceed as for rhubarb sherbet.

12

Pastry

Although the mixer is not suitable for making the richer pastries, such as flaky, puff and rough puff pastry, it is an excellent aid when making those that require the rubbing of fat into flour. These mixtures are always improved by being kept cool, and the mixer cuts to the minimum the use of warm hands. Care must be taken not to overmix, either at the rubbing-in stage, or when the liquid is added. The liquid, of course, should be very cold. Just at the start of mixing, at the slowest speed, when the fat is still in lumps, the flour will tend to fly out of the bowl, so it is a good idea to cover roughly with a cloth.

It is also a good idea to mix a large batch of pastry and store, either the dry mix, pastry ready for rolling, or baked goods which can either be finished, just ready for rewarming, or baked in the form of flan cases or tartlets which are ready for filling when required and will keep some time in an airtight tin. The dry mix, of fat rubbed into flour, will keep a long while in the refrigerator (as long as the fat alone would), and can quickly be brought out, liquid added, and the pastry rolled out when required.

Suet Crust Pastry · Slicer/Shredder and Mixer

The possession of a slicer/shredder must surely encourage the use of butcher's suet, with consequently richer pastry. A lump of suet is bought, any skin or stringy parts are pulled and cut off, and then the suet grated using the finest shredding disc or drum. A larger quantity can be grated than is needed at once, and the remainder will keep in a plastic box in the refrigerator for weeks provided a little flour is mixed in with it.

½ lb. (200 g.) plain flour	4 oz. (100 g.) suet (shredded on
½ teasp. salt	slicer/shredder, or from
1 rounded teasp. baking	packet)
powder	water – probably just less
	than ¼ pt. (125 ml.)

1. Prepare the butcher's suet as above or use packet shredded suet.
2. Weigh all the dry ingredients into the mixer bowl and, with the beaters at slowest speed, pour about two-thirds of the water into the centre, and then add the remaining third more slowly, to give a light and spongy dough which can be rolled out on a floured board. Only mix just long enough to bind the pastry.
3. Use as required for puddings, sweet or savoury, or dumplings.

Steak and Kidney Pudding · Mixer (and Slicer/Shredder)

Serves 6–7

FOR SUET CRUST PASTRY	FOR MEAT FILLING
12 oz. (300 g.) plain flour	1¾ lb. (700 g.) stewing steak
6 oz. (150 g.) suet	4 oz. (100 g.) kidney
1¼–1½ rounded teasp. baking	1 medium onion
powder	1 tbs. plain flour
¾ teasp. salt	1 level teasp. salt
	¼ level teasp. pepper
	4 tbs. stock or water

1. Put the water in steamer or pressure cooker to heat.
2. Remove skin and core from kidney and cut both steak and kidney into small chunks.
3. Mix the flour with the seasonings and toss the meat and kidney into it so that each cube is floured.
4. Peel the onion and if the slicer/shredder is available slice it on the fine slicer, otherwise chop finely.

5. Make the suet crust pastry as on p. 180 and roll out three-quarters of it to line a 2½–3 pint (1½–2 l.) greased pudding basin.

6. Put the meat and onion in layers into the lined basin and add the liquid.

7. Roll out the remaining pastry to make a lid, damp the edges and fold the basin lining down on to it.

8. Cover with greased paper and then securely with foil, and steam for 3½–4 hours. Alternatively this pudding can be cooked in a pressure cooker, putting it in with the lid on but without increased pressure, just to steam for 15 minutes, then increasing the pressure to 15 lb.-pressure and cook for a further 1 hour. Reduce the pressure and serve.

9. The pudding should be served in the basin with a clean napkin pinned round it.

Short Crust Pastry · Mixer

This everyday standby can be made in the mixer in large quantities and then stored in the refrigerator, either as rubbed-in crumbs (in a tightly closing plastic box) or when ready to roll out (in a plastic bag). The former will keep well for weeks, but the latter must be used after a few days.

> 1 *lb.* (400 g.) *plain flour*   combination of fats)
> 4 *oz.* (100 g.) *margarine,*   water to mix (approx. 4 tbs.)
>   4 *oz.* (100 g.) *lard (or other*   ½ teasp. salt

1. Sift the flour and salt into the mixer bowl, and roughly cut the fats into lumps.

2. Mix at the slowest speed until the fats are rubbed in and resemble fine breadcrumbs. Stop at this point *before* the mixture begins to bind together as in shortbread.

3. Still mixing at the slowest speed add the water quickly (about 1 teaspoon per 1 oz. (25 g.) flour) and mix until the pastry just binds together, then stop and do the final kneading by hand. Roll out and use as required. Bake at 400°F (200°C, Gas No. 6)–425°F (220°C, Gas No. 7).

Iced Almond Flan · Mixer

Serves 5

4 oz. (100 g.) flour as shortcrust pastry (p. 181)

2 tbs. jam (raspberry or blackcurrant best)

3 oz. (75 g.) butter (softened)

3 oz. (75 g.) caster sugar

1 large egg

2 oz. (50 g.) ground almonds and 1 oz. (25 g.) cake or biscuit crumbs (p. 60) (or other proportions to make up 3 oz. (75 g.))

1 oz. (25 g.) self-raising flour

1 tbs. milk

few drops of almond essence

ICING

4 oz. (100 g.) sifted icing sugar

1 tbs. sherry

½ oz. (15 g.) flaked almonds, browned in oven

1. Light oven at 425°F (220°C, Gas No. 7).

2. Roll out the pastry and line an 8 in. (20 cm.) flan ring with it, then spread with the jam.

3. At medium speed, cream the butter and sugar together until very light and fluffy.

4. Add the essence, break in the egg and continue beating at medium speed until it is fully incorporated.

5. Add the ground almonds, crumbs and flour and, together with the milk, fold in at the slowest speed.

6. Spoon into the pastry case and spread smooth. Bake for 15 minutes, then turn down to 350°F (180°C, Gas No. 4) for about 30 minutes until brown and firm. Cool.

7. Mix the sherry and the icing sugar to form a stiff icing and spread over the flan – then scatter over it the toasted flakes of almond.

8. Serve as a sweet with cream and cut the remainder into thin fingers for eating at teatime.

Lemon Meringue Pie · Mixer and Blender

Serves 6

5 oz. (125 g.) flour etc. made into
short crust pastry (p. 181) or
flan pastry (p. 184)

FOR FILLING

1½ oz. (40 g.) cornflour ½ pt. (225 ml.) water less 2 tbs.
7 oz. (175 g.) sugar 3 egg yolks
3 lemons

FOR MERINGUE

3 egg whites glacé cherries and angelica
3 oz. (75 g.) caster sugar for decoration

1. Light the oven at 425°F (220°C, Gas No. 7) for short crust pastry or 400°F (200°C, Gas No. 6) for flan pastry, and make the pastry using the mixer.
2. Roll the pastry to line a 7 in. (18 cm.) flan ring and bake it blind (filling centre with baking beans on a paper circle to prevent it from rising). Put in the oven at the appropriate temperature. Remove the beans when the pastry is set and finish cooking the base.
3. When the case is baked, cool on a wire rack and make the filling.
4. Peel the yellow rind thinly from the lemons with a potato peeler or sharp knife, and put with the water into the blender jar. Blend at fast speed until the rind is very fine; this may take up to 2 minutes.
5. Add the cornflour, sugar and lemon juice and blend until smooth, then transfer to a saucepan and bring to the boil slowly, stirring all the time, until the sauce thickens and clears, then boil for 1 minute only.
6. Cool slightly before beating in the egg yolks, then fill into the pastry case.
7. Whisk the egg whites at fast speed to soft peak stage. Add the sugar, one teaspoonful after another, while still whisking fast.
8. Pile the meringue on to the lemon filling, taking care to take the meringue right to the edge of the case. Decorate with cherries and angelica and bake at 325°F (160°C, Gas No. 3) until golden brown all over.
9. Serve hot or cold.

Treacle Tart · Mixer and Blender

Serves 6

6 oz. (150 g.) flour as short crust   2 oz. (50 g.) crustless white bread
   pastry (p. 181)   or breadcrumbs (p. 60)
10 oz. (250 g.) golden syrup (3   rind and juice of ½ large
   generous tbs.)   lemon

1. Light the oven at 425°F (220°C, Gas No. 7).
2. Make up the pastry using the mixer, and roll it out to about ⅛ in. (4 mm.) thickness to line a 10 in. (25 cm.) ovenproof pie plate. Trim and mark the edge.
3. Make the breadcrumbs (p. 60). If liked, the thinly pared yellow rind of the lemon can also be chopped in the blender (with the breadcrumbs), but it is probably better grated finely.
4. Put the syrup into a warm basin, add the breadcrumbs and lemon juice and rind and mix well together.
5. Spoon the mixture into the pastry case, and spread over the centre, then use the trimmings of the pastry to form a lattice or wheel of twisted strands over the top.
6. Bake for 20–25 minutes until the pastry is cooked through and lightly coloured.

Flan Pastry · Mixer

Makes 2 × 8 in. (20 cm.) flan rings or 1 × 8 in. (20 cm.) flan ring and 12 tartlet cases

8 oz. (200 g.) plain flour   2 oz. (50 g.) caster sugar
¼ rounded teasp. salt   2 egg yolks (or 1 yolk with
6 oz. (150 g.) butter or margarine   1 tbs. water)

1. Sift the flour and salt into the mixer bowl, and add the fat and sugar. Mix at the slowest speed until the mixture resembles breadcrumbs. Be careful not to overmix so that the pastry begins to bind into a ball.
2. Drop in the egg yolks, and continue beating at the slowest speed until the pastry binds together.

3. Roll out on a floured board and use to line flan cases and tartlet cases. If baking blind, bake in an oven of 375°F (190°C, Gas No. 5).

Gooseberry Meringue Tart · Mixer and Blender

Serves 5

> *flan pastry (p. 184) or*
>   *shortcrust pastry (p. 181)*
>   *(using 6 oz. (150 g.) flour)*
> 1 *lb. (½ kg.) gooseberries*
> 4 *oz. (100 g.) caster sugar*
>
> ¾ *oz. (20 g.) cornflour*
> 2 *eggs (separated)*
> *few drops of green colouring*
> *glacé cherries and angelica*
>   *for decoration*

1. Make up the chosen pastry using 6 oz. (150 g.) flour, and line a 7 in. (18 cm.) flan ring or sandwich tin. Prick the bottom pastry or weigh it down with a layer of beans on a circle of paper, to prevent it rising.

2. Bake in the oven at 425°F (220°C, Gas No. 7) for shortcrust pastry or 375°F (190°C, Gas No. 5) for flan pastry until the pastry is firm, then remove the paper with baking beans, and finish cooking until the pastry is golden. Cool on wire tray.

3. Wash, top and tail the gooseberries. Stew them gently in a saucepan with 2 oz. (50 g.) sugar and 1 tablespoon of water until they are quite tender.

4. Transfer the gooseberries to the blender and blend at fast speed for about 30 seconds until quite smooth. At this stage the pips can be strained off, if desired, by passing the fruit through a nylon strainer, but it is quite acceptable to allow them to remain.

5. Check that the fruit purée is now only tepid, then add the cornflour and switch on for about 10 seconds until it is completely blended with the fruit.

6. Return the purée to a saucepan, and slowly bring to the boil, stirring all the time. Boil for 2 minutes stirring well. Cool slightly.

7. Add the egg yolks, stirring rapidly, then a few drops of green colouring. Pour the mixture into the pastry case.

8. Whisk the egg whites at fast speed to soft peak stage. Continue whisking while rapidly adding the remaining 2 oz. (50 g.) sugar, one teaspoonful at a time.

9. Pile the stiff meringue carefully on the gooseberry mixture, spreading it right to the edges of the flan case.

10. Decorate with pieces of cherry and angelica and return to the oven set at 350°F (180°C, Gas No. 4) until the meringue is biscuit coloured all over – probably 20–30 minutes.

11. Serve hot or cold.

Crumb Crust · Blender

Serves 6. Lines a 9 in (23 cm.) flan

4 oz. (100 g.) *rich tea biscuit crumbs and 4 oz. (100 g.) stale cake or cake crumbs (p. 60)*

or 8 oz. (200 g.) *digestive biscuit crumbs (p. 60)*
3 oz. (75 g.) *butter*
2 oz. (50 g.) *sugar*

1. Melt the butter and sugar and use them to bind the biscuit and cake crumbs together.

2. Press firmly into a 9 in. (23 cm.) pie plate or a sandwich tin to form a flan case. As the crust is very fragile, it is best to cook it in a dish in which it can be served at table. It is possible to turn it out if it is well chilled.

3. Bake in the oven at 350°F (180°C, Gas No. 4) for 10 minutes, then cool and chill in the refrigerator. Baking can be completely omitted, but the results are not quite so satisfactory.

4. Use the crust as a flan case and fill with a variety of fruits, chiffon pie fillings or icecreams. See Sponge Fruit Flan (p. 155) for fruit filling. As it is rather sweet, it is nicest with sharp fillings such as red- and blackcurrants. Lemon Meringue Pie (p. 183) is very good in this crust.

Cheese Pastry · Mixer (and Slicer/Shredder)

6 oz. (150 g.) *plain flour*
4 oz. (100 g.) *margarine*
4 oz. (100 g.) *finely grated cheese (dry Cheddar or Parmesan)*
½ *level teasp. salt*

good shaking of pepper
pinch of cayenne pepper
1 *egg yolk*
2 *tbs. milk (approx.)*

1. Put the flour and seasonings in the mixer bowl, and add the margarine roughly cut in lumps. Use the mixer at slow speed to rub the fat into the flour until it resembles coarse breadcrumbs.
2. Add the finely grated cheese to the mixture. (This can be grated on a slicer/shredder attachment to the mixer using the finest shredding disc.)
3. At slow speed, mix in the egg yolk and the milk until the pastry just binds together, then stop the motor at once.
4. Using the hands, collect the pastry into a ball and press lightly to eliminate the cracks. Roll out on a floured board and use as required.

Suggestions for using this pastry are given in the following three recipes.

Cheese Straws

These are made from the cheese pastry in the previous recipe, and are a very good way of using up any scraps remaining after the pastry has been rolled for a flan, biscuits etc. If a large quantity is needed, however, a batch of pastry must be made especially for the purpose.

1. Light oven at 350°F (180°C, Gas No. 4).
2. Make the cheese pastry and roll out about $\frac{1}{8}$–$\frac{1}{4}$ in. (3–6 mm.) thick on a floured board. Cut into a neat rectangle either 3 in. or 6 in. (8 or 16 cm.) wide.
3. Transfer this rectangle to a greased baking sheet, and, using a sharp knife, cut into straws 3 in. long × $\frac{1}{4}$ in. (8 cm. × 6 mm.) wide. Separate each straw slightly.
4. Reroll the scraps to cut more straws.
5. Bake until cooked through and a golden colour – about 10 minutes. Cool on a rack.
6. If liked a few hollow circles can be cut out of the pastry using two plain circular cutters, one a little smaller than the other. These can then be used to bundle the straws together.

Cheese Biscuits

Makes 32–36 biscuits

cheese pastry as on p. 186
1 oz. (25 g.) nuts (walnuts,
hazelnuts, almonds, peanuts
etc.)

egg wash (beaten egg and
milk or water)

1. Light the oven at 350°F (180°C, Gas No. 4).
2. Roll out the pastry thinly, about ⅛ in. (3 mm.) thick, on a floured board and cut into circles with a 2 in. (5 cm.) plain cutter.
3. Put the biscuits on a baking sheet, and brush the centre of each with egg wash.
4. Chop the nuts finely, in the blender if possible, and press a little on to the egg-washed centre of each biscuit.
5. Bake until just golden brown – 20–25 minutes. Cool on a rack.

Savoury Cheese Tartlets

Cheese pastry (p. 186) can be used to make tartlet cases which can be baked blind and then filled with a variety of savoury fillings.
1. Light the oven at 350°F (180°C, Gas No. 4).
2. Roll the cheese pastry to about ⅛ in. (3 mm.) in thickness and cut with a circular cutter suitable in size for the tartlet cases (or bun tins) available.
3. Prick over the bottoms of the tartlets with a fork and bake until the pastry is cooked through and golden – about 10–15 minutes.
4. Cool the cases on a rack and either fill at once with a savoury filling, or store away in an airtight tin until needed.

Fillings – a few suggestions; there are many more.
1. Savoury scrambled egg, flavoured with cheese or Marmite.
2. Flaked fish or smoked fish or shell fish (such as shrimps) mixed with a well-seasoned white sauce.
3. Diced ham or tongue in a cheese or plain white sauce.
4. Cooked diced vegetables in a well-flavoured cheese sauce.
In every case grated cheese can be sprinkled on the top and the tartlets browned in the oven or under the grill to serve hot.

Choux Pastry · Mixer

Because it requires so much beating, choux pastry is liable to be a failure when made by hand. The mixer, however, comes into its own here and effortlessly beats air into the mixture with the eggs. A hand-held mixer gives most help as it can be used at both stages in making the mixture.

> 4 oz. (100 g.) plain flour $\frac{1}{4}$ pt. (125 ml.) water
> $\frac{1}{2}$ teasp. salt   4 eggs (4 small eggs)
> 2 oz. (50 g.) butter

1. Put the butter and the water into a small saucepan and bring to the boil.
2. Stir in the flour, beating well with a wooden spoon (or a hand-held mixer at medium speed).
3. Continue cooking and beating until the mixture is sufficiently cooked to leave the sides of the pan and begin to form a ball on the spoon or the beaters, if these are revolving slowly.
4. Transfer from the pan to the mixer bowl and beat in the eggs one at a time at medium speed. It is very important to beat thoroughly, so allow at least 30 seconds between the addition of each egg.
5. When the mixture has been thoroughly beaten, it is ready for use as Eclairs, Cream Buns, Profiteroles etc.

Chocolate Eclairs

Makes 12–14

> choux pastry as in previous recipe   ($\frac{1}{2}$ quantities of recipe on
> $\frac{1}{4}$ pt. (125 ml.) whipped cream   p. 244) or confectioner's
>   or half-price cream,   custard (p. 245)
>   whipped   chocolate glacé icing (p. 242)

1. Light the oven at 400°F (200°C, Gas No. 6).
2. Put the choux pastry in a piping bag with a $\frac{1}{2}$ in. (12 mm.) plain nozzle and pipe on to a well-greased baking tray. Make fingers about 4 in. (10 cm.) long, and allow $1\frac{1}{2}$ in. (4 cm.) between each one.

3. Bake until the eclairs are well risen, firm and golden brown (25–35 minutes). Do not open the oven door for at least 25 minutes. The eclairs can be taken from the oven just before they have finished cooking, split down the side and then returned to the oven to finish baking and to dry off the inside. In any case, they must be cooled on a rack and dried with the side split open. '

4. When cool, fill the eclairs with any of the fillings suggested above; as the choux pastry is not sweetened, the eclairs may be liked better if the cream has icing sugar added.

5. Ice with chocolate glacé icing (p. 242) or with one of the proprietary chocolate icings on the market.

Profiteroles

Make as for eclairs, but with a ½ in. (12 mm.) plain pipe, pipe the mixture on to a well-greased tray, into small rounds about 1 in. (2½ cm.) in diameter, or less. Bake as for eclairs but for only about 20 minutes.

Fill with cream and ice with chocolate or coffee glacé icing.

13

Scones and Cakes

Preparation of cake tins
If cakes are to be in the oven for a long time, lining the tins, some-times with several layers of paper, helps to prevent a hard, dry crust developing before the centre of the cake is fully cooked.

It should be remembered that when making comparatively plain cakes, i.e. those with less than half fat to flour, it is advisable to grease the lining paper, unless using one of the specially treated non-stick silicone papers.

Oven Scones · Mixer

Makes 12–16 scones

PLAIN SCONES

8 oz. (200 g.) plain flour
1 level teasp. bicarbonate soda and 2 level teasp. cream of tartar or 2 rounded teasp. of baking powder
2 oz. (50 g.) fat (lard, butter, margarine, cooking fat or a mixture)

½ oz. (15 g.) sugar
4 oz. (100 ml.) milk approx. (8 tbs.) (sour milk or buttermilk can be used, in which case use only 1 level teasp. of cream of tartar)
¼ level teasp. salt

1. Light the oven at 475°F (240°C, Gas No. 9).
2. Sift the flour, raising agents, salt and sugar into the mixer bowl.

3. Add the fat and mix at the slowest speed until the fat has disappeared and the mixture looks like breadcrumbs.

4. Continue mixing at slow speed and add the milk, sufficient to make a soft dough, switching off the mixer as soon as it is all incorporated.

5. Turn the dough from the mixer on to a floured board and shape:
either a. Divide the dough into 2.

      Shape quickly and lightly into 2 rounds.

      Place on 2 greased tins.

      Cut through each into 6 segments but do not separate.

      Glaze, if desired, with a little egg or milk.

or   b. Roll out to a $\frac{1}{2}$ in. ($1\frac{1}{2}$ cm.) thickness.

      Cut with a small cutter (2 in. (5 cm.) is a good size).

      Glaze with a little milk or egg brushed on.

6. Bake on a greased tin for 8–10 minutes approximately, until risen, golden brown, and no longer sticky in the centre.

VARIATIONS

Cheese Scones

Use the recipe for oven scones but omit the sugar and add the following just before adding the milk:

    3–4 *oz.* (75–100 *g.*) *strong-*   *pepper*
       flavoured grated cheese   1 *level teasp. dry mustard*

1. Roll the dough out to $\frac{1}{2}$ in. ($1\frac{1}{2}$ cm.) thick and cut into triangles, fingers or rounds. Glaze with beaten egg and milk and bake as in previous recipe.

Fruit Scones

Repeat the recipe for oven scones, adding, just before the milk, 2 oz. (50 g.) dried fruit such as one or more of the following: currants, sultanas, raisins, peel.

Scotch Pancakes (Drop Scones) · Blender

Makes 20–24 scones

4 oz. (100 g.) plain flour
½ level teasp. bicarbonate of
  soda
1 level teasp. of cream of
  tartar
1 oz. (25 g.) sugar

3 oz. (75 ml.) milk (6 tbs.) (sour
  milk or buttermilk can be used,
  in which case use only ½ level
  teasp. cream of tartar)
1 egg

1. Heat a girdle or heavy-based frying pan which has been *lightly* greased with lard. This must be hot, and the flame underneath turned to medium intensity.
2. Put the egg and milk in the blender, and add the sifted dry ingredients. Blend at medium speed until completely mixed, then stop the motor immediately.
3. Drop the mixture by the dessertspoonful on to the hot girdle, allowing plenty of room between each for running out.
4. As the bubbles rise to the surface and burst, turn the pancakes over and continue cooking until they are golden brown on both sides – 4–6 minutes in all. Then cook another batch, making sure that the girdle is still hot.
5. Cool in a clean tea towel to keep them moist and serve spread liberally with butter.

Rock Buns · Mixer

Makes 12–14 buns

8 oz. (200 g.) self-raising flour
pinch of salt
½ level teasp. grated nutmeg
½ level teasp. mixed spice
4 oz. (100 g.) dripping or butter
4 oz. (100 g.) demerara or
  granulated sugar

2 oz. (50 g.) currants
1 oz. (25 g.) chopped peel
1 egg
2–3 tbs. milk

1. Light the oven at 425°F (220°C, Gas No. 7) and grease a baking sheet.

2. Sift the flour, salt and spices into the mixer bowl, add the fat, roughly cut into lumps, and mix at slow speed until the fat is rubbed in and the whole resembles breadcrumbs.

3. Add the sugar and fruit and mix for a moment, then break in the egg and continue mixing at slow speed, adding enough milk to make a stiff mixture. Switch off when completely mixed.

4. With a dessertspoon and fork place the mixture in rocky heaps on the baking sheet allowing room for them to spread a little, and bake until set, cooked through and lightly browned – 15–20 minutes.

Rum Truffles · Blender

Makes 16–20 truffles

> 6 oz. (150 g.) *stale cake or biscuits*
> 3 oz. (75 g.) *block chocolate*
> 3 oz. (75 g.) *drinking chocolate powder*
> 1 tbs. *orange juice or frozen concentrated orange juice*
>
> 2½ tbs. *rum (a miniature bottle) or rum flavouring*
> 2 teasp. *apricot jam (no skins)*
> *chocolate vermicelli*

1. Start blender at fast speed and drop alternately pieces of cake or biscuit and pieces of chocolate through the hole in the lid. Continue until they are all very fine.

2. Put all the ingredients except the chocolate vermicelli into a bowl and mix well together. If rum essence is used instead of rum, a little extra orange juice and jam will be needed to bind the mixture into balls.

3. Form the mixture into small balls and roll in chocolate vermicelli. Serve in fluted paper cases.

Sponge Cake (Fatless) · Mixer

The use of the mixer revolutionises the making of this cake, which can be done in a few minutes. There is no need to whisk in a bowl over hot water, as the speed of the mixer brings the eggs to a very stable foam without doing so. Makes 2×7 in. (17 cm.) sandwich cakes

3 *eggs*	*scant 3 oz. (75 g.) of plain flour*
3 *oz. (75 g.) caster sugar*	

1. Light the oven at 375°F (190°C, Gas No. 5) and line the bottoms of the two sandwich tins with paper, then grease the paper and sides of the tins.
2. Whisk the eggs and sugar at fast speed until the mixture is thick and creamy. By this time the bubbles will be very small and the whisk when withdrawn will leave a trail on the surface of the mixture which remains for some moments. It is important that the mixture be whisked until stiff enough, as only then will it be firm enough to hold the flour as it is folded in, and also sufficient air beaten in to make the cake rise well.
3. Sift the flour over the surface of the mixture, one-third of it at a time, while folding it in very gently with a metal tablespoon. Be careful there are no pockets of dry flour, but do not fold longer than absolutely necessary.
4. Turn the mixture into the two prepared tins and bake until risen, brown and resilient to the touch – 20–25 minutes.
5. Turn out, cool on a rack, sandwich with jam and dust with icing sugar, or use in any other way required.

Nut Sponge · Mixer (and Blender)

Make this cake exactly as for sponge cake above, but substitute 3 oz. (75 g.) ground nuts for the flour. Hazelnuts or walnuts ground very fine in the blender can be used, or ground almonds.

This cake has a very delicate flavour, so it should be sandwiched with fresh whipped cream or with vanilla-flavoured butter cream.

Swiss Roll · Mixer

2 *large eggs*	2 *tbs. milk*
2 *oz. (50 g.) caster sugar*	*suitable filling, i.e. jam,*
2 *oz. (50 g.) plain flour*	*lemon curd, butter cream, etc.*

1. Light oven at 450°F (230°C, Gas No. 8).

2. Line a swiss roll roll tin 8 × 12 in. (20 × 30 cm.) and grease it well.

3. Whisk the eggs and sugar at fast speed until they are very thick, pale and creamy, and stiff enough to leave a trail which remains for a minute when the whisk is lifted out.

4. Remove from the mixer, sift the flour over the surface of the mixture, add the milk, and fold all together very gently and quickly with a metal tablespoon.

5. Pour into the prepared tin and bake for 7–10 minutes until brown and resilient to the touch.

6. Remove from oven and turn, while hot, on to a sheet of paper dusted with caster sugar.

7. Roll up while hot as follows:

a. Trim off the crisp sides.

b. Mark a line $\frac{1}{2}$ in. ($1\frac{1}{2}$ cm.) from narrow end by pressing with a palette knife.

c. Start the roll from this indentation and roll up, using the paper as a lever.

d. Hold it rolled up for a minute, then unroll and cool on a rack.

8. When cold, trim the ends, spread with jam or other filling, roll up and cut off the ends of the roll. Dust with icing or caster sugar.

Chocolate Swiss Roll

Use the recipe given for swiss roll above but instead of 2 oz. (50 g.) flour, use $1\frac{1}{2}$ oz. (40 g.) plain flour and $\frac{1}{2}$ oz. (15 g.) cocoa sifted together. Add a few drops of vanilla. It may be filled with chocolate or vanilla butter cream.

Coffee Swiss Roll

Use the recipe given for plain swiss roll, but dissolve 2 teaspoons of instant coffee powder in 2 tablespoons of hot water, and use instead of the milk in the recipe. Fill the swiss roll with coffee butter icing (p. 246).

Genoese Sponge · Mixer

This is a most useful basic cake which is made very similarly to a sponge cake. However, as it contains butter, it is much less dry than a sponge and it keeps better. Although the quantities given here are for only one cake, they can easily be doubled, and a large flat slab baked, which will cut up into many small cakes and can be iced and decorated in a number of ways.

Makes a 7 in. (17 cm.) sandwich cake

2 eggs	2 oz. (50 g.) plain flour (or
2 oz. (50 g.) caster sugar	1½ oz. (40 g.) flour and ½ oz.
1½ oz. (40 g.) butter	(10 g.) cornflour can be used)

The cake can be flavoured by folding in with the flour the finely grated rind of an orange or a lemon, a few drops of vanilla essence, or 2 teaspoons of coffee powder dissolved in 2 teaspoons of hot water.

1. Light the oven at 375°F (190°C, Gas No. 5) and line and grease well 2 × 7 in. (2 × 17 cm.) sandwich tins.
2. Melt the butter and allow to cool.
3. Weigh the flour and stand it in a warm place so that it is completely dry and warm.
4. Whisk the eggs and sugar at fast speed until they are very pale and thick. The whisk should leave a trail which remains some while when it is lifted out of the mixture.
5. Fold in the melted butter and the flour by hand with a metal tablespoon, using the following method. (It is necessary to reach the butter at the bottom of the bowl easily, so if the mixer bowl is very deep it may be better to transfer to a flatter, shallower bowl at this stage.)

Pour one-third of the butter down the side of the bowl, where it will slip down to the very bottom, and gently sift one-third of the flour on to the surface of the mixture. Gently fold the butter and flour into the whisked eggs. Repeat the process twice more, just until the flour and butter are folded in and no longer.

6. Divide the mixture between the two tins and bake for about 20 minutes until risen, brown and resilient to the touch.
8. Allow to cool for a few minutes and to shrink from the sides of the tins before turning out on to a rack to cool.
9. Sandwich with jam or butter cream, and dust with icing or caster sugar.

Angel Food Cake · Mixer

Makes an 8 in. (20 cm.) cake

4 oz. (100 g.) *plain flour*	6 *egg whites*
6 oz. (150 g.) *icing sugar*	4 oz. (100 g.) *caster sugar*
¾ *level teasp. cream of tartar*	¾ *teasp. vanilla essence*
large pinch of salt	*small ¼ teasp. almond essence*

1. Light the oven at 375°F (190°C, Gas No. 5) and have ready an 8 in. (20 cm.) square tin *or* 9 × 5 in. (23 × 13 cm.) loaf tin *or* a 9 in. (23 cm.) ring mould. *Do not grease.*

2. Sift together three times the flour, icing sugar and salt.

3. Whisk the egg whites and cream of tartar, in the largest mixer bowl, at fast speed until they are foamy.

4. Now rapidly add the caster sugar, a teaspoonful at a time, and continue beating until the egg white holds into stiff peaks.

5. Sift the flour/sugar mixture over the meringue very gently, 3 tablespoonfuls at a time, together with the flavouring essences, and very gently cut and fold all together, using a metal tablespoon or a rubber spatula.

6. Spoon the mixture into the prepared tin, and gently press into all the corners. Smooth the top.

7. Bake until the top springs back when lightly touched – about 35–40 minutes.

8. As this cake is so fragile it is important that it should be inverted, and 'hang' while cooling (see Chiffon Cake, p. 199).

9. When cold, cut round the sides with a knife and the cake should fall out when inverted and the tin knocked.

10. This cake can be served dusted with icing sugar, or it can be iced with butter cream of glacé icing. It should be eaten very new, preferably on the day of baking, as it tends to go rubbery on keeping.

Angel Food Pudding

The cake can have a slice cut off the top and the centre hollowed out to be filled with any creamy, fruity filling, or with icecream. The lid is put back and the cake decorated with cream or fruit.

Chiffon Cake · Mixer (and Blender)

Makes 8 in. (20 cm.) cake

4 oz. (100 g.) *flour (plain),*
  well sifted
6 oz. (150 g.) *caster sugar*
1½ *level teasp. baking powder*
½ *level teasp. salt*
5 *tbs. cooking oil*
3 *egg yolks*

6 *tbs. water*
1 *teasp. vanilla*
grated rind of ½ *lemon*
4 *egg whites*
¼ *level teasp. cream of tartar*

1. Light the oven at 350°F (180°C, Gas No. 4) and have ready the 8 in. (20 cm.) square cake tin or a 9 × 5 in. (23 × 13 cm.) loaf tin or 9 in. (23 cm.) ring mould (see note 6). *Do not grease.*

2. Put the sifted flour, salt, sugar and baking powder into the mixer bowl or blender. Add the oil, egg yolks, water, vanilla and lemon rind and mix or blend at medium speed for a very short time until a smooth batter is made.

3. In another large bowl, whisk the egg whites with the cream of tartar at fast speed, until they stand in stiff peaks.

4. Dribble the egg yolk batter over the surface of the whites and very gently use a rubber or plastic spatula to fold the batter in. Continue dribbling over the surface and folding until all the batter is used. Take care to scrape the spatula right across the bottom of the bowl and lift and fold any batter which has collected there.

5. Pour the mixture into the tin, and bake for approximately 45 minutes until the top springs back when lightly touched.

6. As it is so fragile it is important that this cake should be 'hung' while it is cooling. This is easiest done when a ring mould tin is used and can be inverted over a funnel.

   If a cake tin or loaf tin is used this can easily be inverted and two tins or blocks of convenient height used to prop up the sides.

   Hang the cake until it is cold, then loosen the sides with a knife and the cake should fall out when the tin is knocked.

7. This chiffon cake is very good plain, but to make it more festive it can be iced with butter icing (p. 245), vanilla, lemon or orange, or with glacé icing, and decorated.

Victoria Sandwich · Mixer

This is probably the most versatile of all cakes, and the basic recipe given below can be varied in dozens of ways. It can be used as the base for many gateaux and for iced fancies or with other flavours. Only a few of these variations are given below, but the basic method is the same if others are used.

This mixture lends itself very much to making in double or treble quantities and then using for several different types of cake. Flavourings or colourings can be folded into a portion of the mixture after the flour has been added, or a slab of cake can be baked in a large flat tin and it can then be cut up and iced in a number of ways. A cake will quite satisfactorily wait in the refrigerator for oven space before baking.

When making the mixture it is a good idea to make extra and to reserve part of it to make a baked or steamed sponge pudding (e.g. Eve's Pudding, p. 134).

Here then is the recipe for one basic Victoria Sandwich:

4 *oz.* (100 *g.*) *butter (softened)*	2 *eggs*
4 *oz.* (100 *g.*) *caster sugar*	4 *oz.* (100 *g.*) *self-raising flour*

1. Light the oven at 375°F (190°C, Gas No. 5). Line the bottom of two 7 in. (17 cm.) sandwich tins with paper and grease both the paper and the sides of the tins.
2. Beat the sugar and butter slowly until they are mixed and then at medium speed until the mixture is very pale, fluffy and light.
3. Continue beating at medium speed whilst adding the eggs, one at a time. Wait until the first egg is completely incorporated before adding the second. Any flavourings are best beaten in at this stage although they can be folded in after the flour.
4. Stop the mixer, sift in the flour, and fold it in with the mixer at slowest speed.
5. Divide the mixture evenly between the two 7 in. (17 cm.) sandwich tins. Smooth the mixture.
6. Bake with both tins on a middle shelf of the oven, for about 20 minutes until the cakes are firm and resilient to the touch.

7. Turn out and cool on a wire rack, then sandwich together with jam, cream or butter cream, and dredge top with icing or caster sugar, or ice the cake and decorate.

Variations on Victoria Sandwich
Orange Gateau

CAKE BASE

Ingredients as for Victoria Sandwich, together with:
grated rind of one orange, 2 teasp. orange juice, stirred in with the flour or afterwards if a large batch of mixture has been made.

ICING

4 oz. (100 g.) butter (softened) $1\frac{1}{2}$ tbs. orange juice
8 oz. (200 g.) sifted icing sugar   1 teasp. finely grated orange
                                      rind

DECORATION

1 oz. (25 g.) toasted flaked
  almonds
3 oz. (75 g.) orange jelly   (sieved if it has slivers of
  marmalade   peel in it)

1. Bake the cake as for Victoria Sandwich, and cool.
2. Put the butter for the icing into the mixer bowl and sift in the icing sugar. Beat at slow speed until mixed, then increase to medium and continue beating until light and fluffy. Add the orange rind and juice and beat well until they are incorporated.
3. Sandwich the cakes together with a little of the butter icing.
4. Spread butter icing all round the sides of the cake, then roll the sides in the browned, sliced almonds.
5. Cover the top of the cake with a thin layer of butter cream and then spread the jelly marmalade over this.
6. Put the remaining butter icing into a piping bag, and use it to decorate the cake with lines, roses, shells etc. If liked, finish the decoration with angelica, golden balls etc.

Coffee Sandwich Cake
Make as for Victoria Sandwich cake, but beat in with the egg, 2 rounded teaspoons of instant coffee powder dissolved in 1 tablespoon hot water.

When baked and cold, sandwich the two cakes together with coffee butter icing (p. 246) and ice with the same, or with coffee glacé icing. The top can be decorated with piped whipped cream, and/or shelled walnuts, halved or chopped.

Small Cakes using the Victoria Sandwich Mixture

It is easy to mix up a large amount of Victoria Sandwich mixture and make part into small cakes. Alternatively several varieties of small cakes can be made from the same batch of mixture. All these cakes can be iced with glacé icing or butter cream (p. 246) and decorated to give them a more festive appearance. Using the basic quantities for Victoria Sandwich, i.e.

4 oz. (100 g.) *butter*
4 oz. (100 g.) *sugar*
2 *eggs*
4 oz. (100 g.) *self-raising flour*

} *makes 20 small cakes*

for small cakes make the following variations:

Cherry Cakes

Make the Victoria Sandwich mixture and fold in 3 oz. (75 g.) chopped glacé cherries. Put into greased patty tins or paper cases, half-filling each, and bake at 400°F (200°C, Gas No. 6) for 10–15 minutes until resilient and brown.

Queen Cakes

Make the Victoria Sandwich mixture, folding in a teaspoonful of grated lemon rind and 2 oz. (50 g.) currants. Put into greased patty tins or paper cases, half-filling each, and bake at 400°F (200°C, Gas No. 6) for 10–15 minutes until resilient and brown.

Chocolate Cakes

Make the Victoria Sandwich mixture, folding in 8 drops of vanilla essence and 1 oz. (25 g.) sifted cocoa with the flour if possible or adding to a previously prepared mixture. Put into greased patty tins or paper cases, half-filling each, and bake at 400°F (200°C, Gas No. 6) for 10–15 minutes until resilient and brown. Ice with chocolate icing.

Coffee Cakes

Make up the Victoria Sandwich mixture, folding in 2 teaspoonfuls of instant coffee powder dissolved in 1 tablespoon of hot water (*or* 2 teaspoonfuls coffee essence). Put in greased patty tins or paper cases, half-filling each, and bake at 400°F (200°C, Gas No. 6) for about 15 minutes until brown and resilient. Ice with coffee icing.

Orange or Lemon Cakes

Make up the Victoria Sandwich mixture. Grate finely the rind of 1 orange, *or* use 2 teaspoonfuls of finely grated lemon rind and fold these in with the flour if possible, or after making up mixture.

Bake at 400°F (200°C, Gas No. 6) until resilient and brown – 10–15 minutes. Ice with orange or lemon icing.

Butterfly Cakes

Make little cakes using the Victoria Sandwich mixture, either plain, coffee, chocolate, lemon or orange. Cut a circle from the top of each cake and cut it in half to make the butterfly's wings. Put a little butter icing of suitable flavour, or jam, on to the centre of the cake and arrange the wings in it, standing up in a slanting position.

Mocha Sponge Cake · Mixer

4 oz. (100 g.) *butter (softened)*
4 oz. (100 g.) *caster sugar*
2 *eggs*
3½ oz. (90 g.) *self-raising flour*

1½ oz. (40 g.) *powdered drinking chocolate*
1 *rounded teasp. instant coffee powder*

1. Line the bottom of two 7 in. (17 cm.) sandwich tins and grease the sides and paper thoroughly, and light oven at 375°F (190°C, Gas No. 5).
2. Cream the butter and sugar together at medium speed, until they are light and fluffy.
3. Continue beating and add the eggs, one at a time.

4. Sift together the flour and the drinking chocolate, and dissolve the coffee in one dessertspoon of hot water.

5. Fold the flour, chocolate and coffee together into the creamed mixture, either using the mixer turned to the very slowest speed, or by hand using a metal tablespoon. Take care not to overmix.

6. Divide the mixture between the two sandwich tins, and bake for 20–30 minutes, until firm and resilient to the touch.

7. When cooked, cool slightly before turning out of the tins, then cool on a wire tray. When cold, sandwich together with mocha butter cream (p. 246) and ice with mocha icing (p. 242).

Layer Cake · Mixer

Make 7 in. (17 cm.) cake

5 oz. (125 g.) *butter (softened)*	6 oz. (150 g.) *self-raising flour*
5 oz. (125 g.) *caster sugar*	2 tbs. milk
3 eggs (separated)	jam and fillings and icing

1. Line the bottoms of two 7 in. (17 cm.) sandwich tins with paper, and grease the sides and bottoms of the tins. Light oven at 400°F (200°C, Gas No. 6).

2. Cream the butter and sugar together at medium speed, until light and fluffy.

3. Continue beating at medium speed while adding the egg yolks, one at a time.

4. When they are fully beaten in, turn the speed down to slow and fold in the sifted flour and the milk. Use the mixer just long enough to incorporate the flour and no longer.

5. Whisk the egg whites at fast speed to soft peak stage.

6. Use a metal tablespoon to fold the stiff whites into the cake mixture, folding gently for just enough time to make a uniform mixture and no longer.

7. Divide the mixture between the two prepared tins and bake until risen, brown and resilient to the touch – 25–30 minutes.

8. Turn out and cool on a wire rack, and when cold split each cake into two.

9. These four pieces can now be sandwiched with jam or with any butter cream (pp. 245–7) and the cake can be iced with any of a variety of icings (pp. 241–3). The mixture can also be flavoured with the rind of an orange or a lemon, finely grated.

Almond and Coconut Cake · Mixer

A cake with a crisp topping, yet which keeps well, and stays moist.
Makes an 8 in. (20 cm.) cake

CAKE BASE

8 oz. (200 g.) *butter* (or 4 oz.
  (100 g.) *margarine and* 4 oz.
  (100 g.) *butter*) (*softened*)
8 oz. (200 g.) *caster sugar*
4 eggs (3 large eggs) and 1 yolk
½ teasp. vanilla essence

4 oz. (100 g.) *plain flour*
4 oz. (100 g.) *self-raising flour*
1 oz. (25 g.) *ground almonds*
1 oz. (25 g.) *desiccated coconut*

NUTTY TOPPING

1 egg white
3 oz. (75 g.) caster sugar
½ oz. (15 g.) desiccated coconut
1 oz. (25 g.) ground almonds

½ teasp. vanilla
½ oz. (15 g.) almonds (blanched
  and flaked)

1. Line and grease an 8 in. (20 cm.) cake tin – round or square. Light the oven at 350°F (180°C, Gas No. 4).
2. Cream the fat and sugar at medium speed until white and very light and fluffy, and then beat in the vanilla, the egg yolk, and the eggs, one at a time.
3. With mixer at slowest speed, fold in the sifted flours, the ground almonds and the coconut, until the mixture is homogeneous, but no longer.
4. Turn the mixture into the prepared tin and smooth down.
5. Now make the topping:
a. Whisk the egg white in a small mixer bowl, or use a hand-held mixer. If only a large mixer is available, a hand whisk must be used for this small quantity.
b. When the egg white is at the soft peak stage, fold in the sugar,

coconut, ground almonds and vanilla using a metal tablespoon or the mixer running at slowest speed.

6. Smooth the topping over the cake mixture and sprinkle with the flaked almonds.

7. Bake for about 1½ hours. As the topping is crisp, it is impossible to test the cake by touch, so a skewer must be inserted and should come out clean when the cake is cooked.

8. After a few minutes, turn out of the tin and cool on a rack.

Banana Cake · Mixer

A moist and unusual cake which is very popular.
Makes a 7 in. (17 cm.) cake

4 oz. (100 g.) butter (softened)	7 oz. (175 g.) self-raising flour
5 oz. (125 g.) caster sugar	½ level teasp. bicarbonate of
1 egg	soda
10–12 oz. (250–300 g.) ripe	1 tbs. milk
bananas	
(3 average bananas)	

1. Line and grease a 7 in. (17 cm.) cake tin. Light oven at 300°F (150°C, Gas No. 2).

2. Cream butter and sugar at medium speed until they are light and fluffy.

3. Break the egg into the bowl and continue beating at medium speed until it is incorporated, then add the bananas which have been roughly mashed with a fork, and beat them in.

4. Stop the mixer, sift in the flour and baking powder, add the milk and fold all together with the mixer running at its slowest speed.

5. Turn into the prepared tin and bake until firm and resilient to the touch – about 1¼ hours.

6. Turn out and cool on a rack, then ice the top. This can be done with any glacé or butter icing, but lemon flavour seems to go best with the banana. (For Lemon Butter Icing see p. 246). For lemon glazé icing, just moisten sifted icing sugar with lemon juice until the desired spreading consistency is reached.

Banana Tea Bread · Mixer (and Blender)

Makes 1 medium loaf

3 oz. (75 g.) butter (softened)	¼ level teasp. bicarbonate of
6 oz. (150 g.) caster sugar	soda
2 eggs	½ level teasp. salt
1 lb. (400 g.) bananas	4 oz. (100 g.) nuts
7 oz. (175 g.) self-raising flour	

1. Light the oven at 350°F (180°C, Gas No. 4). Grease a loaf tin 8 in. × 4 in. (20 × 10 cm.).
2. Using the blender at slow speed for a few seconds, roughly chop the nuts.
3. Cream the butter and the sugar at slow speed, increasing to medium, until the mixture is light and fluffy. At this stage beat in the eggs one at a time.
4. Peel the bananas and roughly chop into 1 in. (2 cm.) lengths.
5. Drop the lumps of banana one at a time into the bowl, continuing beating at medium speed. This will mash the banana completely.
6. Stop the mixer and sift in the flour, bicarbonate of soda and salt. Add the nuts and fold all together, either using a metal tablespoon or the mixer at very slow speed.
7. Turn the mixture into the prepared tin.
8. Bake on the middle shelf of the oven until risen, browned and resilient to the touch – about 1¼ hours.
9. Turn on to a wire rack after a few minutes and, next day, slice for buttering.

Chocolate Cake · Mixer

A quick, one-stage cake, moist and delectable

8 oz. (200 g.) self-raising flour	8 oz. (200 ml.) milk
2 oz. (50 g.) cocoa powder	3 eggs
6 oz. (150 g.) caster sugar	1 tbs. black treacle
½ level teasp. salt	½ teasp. vanilla essence
4 oz. (100 g.) luxury margarine	

1. Light the oven at 300°F (150°C, Gas No. 2) and line and grease an 8 in. (20 cm.) cake tin (square or round).

2. Sift the flour, cocoa, sugar and salt into the mixer bowl.

3. Add the margarine, milk, eggs, treacle and vanilla essence, and mix at slow speed until all is homogeneous, but no longer. Make sure that the margarine is completely beaten in.

4. Turn the mixture into the prepared tin, and bake for about $1\frac{1}{4}$–$1\frac{1}{2}$ hours until the cake is firm and resilient to the touch.

5. Turn out and cool on a wire rack, and when cold split and sandwich with Chocolate Butter Icing (p. 246) and/or ice with Chocolate Glacé Icing (p. 242).

Christmas Cake · Mixer

Makes an 8 in (18 cm.) square or 9 in. (20 cm.) round cake, proportionately smaller with metric measures.

$\frac{1}{2}$ lb. (200 g.) butter (softened)	pinch of bicarbonate of soda
$\frac{1}{2}$ lb. (200 g.) soft, dark brown sugar	2 tbs. sherry
	few drops of gravy browning
4 eggs (3 large eggs)	1 lb. (400 g.) currants
1 tbs. black treacle	12 oz. (300 g.) sultanas
$\frac{1}{2}$ lb. (200 g.) plain flour	6 oz. (150 g.) seedless raisins
1 oz. (25 g.) ground almonds	2 oz. (50 g.) mixed peel (chopped)
$\frac{1}{2}$ level teasp. mixed spice	$2\frac{1}{2}$ oz. (70 g.) mixed nuts (almonds and walnuts etc.)
$\frac{1}{2}$ level teasp, ground nutmeg	
rind of $\frac{1}{2}$ lemon grated	4 oz. (100 g.) glacé cherries

1. Line the cake tin with a double layer of newspaper and then a layer of greaseproof paper, cutting all 2 in. (5 cm.) above the top of the tin. Light the oven at 300°F (150°C, Gas No. 2).

2. Weigh and prepare the fruit as follows:

Currants: Wash (if necessary) and remove any stalks.

Sultanas and Raisins: As with currants and then chop roughly on a board using a sharp knife – chopping these keeps the cake moist but it cannot be done in the blender as the fruit goes sticky almost immediately.

Mixed Peel: Chop into small dice.

Nuts: Chop with a sharp knife or in the blender. If in the latter, put in the jar and switch on/off at maximum speed for the minimum time so that some fair-sized pieces of nut remain.

Glacé Cherries: Cut into four.

3. Sift together the flour, spices and ground almonds.

4. Cream the butter and sugar at medium speed until light and fluffy.

5. In another basin beat the eggs, treacle, browning and bicarbonate of soda and continuing with the mixer at medium speed, slowly add this mixture to the creamed butter and sugar, allowing each portion to become completely absorbed before adding the next. Unless this is done very carefully it may be that the mixture will begin to curdle. This is not as disastrous as it might be in another cake, as such a rich mixture, in any case, will not rise much.

6. Add all the fruit and dry ingredients, the lemon rind, finely grated, and the sherry, and with the mixer at slowest speed, fold all together. If the mixer is a small one it may be necessary to do this last stage by hand in a bigger bowl.

7. Turn into the prepared tin and bake for $3\frac{1}{2}$–4 hours, then test with a skewer to see if the cake is cooked right through. Cool in the tin and remove the papers when cold.

8. Cover the cake with almond paste and finally with royal icing (p. 243). A series of holes can be made with a skewer at intervals of 1 in. (3 cm.) before covering with almond paste, and half a teaspoonful of rum or sherry run into each to make the cake more moist.

Wedding Cake or an Anniversary Cake

The very rich, dark fruit cake mixture given above is equally suitable for a 'special occasion' cake and can be made in much larger quantities. In this case it will certainly be necessary to mix in the dry ingredients by hand, but the heaviest work of creaming and beating in the eggs can still be done by the mixer. Just as a guide, 5 times the quantities given for Christmas cake will make a 3-tier cake with a 12 in. (30 cm.) square bottom, 9 in. (23 cm.) square middle and 6 in. (15 cm.) square top tier.

The cakes should be covered with almond paste and royal icing, and decoration added as liked.

Plain Orange Cake · Mixer

Makes 1 medium loaf

7 oz. (175 g.) plain flour	1 egg
2½ level teasp. baking powder	1 tbs. orange juice
½ level teasp. salt	1 tbs. lemon juice
2 oz. (50 g.) butter (softened)	grated rind of 1 orange
6 oz. (150 g.) caster sugar	2 tbs. milk

1. Line a loaf tin 8 × 4 in. (20 × 10 cm.) with paper and grease the paper thoroughly. Light the oven at 375°F (190°C, Gas No. 5).
2. Cream the butter and sugar, starting at slow speed and increasing to medium. Continue beating until the mixture is light and fluffy.
3. Beat in the egg, followed by the juices and rind.
4. Sift together the flour, baking powder and salt, and with the milk fold them into the creamed mixture using the mixer at very slow speed for a short time.
5. Turn the mixture into the prepared tin and bake for 30–40 minutes, until brown and resilient to the touch.
6. Turn out and cool on a rack. When cold the cake can be split and sandwiched with orange butter cream (p. 246) or it can be eaten plain when fresh, and, as it becomes staler, it is very pleasant with butter, sliced as a tea bread.

Orange and Walnut Cake · Mixer (and Blender)

8 oz. (200 g.) self-raising flour	grated rind of 1 orange
5 oz. (125 g.) butter (softened)	2 oz. (50 g.) walnuts
3 oz. (75 g.) caster sugar	2 eggs (separated)
4 tbs. water	additional walnuts for
2–3 tbs. marmalade (well flavoured)	decoration

1. Light the oven at 350°F (180°C, Gas No. 4). Prepare a 7 in. (17 cm.) cake tin, by lining the bottom and sides with paper.

2. Blend the nuts at slow speed for a few seconds, until they are roughly chopped. Do not chop too much as the cake is pleasant with some large pieces of nut in it.

3. Cream the butter and sugar, first slowly and then at medium speed, until the fat and sugar are fully creamed, light and fluffy. Add the orange rind at the end of creaming.

4. Beat the egg yolks into the creamed mixture, one at a time.

5. Reduce the speed of the mixer to slow and fold in the marmalade, nuts, flour and water.

6. Whisk the egg whites at fast speed to soft peak stage.

7. Gently fold the beaten egg whites into the cake mixture with a metal tablespoon and then turn into the prepared tin.

8. Bake for $1\frac{1}{4}$–$1\frac{1}{2}$ hours, until firm and resilient to the touch.

9. Turn out of the tin, and when cold ice either with orange water icing (p. 241) or with orange butter cream (p. 246). In addition, the cake can be split and sandwiched with orange butter cream. Decorate with shelled half walnuts.

Old-fashioned Seed Cake · Mixer

Makes 7 in. (17 cm.) cake

8 oz. (200 g.) butter (softened)	2 oz. (50 g.) ground rice
8 oz. (200 g.) caster sugar	3 level teasp. caraway seeds
4 eggs (separated)	$\frac{1}{4}$ level teasp. grated nutmeg
8 oz. (200 g.) self-raising flour	pinch of salt

1. Light oven at 325°F (160°C, Gas No. 3) and line a 7 in. (17 cm.) cake tin with paper.

2. Cream the butter and sugar, first at slow speed and then increasing to medium, until the mixture is very pale, fluffy and light.

3. Add the egg yolks one at a time to the creamed mixture, beating them in well, with the mixer at medium speed.

4. Beat in the caraway seeds.

5. Turn the mixer to its slowest speed and fold in the sifted flour, salt, ground rice and nutmeg until they are just incorporated.

6. Whisk the egg whites at fast speed to soft peak stage.
7. Fold the whites into the cake mixture, using a metal tablespoon, and turn into the prepared tin.
8. Bake until firm and resilient to the touch – about 2 hours.

(If there is any difficulty in buying caraway seeds at the grocer's shop, they may be obtained at the chemist.)

Sultana Cake · Mixer

Makes a cake 7 in.–8 in. (18 cm.) diameter.

This cake keeps well, remaining moist, and the recipe is very versatile, because other fruits can be substituted for the sultanas to give a variety of cakes. Hence a double quantity could be mixed in one batch and divided into two at the last, and different fruits folded in to each half to give two differently flavoured cakes.

½ lb. (200 g.) butter (softened)
½ lb. (200 g.) caster sugar
3 eggs
12 oz. (300 g.) self-raising flour
2 oz. (50 g.) ground almonds
½ lb. (200 g.) sultanas

1. Line a 7 in. or 8 in. (18 cm.) cake tin, and light oven at 350°F (180°C, Gas No. 4).
2. Cream the butter and sugar until light and fluffy, starting at slow speed and increasing to medium once the sugar is incorporated.
3. Break in the eggs, one at a time, beating all the while.
4. Stop the mixer, add the almonds, the sifted flour, and the sultanas, and fold these in with the mixer running at the slowest speed, or by hand.
5. Transfer to the prepared cake tin and bake until firm (about 1½ hours).

VARIATIONS

Cherry Cake
Substitute 6–8 oz. (150–200 g.) glacé cherries, cut in quarters, for the ½ lb. (200 g.) sultanas. (If only cut in halves the cherries are more likely to sink to the bottom of the cake.)

Currant Cake

Substitute 8 oz. (200 g.) cleaned currants and finely grated rind of a lemon for the sultanas.

Date and Walnut Cake

Substitute 3 oz. (75 g.) coarsely chopped walnuts and 6 oz. (150 g.) chopped dates for the sultanas.

Swiss Meringues · Mixer

Makes 16 large meringue shells or 40 small meringue shells

> 4 egg whites (separated)   whipped cream for serving
> 8 oz. (200 g.) caster sugar

1. Whisk the egg whites at fast speed to soft peak stage. If the whites are whisked further, until the peaks are very stiff and the white becomes dry-looking, the foam will not hold the sugar so well and the meringues will be disappointing in volume.
2. Once the required stiffness has been reached add 4 oz. (100 g.) of the sugar, by rapidly putting in one teaspoonful after another, while continuing to whisk at fast speed.
3. When half the sugar has been added in this way, stop the mixer, and sift the other 4 oz. (100 g.) over the surface of the meringue; fold it in very gently with a metal tablespoon.
4. Have ready a large baking sheet, covered with paper which has been well oiled with cooking oil. Wipe off any excess oil with a screw of crumpled paper. On to this sheet shape the meringues using two wet tablespoons or with a pipe and bag. A pipe of $\frac{1}{2}$ in.– $\frac{5}{8}$ in. ($1\frac{1}{2}$ cm.) diameter is best and it can be either plain or star shaped. The meringues may be large, or very small if required for a dainty tea party. Pipe them close together so as to be almost touching.
5. Bake in the oven at its lowest setting, 180°–210°F (80–100°C). On some cookers this may not be low enough and the meringues will turn biscuit coloured. In this case the door can be propped very slightly ajar with a folded towel, and on a gas cooker, the gas tap turned only half on, to keep the temperature down (should take 4–5 hours).

6. Dry out completely until firm to pressure on the base, then cool.

7. Store in an airtight tin, where they will keep well for 1–2 weeks.

8. When required, sandwich the shells together with whipped cream. This must be done immediately before serving as in an hour or two the meringues will go soft.

Italian Meringues · Mixer

This meringue mixture makes harder meringues with a closer texture than the conventional Swiss meringues. It therefore keeps better, is easier to pipe and is capable of holding chopped fruit and nuts, to give fancy meringues. It should be dried for a longer time at a cooler temperature.

Plain Italian Meringues

Makes 36 small meringues

3 egg whites
9 oz. (250 g.) icing sugar

whipped cream to sandwich

1. In a well-warmed mixer bowl, whisk the egg whites and the sifted icing sugar. Use medium speed to begin and, increasing to fast, continue whisking until the meringue is very white and stands in *stiff* peaks when the whisk is lifted out. This may take up to 10 minutes.

2. Pipe with a plain pipe $\frac{5}{8}$ in. or $\frac{3}{4}$ in. (1½–2 cm.) diameter, on to a baking sheet covered with a well-oiled paper. Large or small round meringues may be made, or fingers.

3. Dry the meringues very slowly, either in the oven with the lowest possible setting, and with the door propped slightly open with a towel (5–6 hours), or preferably in a hot cupboard or other similar warm place for 12–18 hours (overnight).

4. When dry, sandwich in pairs with whipped cream or store in airtight containers until required.

MERINGUE FANCIES

The above basic mixture can be flavoured in a variety of ways to give more festive cakes. These can be served on their own or sandwiched together with whipped cream or butter cream.

Coffee

Add 2 level tablespoons instant coffee powder to the eggs and sugar and whisk and pipe as 1–4 above. Using a star pipe of similar diameter will give attractively shaped meringues. Finish each one with a chocolate polka dot or with a few flaked almonds. Sandwich with whipped cream or with coffee butter cream.

Cherry and Coconut (or Walnut)

Add to plain meringue mixture:

> 3 oz. (75 g.) *glacé cherries*
> 1½ oz. (40 g.) *desiccated coconut or chopped walnuts*

Follow the method as given for the Italian meringues as far as the end of stage 3, then fold the chopped cherries and nuts into the stiff meringue mixture, using a metal spoon. Pipe as for plain meringues, or use a wet tablespoon to shape the mixture. Top each meringue with a half glacé cherry.

Ginger

Add 2–3 oz. (50–75 g.) crystallized ginger. Follow the method as given for the Italian meringues as far as the end of stage 3, then fold in the finely chopped ginger with a metal tablespoon. Save a small slice of ginger to top each meringue before drying.

Nuts

Add 1½–2 oz. (40–50 g.) browned chopped nuts.

Follow the method as given for the Italian meringues as far as the end of stage 3, then fold in the browned chopped nuts (they can be chopped in the blender), using a metal tablespoon. Top each meringue with a browned hazelnut, almond or walnut before drying.

Coconut Meringues · Mixer

Makes 12–16 meringues

2 egg whites
5 oz. (150 g.) caster sugar
4 oz. (100 g.) desiccated coconut

colouring – a few drops of
red or green to give a
delicate colour if desired

1. Light the oven at 300°F (150°C, Gas No. 2) and prepare a baking sheet by covering it with oiled paper.
2. Whisk the egg whites at fast speed to soft peak stage.
3. Continue whisking at fast speed while adding half the sugar rapidly, a teaspoonful at a time.
4. Turn the mixer to the slowest speed and fold in the remaining sugar, the coconut and any colouring. It is perhaps nicest to colour half the mixture with a few drops of colouring and leave the other half plain.
5. Either pipe with a ½ in. (12 mm.) plain nozzle or drop from a spoon into rocky circles on to the prepared tin.
6. Bake for 40–45 minutes until the white meringues are tinged a delicate biscuit colour.
7. When slightly cooled transfer to a wire rack, and store in an airtight tin. When required sandwich with whipped cream or with butter icing as desired, or serve plain.

14

Biscuits

කිරිකිරිකිරිකිරිකිරිකිරිකිරිකිරිකිරිකිරිකිරිකිරි

Biscuits – A Basic Recipe with Variations · Mixer

Make a large batch and flavour in a variety of ways then store in airtight tins. Makes 36 (30) biscuits

8 oz. (200 g.) plain flour
4 or 5 oz. (100–125 g.) butter
  (softened)
4 oz. (100 g.) caster sugar
1 small egg
choice of flavouring –
  grated rind of 1 lemon
or 2 oz. (50 g.) walnuts,
  coarsely chopped in blender
or 1 level teasp. ground
  cinnamon
or 2 oz. (50 g.) currants
or ½ oz. (15 g.) carraway seeds
or 3 oz. (75 g.) desiccated coconut

1. Light the oven at 350°F (180°C, Gas No. 4). Cream the butter and sugar in the bowl at medium speed, until they are light and creamy.
2. Still at medium speed, gradually beat in the egg. If a large egg must be used, do not add it all, but retain some which can be used for egg wash.
3. Turn the mixer to slow speed, add the flour, and continue mixing until the mixture binds together.
4. At this stage mix the flavouring, either to all, or part of the mixture.
5. If the dough is very soft, allow it to relax and cool in the refrigerator until it is firm enough to roll. Roll out thinly about ⅛ in. (3 mm.) thick in a floured board, and cut into fancy shapes.
6. Place on a greased baking sheet and bake for about 10 minutes (or

longer depending on the size of the biscuit), until they are firm, and very lightly browned. While warm dredge with caster sugar if desired.

Imperial Biscuits

Bake the above recipe without any additional flavouring, shape by using a 2 in. (5 cm.) plain cutter, but cut a small circle from the centre of half the biscuits with a small round cutter. When they are cooked sandwich the biscuits together in pairs with jam so that the jam shows through the hole. The top circle can be iced with water icing (p. 241) or dusted with icing sugar if desired, before sandwiching the biscuits together.

Traffic Light Biscuits – A great favourite at children's teatime.

Make as for Imperial Biscuits above, but use a larger plain cutter, about 4½ in. (12 cm.), and cut three small holes about 1 in. (2½ cm.) in diameter. Drop teaspoonfuls of each of seedless red, seedless yellow and seedless green jam on to the bottom biscuit so that they show through the holes when the top is put on. It will probably be necessary to add additional colouring essence to the jams to make them distinctive and if no greengage jam is available, it is possible to add green colouring to a yellow jam.

Cats' Tongues · Mixer

Makes 32 (30) biscuits

4 oz. (100 g.) *butter (softened)*   2 *egg whites*
4 oz. (100 g.) *caster sugar*   ¼ *teasp. vanilla essence*
4½ oz. (120 g.) *plain flour*

1. Light the oven at 340°F (170°C, between No. 3 and No. 4 Gas).
2. Cream the butter and sugar at medium speed until light and fluffy.

3. Add the egg whites, one at a time, beating well between additions. Beat in the vanilla.

4. At slowest speed fold in the sifted flour for the minimum time necessary.

5. Scrape the mixture into a piping bag (fitted with a $\frac{1}{4}$ in. (6 mm.) plain pipe) and pipe $2\frac{1}{2}$–3 in. (6–8 cm.) lengths on to a greased baking sheet. The biscuits must be 2 in. (5 cm.) apart as they will run out flat.

6. Bake until pale brown at the edges – 15–20 minutes – and remove from the tray to a cooling rack while they are still warm, using a palette knife.

Choco–Walnut Bars · Blender

A wonderful way of using up broken or stale biscuits, or stale cake. Keeps for several weeks. Makes 24 small bars

6 oz. (150 g.) broken biscuits or cake (preferably including 2 oz. (50 g.) digestive biscuits)
2 oz. (50 g.) walnuts
1 generous tbs. golden syrup
2 oz. (50 g.) cocoa
1 oz. (25 g.) caster sugar
$3\frac{1}{2}$ oz. (90 g.) butter
chocolate icing (see method stage 5)

1. Start the blender at maximum speed, then gradually drop the biscuits or pieces of cake through the hole in the lid. Wait until each piece is broken up before adding another.

2. Meanwhile warm together the butter, syrup and sugar, just to melt and amalgamate them, then stir in the crumbs and the sifted cocoa.

3. Chop the nuts, very roughly, by putting in the blender and just switching on and off to maximum speed three times. This should leave largish pieces of nut which form a pleasant contrast to the smooth texture of the chocolate cake.

4. Mix the nuts into the chocolate mixture, and press it all into a shallow, square baking tin 9 × 9 in. (23 × 23 cm.) or a 9 in. (23 cm.) flan ring. Smooth the surface down well, and put in a cold place to set firmly (a refrigerator is ideal).

5. When set, ice with *chocolate icing,* either one of the proprietary brands, or with the following:

2 oz. (50 g.) *cooking chocolate*   ½ oz. (15 g.) *butter*
2½ oz. (60 g.) *icing sugar*

Melt the chocolate with the butter in a bowl over hot water, then stir in the sifted icing sugar and beat. The icing can be smoothed over or roughed up with a fork.

6. When the icing is set, cut the cake into fingers.

Melting Moments · Mixer

Makes 20 (18)

8 oz. (200 g.) *butter (softened)*   ½ teasp. vanilla essence
2 oz. (50 g.) *icing sugar, sifted*   *glacé cherries, angelica,*
6 oz. (150 g.) *plain flour*   *chopped nuts for decoration*
2 oz. (50 g.) *cornflour*

1. Light oven at 375°F (190°C, Gas No. 5).
2. At medium speed cream together the butter, vanilla and icing sugar until well mixed and soft.
3. Sift in the flour and cornflour, and with the mixer at slow speed fold them in thoroughly.
4. Transfer the mixture to a piping bag fitted with a star pipe, and pipe rosettes on to a baking sheet – leaving space between for the biscuits to spread slightly. For quickness the mixture can be dropped in teaspoonfuls on to the baking sheet, but the results are not so attractive.
5. Decorate the centre of each biscuit with cherry and angelica or with nuts, pressed on. Cherries of several different colours are attractive here.
6. Bake until cooked through and only lightly coloured – probably about 10 minutes.

Nut and Cherry Meringue Slice · Mixer (and Blender)

Makes 16 (14) large fingers

3 oz. (75 g.) *soft brown sugar*	1 oz. (25 g.) *nuts – chopped*
3 oz. (75 g.) *butter (softened)*	*medium fine in the blender*
2 eggs *(separated)*	2 oz. (50 g.) *chopped glacé cherries*
6 oz. (150 g.) *self-raising flour*	4 oz. (100 g.) *caster sugar*

1. Light the oven at 325°F (160°C, Gas No. 3). Grease a 12 × 8 in. (30 × 20 cm.) Swiss roll tin.
2. Cream the butter and brown sugar at medium speed (start at slow speed until the sugar is incorporated in the fat).
3. Cream until the fat is light and fluffy, beat in the egg yolks one at a time, then turn the mixer down to the slowest speed, and fold in the sifted flour, using the beaters for the shortest possible time.
4. Spread the mixture smoothly over the bottom of the prepared tin.
5. Cover with the chopped glacé cherries and most of the chopped nuts, reserving a few to scatter over the surface of the meringue.
6. Whisk the egg whites at fast speed to soft peak stage.
7. Continue to whisk at fast speed adding 2 oz. (50 g.) caster sugar slowly, one teaspoonful after another, then stop the beaters. Fold in the remaining 2 oz. (50 g.) sugar by hand, with a metal tablespoon.
8. Spread the meringue carefully over the cherries and nuts, sprinkle with the remaining chopped nuts and bake very slowly for 15 minutes, then turn the oven down to 300°F (150°C, Gas No. 2) and continue baking for 35 minutes in all, until the meringue is crisp and biscuit coloured and the underlying cake mixture firm.
9. Allow to cool in the tin, and when cold cut into fingers or squares with a sharp knife.

Shortbread · Mixer

The quickest and easiest of teatime favourites, which stores very well in an airtight box, and can be made well before the day it is needed. Makes 2 × 7 in. (2 × 17 cm.) rounds.

10 oz. (250 g.) plain flour   (gives an infinitely better
2 oz. (50 g.) rice flour or ground   flavour than margarine)
   rice   4 oz. (100 g.) caster sugar
8 oz. (200 g.) softened butter

1. Light the oven at 350°F (180°C, Gas No. 4).
2. Put the flours in the mixer bowl with the sugar, add the softened butter roughly cut into lumps, and mix into the flour with the machine running at the slowest speed, until all the ingredients are amalgamated into one lump – usually 2–3 minutes.
3. Divide the mixture into two equal portions, and either press into a well-floured 7 in. (17 cm.) shortbread mould and turn on to a baking sheet, or press into two 7 in. (17 cm.) sandwich tins (*not* lined or greased) and mark edges and prick centre with a fork.
4. Bake on centre shelf until the shortbread is firm, and golden brown at the edges – about 45 minutes. Sprinkle with caster sugar.
5. Cool for a short while, but when still warm cut the rounds into suitably sized pieces, marking with the knife almost through to the bottom. Do not turn out of the tin until quite cold.

Shortbread Biscuits

This mixture is also excellent if rolled out ⅛ in. (3 mm.) thick on floured board and cut into fancy biscuit shapes. These should be baked at 350°F (180°C, Gas No. 4) for about 15 minutes, until lightly coloured, and then sifted with caster sugar.

Butterscotch Shortbread · Mixer

Makes 16 squares

4 oz. (100 g.) butter   2 oz. (50 g.) caster sugar
6 oz. (150 g.) plain flour   1 level teasp. baking powder

BUTTERSCOTCH TOPPING
3 oz. (75 g.) butter   1 small tin sweetened
2 oz. (50 g.) soft brown sugar   condensed milk
1 tbs. golden syrup

ICING, OPTIONAL
3 oz. (75 g.) plain chocolate

1. Light the oven at 350°F (180°C, Gas No. 4).
2. Sift the flour and baking powder into the mixer bowl, and add the sugar and butter, roughly cut into lumps.
3. Mix at slow speed and continue until the fat is rubbed into the flour and all binds together into one lump.
4. Press this shortbread mixture into a thin layer in an 8 × 12 in. (20 × 30 cm.) Swiss roll tin, and bake until golden brown – 20–30 minutes.
5. Melt the ingredients for the topping in a pan very slowly, stirring all the time. Boil for 5 minutes while still stirring until the mixture changes colour and texture, and clings to the spoon.
6. Pour the topping, while still warm, over the shortbread, and when cold cover with melted plain chocolate if liked. Cut into squares with a sharp knife.

Strawberry Shortbread Slice · Mixer

Makes 10 slices

SHORTBREAD (This can be prepared some days before use and stored in an airtight tin)
3 oz. (75 g.) plain flour
1 oz. (25 g.) ground rice
3 oz. (75 g.) butter
2 oz. (50 g.) caster sugar

TOPPING
1 oz. (25 g.) butter (softened)
1 oz. (25 g.) caster sugar
4 oz. (100 g.) cream cheese
1 tbs. top of milk
grated rind of 1 lemon
½ lb. (250 g.) strawberries, hulled and sliced. (Smaller fruit are best as then the berries need only be sliced in half)
icing sugar

1. Light oven at 375°F (190°C, Gas No. 5).
2. Put all the ingredients for the shortbread into the mixer bowl and mix at slow speed until all are amalgamated.
3. Either press the shortbread mix into a shallow square tin 7 × 7 in. (17 × 17 cm.) or mark a 7 in. (17 cm.) square on greaseproof paper, place on a baking sheet and press the shortbread mixture evenly over it. This way makes the shortbread easier to manage after baking.

4. Bake until crisp, and just coloured – 20–25 minutes.

5. Cool for a few minutes and then mark (but not cut) into slices with a knife.

6. Turn out of the tin carefully when quite cold.

Topping

7. Cream the butter and sugar at medium speed until they are white and fluffy.

8. Continue beating at medium speed while adding the cheese, the top of the milk and the lemon rind, until all are mixed in.

9. Just before serving, spread the creamy mixture over the short-bread and completely cover with a layer of strawberries. Dust with sieved icing sugar.

10. Cut into 10 slices using the marks already made on the short-bread.

(The shortbread will go very soft if left with the cream mixture for more than a few hours.)

15

Yeast Mixtures

ᖳᖰᖳᖰᖳᖰᖳᖰᖳᖰᖳᖰᖳᖰᖳᖰᖳᖰᖳᖰᖳᖰᖳᖰᖳᖰᖳᖰᖳᖰᖳᖰᖳᖰᖳᖰ

YEAST COOKERY

In this day of multiple bakeries there is nothing which so enhances a cook's reputation or gives her more satisfaction than a freshly baked batch of homemade bread, rolls and teatime delicacies. There are many recipes and suggestions available for yeast cookery so only a few representative mixtures are given here, but the methods can be used for many other yeast recipes.

When using yeast in cookery it is important to have a strong, plain 'bread' flour as opposed to the 'soft' plain flour used for pastry and cakes. The former has a much higher content of gluten, the flour protein, which develops during kneading to give the elastic network which characterizes the structure of bread. It is for this development of the gluten that thorough kneading is so important to give a loaf of good volume.

The mixer is used to mix the dough initially and it is helpful here, but by far its greatest value is to take the time and effort from the kneading of the dough. The machine is fitted with the dough hook (or hooks) in place of the whisks or beaters and is switched on at slow speed to knead the dough, for 2–3 minutes – that is until a rather sticky dough has become firm and rubbery. If a fairly 'soft' flour has been used, rather than a 'strong' bread flour, it will require much longer kneading as the smaller quantity of gluten must be developed to the maximum.

Just as the action of kneading is tiring to the hands, so it is a strain on the motor of the mixer, and is not possible at all with many of the smaller mixers. Some manufacturers do provide dough hooks with small motors, but these must be used warily, and if the motor seems to be labouring it must be switched off immediately. For this reason also, manufacturers give instructions as to how much dough may be kneaded at any one time, and this quantity must be adhered to most carefully.

However, a batch of two or three times the permitted weight can be mixed, and kneaded in several batches, as each kneading will only take 2–3 minutes. There are seven stages in the making of most yeast mixtures, and in between handling, the dough must be covered with a damp cloth, or better still a sheet of plastic, or put inside a large, oiled, plastic bag. This prevents drying and a tough skin forming on the outside, which would in turn prevent rising.

1. **Mixing:** For this the mixer is fitted with the ordinary beater. All the ingredients can be put together at one time. This is called the straight dough mix and is the easiest and quickest method. Better results are obtained, however, if the mixing is carried out in two parts, the yeast batter mix and the dry mix.

a. the yeast batter mix: collect in a jug all the liquid, the yeast, sugar, eggs and one-third of the flour in the recipe. Mix these well together and stand in a warm place to ferment until the batter is light and spongy. This mixing can very well be done in the blender, but as the batter will double in size it may be necessary to transfer it to a larger vessel for fermentation.

b. the dry mix: into the mixer bowl can be collected the remaining two-thirds of the flour, the salt and spices, fat or oil and any fruit or nuts. If the fat must be rubbed into the flour, this can be done by the beater of the mixer working at the slowest speed. When the yeast batter is fully sponged, start the mixer beaters at slowest speed and rapidly pour the batter into the mixer bowl until the dough is fully mixed. This mixing of the liquid into the bulk of the flour should be done all at once, rather than in dribs and drabs, and a rather soft dough should be made in preference to a dry one. A softer dough will give a more successful finished product, and as with the mixer the handling of the dough is reduced to a minimum, the dough can start more sticky than if the kneading were done by hand. The subsequent vigorous kneading with the dough hook will cause the dough to absorb more liquid and the gluten network to become stronger.

2. **Kneading:** Once the dough is mixed together, immediately change the beater for the dough hook and continue with the motor running at slow speed for 2–3 minutes. If it has been necessary to use 'soft' cake flour for the yeast mixture, then the kneading must be longer than this to make the dough resilient. Again, this process is very wearing on the motor of the mixer, so it is important not to continue it longer than the minimum necessary.

3. **Rising:** Once the dough has been kneaded it should be put to rise, either in a warm or a cold place.

Formerly it was thought that dough must rise in a warm place, but recently it has been realized that just as good a rise, if not better, can be obtained by putting the dough in a cool place (larder) or even in a domestic refrigerator, but of course for a longer time. This can be extremely convenient, for the dough can be mixed and given the initial kneading, then covered and put to rise cold for a number of hours, perhaps overnight, and then given the final kneading and shaping just before baking fresh for a meal.

Here then are the rising times:

a. In a very warm place, e.g. airing cupboard $\frac{1}{2}$ hour
b. On the table in a warm kitchen or on a
    hot summer's day   1 hour
c. In a cool place such as a larder   4 hours
d. In a refrigerator   12 hours approx.
                          or overnight

It is worth repeating that it is most important to prevent a skin forming by drying and this can best be done by putting the dough in a large, oiled, plastic bag, with plenty of room to rise. Wherever the dough is rising, it will eventually double its size and spring back and feel elastic when dented with a floury finger. This is the point at which to proceed to the next stage, but as the rising time will vary according to the conditions, the dough must be tested for fully rising first.

4. **Knocking Back or Second Kneading:** The dough is again kneaded with the dough hook for about 2 minutes. If a large batch has been made it will be necessary to divide it into several portions, according to the manufacturer's instructions as to the weight of dough which can be kneaded at any one time.

5. **Shaping:** After knocking back, the dough must be shaped, by hand, into loaves or rolls etc. and put into greased and floured tins.

6. **Final Proving:** Again the loaves must be covered and allowed to rise in a warm place until they are fully puffed up with bubbles visible just below the surface.

7. **Baking:** Yeast mixtures require hot ovens so that the heat may penetrate the dough and kill the yeast. 425–450°F (210–220°C, Gas No. 7–8) is usual for plain bread and rolls but 375–400°F (190–200°C, Gas No. 5–6) is sometimes used for richer mixtures containing more fat, eggs, sugar, fruit.

A much better crust is obtained if the air in the oven is moist for a short while at the beginning. This can be done by putting a flat meat tin of water in the bottom of the oven. This will keep the crust soft so that the loaf can continue rising for a few minutes after it is put in the oven. When the loaves or rolls are fully cooked they have a good golden-brown colour, they shrink from the sides of their tins and give out a hollow sound when knocked with the back of a finger.

Yeast goods should be cooled on a wire rack after leaving the oven, to prevent the steam from softening the crust.

Brown Bread and Rolls · Mixer fitted with Dough Hooks

This bread is very quick to make as it requires so little kneading and rising. It can be made with wholemeal flour only, but a mixture of wholemeal with a strong, plain, white flour gives the best rise and flavour. Makes 4×1 lb. ($4 \times \frac{1}{2}$ kg.) loaves.

YEAST MIX

½ pt. (250 ml.) warm water   2 oz. (50 g.) fresh yeast or 2 level
1 teasp. sugar   tbs. dried yeast
1 teasp. flour

DRY MIX

1½ lb. (750 g.) wholemeal   1½ level tbs. salt
  (brown) flour   1 level tbs. sugar
1½ lb. (750 g.) plain white   2 tbs. oil
  (bread) flour

                              1 pt. (500 ml.) water

1. Assemble the ingredients for the yeast mix in a jug and stand in a warm place until it is frothy.

2. Put all the ingredients for the dry mix into the mixer bowl and beating at slow speed, add the frothy yeast mix and the water (warm or cold depending on the place chosen for rising). Add the liquid rapidly so that the dough is quickly mixed.

3. Change the beater for the dough hook as soon as the dough is mixed, and continue using the dough hook with the mixer running at slow speed for 2 minutes. This is all the kneading that is necessary for this bread.

4. Divide the dough into four and shape the loaves or rolls on a floured board as follows:

a. Tin loaves. Roll into 9 in. (23 cm.) roll. Tuck the ends under and place in a 1 lb. (½ kg.) greased loaf tin.

or b. Cobs. Shape each piece into a large bun, pulling down the sides and tucking under tight to make a neat shape, then place on a greased, floured baking sheet.

or c. Batons. Roll the dough into an 8 in. (20 cm.) roll with pointed ends – again place on a greased, floured baking sheet.

or d. Rolls. A quarter of the quantity in this recipe will divide into 9 rolls. Divide the dough and roll each piece individually on the table under the palm of the hand to make a small ball. Place on a greased and floured baking sheet, ¼ in. (5 mm.) apart if soft-sided rolls are wanted, and 1 in. (2½ cm.) apart for crusty rolls.

5. Whatever way of shaping is chosen cover the dough immedi-

ately, preferably by putting the tin in a polythene bag or under a polythene sheet, and leave to rise in a place chosen so that the baking takes place at a convenient time (p. 227).

6. When the dough is doubled in size and springs back when dented with a floury finger either:

a. For a soft-crusted loaf or rolls brush with oil and dredge with flour.

b. For a crisper crust on the loaf or rolls spray or brush with very salty water (1 rounded teaspoon salt to 1 tablespoon water).

7. Bake at 450°F (230°C, Gas No. 8) until the loaves or rolls are a good golden-brown colour, shrink from the tins and sound hollow when knocked on the base – loaves 40–45 minutes, rolls 20–25 minutes.

White Bread and Rolls · Mixer fitted with Dough Hooks

This same dough, after the first rising, can have additions made and be used to shape other yeast goods such as dough cake (p. 233), croissants, fruit breads and pizza. Makes 4×1 lb. ($4 \times \frac{1}{2}$ kg.) loaves or 2×1 lb. ($2 \times \frac{1}{2}$ kg.) loaves and 20 rolls.

YEAST MIX

$\frac{1}{2}$ pt. (250 ml.) *warm water*
1 *teasp. sugar*
1 *teasp. flour*

$\frac{1}{2}$ oz. (15 g.) *dried yeast*
or 1 oz. (25 g.) *fresh yeast*

DRY MIX

3 lb. ($1\frac{1}{2}$ kg.) *strong plain flour*
1 oz. (25 g.) *lard (this can be omitted)*
1 *level teasp. salt*

1 pt. (500 ml.) *warm water (if some milk is included milk bread can be made)*

1. Put the ingredients for the yeast mix in a jug, mix well with a spoon to break up the yeast and leave in a warm place until it becomes frothy.

2. Put the ingredients for the dry mix into the mixer bowl and, using the beaters, rub the lard into the flour at slow speed.

3. Continue mixing at slow speed while pouring the yeast mix into the dry mix and add additional 1 pint (500 ml.) of liquid. The dough should be slightly sticky, so that by the time the kneading is finished it is firm and soft and leaves the sides of the bowl clean.

4. As soon as the liquid is mixed in, change the beaters for the dough hooks. This will be too much mixture for kneading at one time, so divide into batches and knead each at slow speed for 2 minutes with the dough hooks.

5. Put the dough to rise inside an oiled polythene bag in a suitable place, depending on how long it will be before it is required for baking (p. 227).

6. When it has risen to twice its size and springs back when dented, then knead with the mixer again in batches, for 1 minute each.

7. Divide the dough into four and shape the loaves or rolls on a floured board, as required.

Tin loaf: Roll 1 lb. ($\frac{1}{2}$ kg.) dough out into a strip, then roll up like a Swiss Roll and put in a greased 1 lb. ($\frac{1}{2}$ kg.) loaf tin, tucking the ends under.

Plait: Divide 1 lb. ($\frac{1}{2}$ kg.) dough into three and roll each one into a long sausage of 12–14 in. (30–35 cm.). Pinch the ends together and plait, then pinch the other ends together. Put to rise on a floured baking sheet.

Rolls: Divide 2 lb. (1 kg.) of dough into 20 pieces, and roll each one on the floured table under the cupped hand. Give some pressure, and then lift the centre of the palm slightly, to give a round roll. Put on a floured tray, $\frac{1}{4}$ in. (6 mm.) apart if soft-sided rolls are required, or 1 in. ($2\frac{1}{2}$ cm.) apart for rolls crusty all round.

8. Brush the tops of bread or rolls with oil, and put to finally rise, well covered with oiled polythene.

9. When loaves or rolls are well puffed up and spring back when dented they are ready to be baked and should be sprayed with salty water. If soft rolls are required, brush instead with oil and dredge with flour.

10. Bake at 450°F (230°C, Gas No. 8) until brown and hollow-sounding when tapped on the base. Loaves will take 40–45 minutes, rolls 20–25 minutes.

Bridge Rolls, Baps or a Poppy-Seed Plait made from Enriched White Dough · Mixer, fitted with Dough Hooks (and Blender)

The same dough is made up for all three items, and shaped in a variety of ways. It has a soft crust and a light, soft crumb. Makes 24 bridge rolls *or* 14 baps *or* 1 good-sized plait

1 lb. (500 g.) *strong plain white flour*	½ oz. (15 g.) *fresh yeast*
1 *teasp. salt*	2 oz. (50 g.) *butter*
½ *teasp. sugar*	1 *egg*
2 *level teasp. dried yeast or*	½ pt. (250 ml.) *milk* (*warm*)

1. Blend the milk, egg, yeast, sugar and 5 oz. (125 g.) of the flour at fast speed for a few moments until a smooth batter is made. Stand in a warm place to rise for about 20 minutes. If the blender is not available this batter can easily be mixed in a jug.
2. Put the remaining 11 oz. (375 g.) of the flour into the mixer bowl and add the salt and butter. Using the beaters at slow speed, rub the butter into the flour.
3. Continuing to mix at slow speed, pour the frothing batter into the flour until a soft sticky dough is made. Switch off and change the beaters for the dough hooks, then knead the dough for 1–2 minutes at slow speed, until it becomes firmer.
4. Put the dough to rise in a covered container wherever is convenient (p. 227) until it has doubled in size and springs back if lightly dented with a finger.
5. Put in the clean mixer bowl again and knock back with the dough hooks running at slow speed for 1–2 minutes. The dough is now ready for shaping into either:

Bridge Rolls
6. Divide the dough into 24 pieces and roll each one into a little sausage with rounded ends. Place on a greased baking tray ¼ in. (6 mm.) apart.

7. Brush with egg wash, cover with a sheet of oiled plastic, and put to rise until the rolls are doubled in size.

8. Bake in the oven at 425°F (220°C, Gas No. 7) for about 15 minutes until golden brown; cool on a rack and pull apart.

Baps

6. Divide the dough into 14 pieces, and shape each under the palm of the hand into a round roll, then flatten slightly with a rolling pin.

7. Put on a greased and floured tin, $\frac{1}{4}$ in. (6 mm.) apart, brush each bap with oil and cover with a sheet of oiled plastic. Put to rise and when doubled in size and fully risen brush with salt water and dredge with flour. Bake at 400°F (200°C, Gas No. 6) for about 20 minutes, then cool and pull apart.

A Poppy-Seed Plait

6. Divide the dough into 3 and roll each into a sausage 12–14 in. (30–35 cm.) long. Lay side by side on the table and make into a fat plait. Pinch the ends together firmly, then lift the loaf carefully on to a greased and floured baking tin.

7. Cover with oiled plastic and leave to rise until doubled in size, and the dough springs back when dented with the finger.

8. Brush with beaten egg containing a pinch of salt, and sprinkle with poppy seeds.

9. Bake in the oven at 375°F (190°C, Gas No. 5) for about 45 minutes until it is golden brown and sounds hollow when knocked on the base.

Dough Cake · Mixer fitted with Dough Hooks

1 lb. (400 g.) risen white dough	1 egg
3 oz. (75 g.) butter	9 oz. (225 g.) mixed dried fruit
4 oz. (100 g.) sugar	

1. Make the white dough as in recipe on p. 230 and when it is well risen, cut off and weigh 1 lb. (400 g.).

2. Put the dough, together with all the other ingredients, into the mixer bowl, and using the dough hooks and with the machine at

slow speed knead until all the added ingredients are incorporated into the dough.

3. Transfer to a loaf tin $7\frac{1}{2} \times 5$ in. (18 × 12 cm.) or a 7 in. (17 cm.) round cake tin, greased well and floured. Stand in a warm place to rise, covered, until the cake is spongy and reaches the top of the tin, then spray the top with warm water.

4. Bake at 350°F (180°C, Gas No. 4) on the middle shelf until brown and shrinking away from the sides of the tin. It will then sound hollow when knocked. To glaze, brush with a wet brush dipped in honey, and cool on a wire rack.

5. Serve cut in thick slices when new, and as it becomes staler, cut the pieces thinner and butter liberally. In this way it can be enjoyed for about a week.

Doughnuts and Currant Buns · Mixer fitted with Dough Hooks

These yeast buns can both be made from the same basic rich dough, with the addition of jam or currants. Probably the best plan is to make up the whole quantity of dough given here and then use half for currant buns and fry the other half for doughnuts. This is a considerable economy, particularly in the case of doughnuts. Of course the quantities can be varied to suit the circumstances. Makes 24

BASIC BUN DOUGH

$1\frac{1}{2}$ lb. (750 g.) plain flour

2 oz. (50 g.) fresh yeast or $1\frac{1}{4}$ oz.
  (35 g.) dried yeast

1 egg

milk – sufficient to make the
  egg up to $\frac{1}{2}$ pt. (250 ml.)

3 oz. (75 g.) lard

3 oz. (75 g.) sugar

add 5–6 oz. (125–150 g.) currants
  for 24 currant buns

or 5 tbs. jam for 24
  doughnuts

1. Mix the milk, warmed to blood heat, with the yeast and the egg, either with a fork or in the blender at fast speed for a few seconds, and stand in a warm place for 10 minutes, until frothy.

2. Put the flour, sugar and lard cut roughly into lumps, in the mixer

YEAST COOKERY

bowl and using the beater attachment running at slow speed, rub
the lard into the flour.
3. Still using the beater at slow speed, gradually pour in the yeast
liquid until a soft, sticky dough is mixed.
4. Change the beater for dough hooks, and using these at slow
speed knead the dough for 2 minutes.
5. Leave the dough to rise in the mixer bowl covered with a sheet of
plastic, or in a large plastic bag. Since it is a dough with plenty of
yeast it must rise in a cool place.
a. on a cool shelf in the kitchen – 2 hours.
or b. overnight, 12 hours in the refrigerator.
When it is risen it will be doubled in size, with bubbles right to the
surface of the dough.
6. At this point add currants to some or all of the dough. This is
best done by rolling in when kneading by hand.
7. Give each portion of the dough, currant buns and/or doughnuts
two minutes' kneading with the dough hooks running at slow speed,
then divide and shape into 24 buns, by rolling under the palm of the
hand on a slightly oiled surface. Keep all the buns from forming a
dry skin by covering with a plastic sheet or a damp tea-towel. The
doughnuts must be flattened, a small teaspoonful of jam placed in
the centre of each and the edges of the bun folded up together and
sealed firmly. Unless the buns are sealed firmly the jam will burst
out during frying, so if preferred the jam can be omitted at this stage,
and the doughnuts split open after cooking and jam and cream
piped in.
8. Place currant buns, 1 in. (2½ cm.) apart and tops brushed with oil,
or doughnuts, 2 in. (5 cm.) apart, on a greased baking tray – cover
with a polythene sheet. Stand in a warm place until well risen and
with a 'domed' top, about 20 minutes, then cook as follows:

Currant Buns
9. Spray the buns with warm water and bake on the middle shelf of
the oven at 400°F (200°C, Gas No. 6) for about half an hour, until
firm and hollow-sounding when knocked underneath.
10. Glaze by brushing with sugar boiled with milk, and cool on a rack.

235

Doughnuts

9. While they are rising for the second time, heat up the deep fat bath to a temperature of 330°F (170°C) (lower than for chips as the doughnuts need more time to cook right through).

10. Drop the doughnuts into the hot fat, taking care they do not touch, and fry for 12–15 minutes. Drain on crushed absorbent paper and roll immediately in caster sugar. Cool on a rack. Reheat the fat before frying a second batch.

Hot Cross Buns · Mixer fitted with Dough Hooks (and Blender)

Makes 24 buns

INGREDIENTS FOR BUNS

1½ lb. (600 g.) plain flour	2 oz. (50 g.) chopped peel
3 oz. (75 g.) lard	1 rounded teasp. mixed spice
2 oz. (50 g.) sugar	1 or 2 egg yolks
½ oz. (15 g.) milk powder or 1 tbs. condensed milk	1 pt. (500 ml.) warm water (approx.)
6 oz. (150 g.) currants	1¼ oz. (30 g.) dried yeast or 2 oz.
2 oz. (50 g.) sultanas	(50 g.) fresh yeast

INGREDIENTS FOR BATTER
(for Crosses)

4 oz. (100 g.) bread flour	pinch of salt
6 oz. (150 ml.) warm water	1 teasp. sugar
1 tbs. oil	1 teasp. dried yeast or ¼ oz. (10 g.) fresh yeast

1. Mix the yeast with the warm water and the egg yolk, and stand in a warm place for 10 minutes.

2. Put all the other ingredients for the buns in a large bowl and mix in the yeast liquid. If the mixer bowl is large enough use it and the dough hooks, otherwise use the hand to mix a soft, sticky dough, adding a little more water if necessary. Then divide into portions small enough to be handled by the dough hooks and knead each for 1 minute with the mixer running at slow speed.

3. Put the dough to rise, in a polythene bag or in a saucepan with a lid (oiled to prevent sticking) on the kitchen table, or a cool place.

As a lot of yeast has been used it must *not* rise in a warm place. It should double in size and spring back when touched with a finger. It will probably take at least 1½ hours.

4. Knead the dough in batches, using dough hooks, for 1 minute at slow speed.

5. Divide the dough, on an oiled surface, into 24 pieces and roll each one to a round ball, using the palm of the hand to give pressure on to the table.

6. Put the buns on a greased baking sheet, 1 in. (2½ cm.) apart and covered with a sheet of polythene. Put to rise in a warm place until they are well risen with a 'domed' top (probably 20–30 minutes).

7. Meanwhile make the yeasted batter for piping the cross on the buns. Blend all ingredients for the batter at fast speed, until smooth. Stand for 10 minutes before piping.

8. When the buns are fully risen, pipe the batter crosses gently on the top, using a plain ¼ in. (6 mm) pipe and either a forcing bag or a greaseproof paper cone, spray with warm water and bake on the middle shelf of the oven at 400°F (200°C, Gas No. 6) for about 30 minutes.

9. Glaze by brushing the buns when hot, either with a glaze of milk and sugar, or condensed milk, mixed with hot water. Cool on a rack.

10. To reheat the buns, heat in a very low oven, or in a saucepan with a tight lid, over a low heat.

Pizza · Mixer fitted with Dough Hooks (and Slicer/Shredder)

This dish, typical of the Italian countryside, is ideal for a light lunch or supper, and although it can be made with pastry or a scone mixture, neither makes such a good contrast to the rich filling which tops it as dough. Serve with a green salad or celery. Serves 4–6

1 *lb.* (500 g.) *risen white dough*
  (*p. 230*)
12 *oz.* (375 g.) *grated cheese* (*use*
  the slicer/shredder if possible)
4 *tomatoes, skinned and sliced,*
  or 1 *small tin tomatoes*
  drained

4 *oz.* (100–125 g.) *luncheon meat*
  in thin slices
4 *oz.* (100–125 g.) *streaky bacon*
mixed dried or fresh herbs, or
  fresh thyme or majoram or
  chives, finely chopped
olive oil
about 12 *black olives*

1. Make the dough as on p. 230, and when it is well risen, cut off and weigh 1 lb. (500 g.).
2. Put the dough in the mixer bowl and with the dough hooks knead for about 2 minutes on the slowest speed.
3. Take out and shape into a large ball, then press this by hand on to a well-oiled baking sheet until it forms a large circle about 12 in. (30 cm.) diameter and ¼ in. (6 mm.) thick.

Alternatively 4 individual pizzas can be made if the dough is divided into 4 after kneading, and flattened in 4 well-oiled sandwich tins of 5 in. (12 cm.) diameter.

4. Brush the dough with olive oil, then cover it to the edge with layers of the savoury fillings as follows:
a. Grated cheese – of any well-flavoured variety
b. Sliced luncheon meat, salami, ham or tuna fish
c. More grated cheese
d. Tomatoes, sliced or tinned ones squashed, and chopped herbs
e. Yet more grated cheese
f. Bacon, cut into thin strips and made into a lattice over the cheese.
g. Olives arranged in the holes in the bacon lattice to decorate. Capers or pickled walnuts can be used instead.
5. Leave the pizza standing in the warm kitchen for 30 minutes or so, until the dough is puffed up.
6. Bake in an oven at 450°F (230°C, Gas No. 8) at the top until the dough is firm and brown – approximately 20–30 minutes.
7. Serve hot, decorated with watercress or parsley.

Rum Baba · Mixer

So easy to make with a mixer and so good to eat. Serves 6–8

YEAST MIX	¾ oz. (20 g.) fresh yeast or 3 teasp.
5 tbs. warm milk	dried yeast
3 tbs. warm water	1 teasp. flour
1 teasp. sugar	2 large eggs (2 standard
	eggs)

DRY MIX
8 oz. (200 g.) *strong bread flour*
3 oz. (75 g.) *butter*

1 oz. (25 g.) *sugar*
1 *level teasp. salt*
2 oz. (50 g.) *currants*

1. Put the yeast mix in a jug in a warm place until frothy.
2. Put the dry mix into the mixer bowl, and rub the butter into the flour, using the beater at slow speed.
3. When the yeast mix is thoroughly frothy add the eggs and just stir in, then add to the dry mix while continuing to beat at slow speed.
4. Continue to beat the batter at slow speed with the mixer for 1–2 minutes more. The dough hooks can be used at this stage, but as the mixture is so wet, the beaters should be able to cope with it more satisfactorily.
5. Pour the mixture to half-fill the moulds, greased and dusted with ground rice. The moulds can be either individual dariole moulds (about 16) or a 2 pint (1 l.) large mould.
    Light the oven at 400°F (200°C, Gas No. 6), or put on the steamer.
6. Put the moulds in plastic bags for the dough to rise to double its size, by which time bubbles will be rising to the surface.
7. Bake for 30–40 minutes or steam for 1 hour if in a large mould, if in small ones only 15 minutes to bake or $\frac{1}{2}$ hour to steam.
8. Turn out on to a hot dish and soak in the following hot syrup:

RUM SYRUP
4 oz. (100 g.) *sugar*, $\frac{1}{2}$ *pt.*
    (250 ml.) *water or* 2 oz. (50 g.)
    sugar, $\frac{1}{4}$ *pt.* (125 ml.) *water and*

$\frac{1}{4}$ *pt.* (125 ml.) *fruit syrup*
1 *tbs. lemon juice*
2–4 *tbs. rum or* 2 *tbs. liqueur*

Put all the ingredients in a saucepan and bring to the boil, stirring to dissolve the sugar.

Savarin · Mixer

The yeast cake base of the savarin can be made 2–3 days before use, and stored in an airtight tin. It is then ready for the addition of syrup, almonds, fruit and cream when required.

239

Yeast cake base (use exactly the same ingredients as for rum baba, but omit the currants).

Apricot glaze
Browned almonds
Fruit salad of fresh or tinned fruits or one type of fruit.
Whipped Cream
Syrup as for rum baba, made with fruit syrup from tinned fruit and rum or a liqueur.

1. Make the yeast cake base exactly as rum baba, but put to rise in an 8 in. (20 cm.) ring mould, greased and dusted with ground rice.
2. When fully risen bake in an oven at 400°F (200°C, Gas No. 6) for 30–40 minutes, or steam for 1 hour.
3. Make the syrup and heat, then turn out the savarin and saturate it in the hot syrup.
4. Brush the savarin with apricot glaze and spike with the split browned almonds.
5. When cold fill the centre of the savarin with either fruit salad or other tinned or fresh fruit, and decorate with piped whipped cream.

16

Icings and Creams

෴෴෴෴෴෴෴෴෴෴෴෴෴෴෴෴෴෴෴

Glacé Icing (Water Icing) · Mixer or Blender

Sufficient for top of 7 in. (17 cm.) cake

    4 oz. (100 g.) *sifted icing sugar*   4–6 *teasp. hot water or other*
                                               liquid

1. This icing mixes equally well in mixer or blender. If granulated sugar must be used, blend it at medium speed and grind until as fine as possible, then blend in the liquid to make the icing. If the mixer is being used put the icing sugar in the bowl and add the liquid, mixing first at slow speed, then at medium. More or less liquid may be used according to the consistency required.
2. Add colouring and any flavour essences and use immediately.

VARIATIONS ON GLACÉ ICING

Lemon or Orange Glacé Icing
Use lemon juice or orange juice as the liquid in the icing instead of water.
  Colour with a few drops of lemon or orange colouring essence if desired.

Coffee Glacé Icing
Dissolve 3 teaspoons instant coffee powder in 1 tablespoon hot water and add to icing sugar in mixer or blender, in place of water.

Chocolate Glacé Icing · Blender

2 oz. (50 g.) block chocolate (or
plain chocolate)

4 oz. (100 g.) icing sugar
2 tbs. hot water

1. Cut or break the chocolate into rough pieces and drop through the hole in the lid with the blender at slow speed.
2. When the chocolate is chopped to a fine powder, stop the blender and add the icing sugar and the water.
3. Blend at fast speed until quite smooth. It will probably be necessary to stop and scrape down the sides once or twice. (A little more water can be added if desired.) Use immediately.

(The mixer can be used to blend the icing, with the beaters working at medium speed, but the chocolate must then be grated first.)

Mocha Icing · Mixer

Sufficient for 7 in. (17 cm.) cake

2 tbs. icing sugar
1 tbs. drinking chocolate
powder

1 teasp. instant coffee powder
boiling water

1. Sift all the dry ingredients into the mixer bowl.
2. Add a drop of boiling water and beat at slow speed. Add more water gradually, until the icing is of spreading consistency and all the sugar is incorporated. Use immediately.

American Frosting · Mixer

Sufficient to ice 2 × 8 or 9 in. (20 or 23 cm.) cakes

1 lb. (500 g.) granulated sugar
¼ pt. (125 ml.) water
pinch of cream of tartar
2 egg whites

a few drops of colouring
essence and flavouring if
desired

1. Mix the sugar, water and cream of tartar in a small saucepan, and dissolve, stirring over a gentle heat.

2. When it boils continue to heat gently until the syrup reaches 240°F (115°C), or forms a soft ball when a little is dropped into cold water.

3. Meanwhile whisk the egg whites at fast speed to soft peak stage.

4. Continuing to whisk at fast speed, pour the boiling syrup into the bowl near the beaters in a slow, steady stream until the mixture is stiff and stands in peaks if the whisk is withdrawn. Beat in any colouring or flavouring.

5. Pour over the cake at once, and have any decorations ready for use immediately.

Soft American Frosting · Mixer

This icing always remains soft and can be finished attractively with swirls made by the spatula, or by pulling out into peaks. Makes sufficient for 3 × 7 in. (17 cm.) cakes or 2 × 8 or 9 in. (20 or 23 cm) cakes.

Using the method given for American frosting, substitute the following ingredients.

$\frac{1}{4}$ lb. (120 g.) sugar   2 egg whites

2 tbs. water $\frac{1}{2}$ teasp. vanilla

2 scant tbs. golden syrup

Royal Icing · Mixer

1 lb. (500 g.) sifted icing sugar   1 oz. (25 g.) glycerine
  (approx.)   1 teasp. lemon juice

2 egg whites

1. Beat the egg whites, lemon juice and the glycerine for a short time at fast speed.

2. Turn down to medium speed and spoon in the sugar until the desired consistency is reached. Should the sugar fly about turn down to slow speed. Beat for a minute or two at medium speed to improve the consistency and colour.

3. Use the icing as desired. It should be very stiff for coating, but

243

slightly less so for piping edges, and quite soft if a fine writing pipe is to be used. When used for coating a cake the air bubbles in the icing may make a smooth finish difficult. The icing is much improved with standing, preferably overnight, in a covered container, when the bubbles will mostly rise to the surface.

Half-Price Cream (Method I) · Blender and Mixer

For many uses this substitute double cream is hardly distinguishable from the true commodity.

$\frac{1}{2}$ pt. (250 ml.) milk   1 rounded teasp. gelatine
$\frac{1}{2}$ lb. (250 g.) unsalted butter

1. Warm the milk.
2. Put the gelatine in a cup with a little warmed milk and stir thoroughly until it is dissolved.
3. Put the butter into the saucepan with the remaining milk, and stir till it is melted.
4. Blend all the ingredients at fast speed for 10 seconds only.
5. Pour into a covered container, and *keep in a cool place* (preferably a refrigerator) *overnight*. Stirred, it is then ready for use as thick double cream. It can be whipped for piping, but care must be taken not to overwhip, as it quickly returns to the 'buttery' state.

Half-Price Cream (Method II) · Blender and Mixer

Another method, quicker than above, but it only produces whipped cream.

$\frac{1}{2}$ lb. (250 g.) unsalted butter $\frac{1}{2}$ pt. (250 ml) milk

1. Melt the butter in the milk and then blend at fast speed for 1 minute.
2. Put into the refrigerator for at least 1 hour until quite cold.
3. Whisk in the mixer bowl at fast speed until stiff and frothy. It is important to watch the process carefully as the cream changes

rapidly from not quite whipped to 'buttery', and must be stopped between the two.

Crème Patissière (Confectioner's Custard) · Blender

2 oz. (50 g.) sugar	½ pt. (250 ml.) milk
2 egg yolks	flavouring – usually 4–5 drops
¾ oz. (20 g.) plain flour	vanilla essence
1 rounded teasp. cornflour	

1. At medium speed, blend the sugar, yolks, flour, cornflour and 2 tablespoons of the milk until smooth.
2. Boil the remaining milk and pour through the hole in the lid of the blender, while still blending at medium speed.
3. Return the whole mixture to the saucepan and gently heat to boiling point, stirring continuously. Boil for 2–3 minutes, continuing to stir. The crème should thickly coat the back of the spoon at this stage.
4. Beat in the flavouring. Grand Marnier or other liqueurs, rums, or almond essence, can all be used instead of vanilla.
5. Cover and when cool use for filling gateaux, pastries or flans.

Butter Icing · Mixer

This most useful icing can be used both as a sandwich layer inside cakes, or spread on top, and as it pipes easily it is excellent for decoration. It keeps very well for several weeks in a covered container in the refrigerator, so lends itself to being made up in a large batch, unflavoured, and then flavoured as required for use. Makes enough for 4 layers in a 7 in (17 cm.) cake

Butter Icing

4 oz. (100 g.) butter (softened)	2 teasp. boiling water
6–8 oz. (150–200 g.) sifted	½ teasp. vanilla essence or
icing sugar	other flavouring – optional

1. Mix the butter and sugar at slow speed until they begin to amalgamate.

2. Switch to medium speed, add the water and any flavouring, and continue beating until the icing is creamy and fluffy.

Chocolate Butter Icing

2 oz. (50 g.) plain chocolate (melted in a basin over hot water) beaten in. Alternatively, but not so good, 1 level tablespoon of cocoa can be mixed with the water and beaten in. In both cases include vanilla essence.

Coffee Butter Icing

3 rounded teaspoons of instant coffee powder dissolved in the 2 teaspoons of boiling water and beaten in. Include vanilla in this recipe.

Lemon Butter Icing

Add the finely grated rind of 1 lemon and 1 tablespoon of its juice to the creamed butter and sugar. Omit the water and vanilla.

Orange Butter Icing

Add the finely grated rind of 1 orange and 1 tablespoon of its juice (or 1 tablespoon of Cointreau) to the creamed butter and sugar. Omit the water and vanilla. 1 tablespoon of frozen concentrated orange added instead gives an even stronger flavour.

Rum Butter Icing

Add 1 tablespoon of rum instead of the water, or use a few drops of rum essence. Omit vanilla.

Mocha Butter Cream · Mixer

Makes enough for 2 layers in a 7 in. (17 cm.) cake

4 oz. (100 g.) icing sugar	2 tbs. drinking chocolate
2 oz. (50 g.) butter (softened)	powder
	2 teasp. instant coffee powder

1. Sift together the sugar and chocolate powder into the mixer bowl.

2. Dissolve the instant coffee in a very little boiling water.

3. Mix all the ingredients together starting at a slow speed until the sugar is incorporated. Then continue creaming at medium speed, until light and fluffy. It necessary, add a drop of boiling water.

17

Savoury Spreads and Butters

SAVOURY SPREADS

Cheese Spread · Blender (or Slicer/Shredder)

An excellent spread for sandwiches or biscuits, or if spread thickly on toast and browned under the grill it makes a very good toasted cheese. Dry or stale cheese can be used up and it keeps very well. Makes just over $1\frac{1}{4}$ lb. (550 g.)

$\frac{1}{2}$ lb. (200 g.) well-flavoured cheese	2 level teasp. dry mustard
2 oz. (50 g.) butter	2 tbs. vinegar
6 oz. (150 ml.) milk ($\frac{1}{4}$ pt. (125 ml.) + 2 tbs.)	$\frac{1}{2}$ oz. (10 g.) cornflour (2 rounded teasp.)
2 eggs	pepper

1. Melt the butter gently in a saucepan.
2. If using the blender, cut the cheese into rough cubes and blend it with all the other ingredients at medium speed until quite homogeneous – probably about 30 seconds.
or If using the slicer/shredder, grate the cheese coarsely. Mix the cornflour and the mustard to a smooth paste with some of the milk, then stir in all the other ingredients – the eggs broken with a fork.
3. Pour the cheese mixture on to the melted butter and cook over a gentle heat, stirring all the time with a wooden spoon until it thickens. It should have the consistency of thick cream, and coat the back of the spoon thickly. Stir very vigorously as this point is reached.

4. Pour into clean jars, cover and store in a cool place. It will keep very well in a cool larder, and longer still in a refrigerator.

Green Cheese Party Dip · Blender

4 (3 oz.) (75 g.) *packets*
    Philadelphia cream cheese or
    12 oz. (300 g.) *other cream* or
    firm curd cheese
3 *tbs. mayonnaise*

2 *tbs. cream*
½ *teasp. salt*
½ *small onion*
2 *teasp. Worcester sauce*
green colouring

1. Blend the cheese, mayonnaise, cream, salt and Worcester sauce at fast speed until quite smooth.
2. Peel and cut the onion into several pieces, and then drop them one at a time into the centre of the mixture as it is blending, so that the onion is carried on to the knives and becomes homogenized with the cheese.
3. Finally put in a few drops of green colouring to give the dip a delicate pale green colour.
4. Store in the refrigerator and serve chilled in a bowl surrounded by suitable foods to dip in – e.g. small biscuits, crisps, fingers of toasted bread, celery sticks etc.

Devilled Meat Paste · Blender

This is an excellent way of using up the tag ends of the Sunday joint.

8 oz. (250 g.) *boiled bacon with*
    fat (a knuckle is very suitable)
8 oz. (250 g.) *cold roast beef or*
    roast mutton

1 *level teasp. paprika*
½ *level teasp. powdered mace*
¼ *level teasp. cayenne pepper*
salt if necessary

1. Remove any gristle from the meat, but retain the fat. Cut roughly into cubes.
2. Start the blender at fast speed, then drop the chunks of meat, a few at a time, through the hole in the lid on to the blades.

3. Blend until chopped and finally beginning to form a paste, stopping and scraping the meat down the sides once or twice.

4. It will probably be necessary to chop more than one batch, as the meat should only just cover the blades. Blend the spices into the last batch.

5. Put each batch as it is chopped into a bowl, and when all is done mix very well together. Press into a pot and store in the refrigerator.

Egg Sandwich Spread · Blender

4 *hard-boiled eggs*
1½ *oz. (40 g.) butter*
3 *tbs. mayonnaise or salad dressing*

salt and pepper
1 *thin slice of onion (optional)*

1. Blend all the ingredients except the eggs at medium speed until they are mixed and soft and the onion has disappeared.

2. Through the hole in the lid drop the halved eggs, waiting until one piece is fully blended before adding another. Stop and scrape down the sides when necessary.

3. When fully blended, refrigerate the spread to make it firmer, and use in sandwiches or on savoury biscuits.

Salmon and Egg Spread · Blender

2 *hard-boiled eggs*
1 × 7 *oz. (175 g.) tin of salmon (pink or red)*
2 *oz. (50 g.) butter*

2–3 *tbs. milk*
1½ *tbs. lemon juice*
salt and pepper
red colouring

1. Remove any dark skin from the salmon but put everything else from the tin, including the liquid and the bones, into the blender.

2. Add the hard-boiled eggs, the lemon juice, the butter (either very soft or melted), the seasoning and 2 tablespoons of milk. Blend at medium speed until the mixture is smooth. If it will not blend properly, add a little more milk, but switch off and scrape down sides

with a rubber spatula if necessary. Add a drop or two of red colouring if the mixture is very pale, and blend it in.

3. Turn into a bowl and cool in the refrigerator. Use as a sandwich spread, or on toast.

Salmon and Egg Dip
A little more milk added when blending Salmon and Egg Spread (above) turns it into a very tasty dip for parties.

Sardine Spread · Blender

1 *tbs. salad dressing*	1 *hard-boiled egg*
2 *teasp. made mustard*	1 *tin sardines (approx. 4 oz.)*
2 *teasp. lemon juice or vinegar*	*(100 g.)*
1 *small onion, sliced*	*salt to taste*

1. Blend the salad dressing, mustard and lemon juice at slow speed.
2. Drop in the slices of onion and continue blending until they are chopped very small.
3. Add the egg, quartered, and the whole tin of sardines including the oil. Continue blending at slow speed until smooth.
4. Taste and add salt and pepper if necessary, then put in a pot and refrigerate before using to spread on biscuits or toast, or in sandwiches.

Tuna Spread · Blender

This is excellent spread on biscuits or toast for party savouries. Add a little extra sauce to make a savoury dip. Makes approx. ¾ lb. (400 g.)

1 *large tin of tuna fish (7 oz.)*	1½ *tbs. lemon juice*
(200 g.)	*salt and pepper*
3 *tbs. thick white sauce*	
1½ *oz. (40 g.) butter*	

1. Blend all the ingredients at fast speed until the spread is quite smooth.
2. Store in covered containers in the refrigerator.

SAVOURY BUTTERS

Mixer or Blender

These are usually served with meat or fish or used to spread on
biscuits or toast for cocktail savouries. They keep well and can be
made in advance and stored in the refrigerator. The mixer is
probably the better tool for the job, although the blender is very
useful if there are other ingredients to be chopped or puréed.

Anchovy Butter

about 6–8 fillets of tinned   4 oz. (100 g.) butter
  anchovy (blender)   red colouring if necessary
or 2 teasp. anchovy essence
  (mixer)

1. Use very soft butter. Blend or mix the butter at medium speed
to cream it.
2. Mix in anchovy essence or, if using the blender, drop the anchovy
fillets one at a time on to the revolving knives and continue blending
until smooth. Add a little colouring to give a delicate pink colour.
Stop motor and scrape down the sides when necessary.
3. Scrape the butter mixture on to a piece of wet greaseproof
paper, and roll into a sausage. Twist the ends. Refrigerate until hard,
then cut into neat slices. It will keep some weeks like this.

Maître d'Hôtel Butter

4 oz. (100 g.) butter   2 teasp. lemon juice
  softened)   salt and pepper
4 tbs. parsley leaves

1. Wash the parsley and drop on to the fast-revolving knives of the
blender to chop.
2. Either add the well-softened butter and cream in the blender at
medium speed, or cream the butter in the mixer bowl at medium
speed and add the chopped parsley.

3. Continue creaming while adding the lemon juice and seasoning.
4. Refrigerate as for anchovy butter.

Lemon Butter

4 oz. (100 g.) butter (softened)   salt
rind and juice of 1 lemon

1. Cream the butter in the blender or mixer at medium speed.
2. Beat in the *finely* grated lemon rind and 1 tablespoon of juice.
3. Season, then refrigerate as for anchovy butter.

Devilled Butter

4 oz. (100 g.) butter (softened)   1 teasp. Worcester sauce
1 teasp. curry powder   salt and pepper
1 teasp. lemon juice

1. Cream the butter in the blender or mixer, then blend or mix in
the other ingredients.
2. Refrigerate as for anchovy butter.

18

Drinks – Hot and Cold

රාශ්රාශ්රාශ්රාශ්රාශ්රාශ්රාශ්රාශ්රාශ්රාශ්රාශ්රාශ්රාශ්රාශ්රාශ්

Coffee · Coffee Grinder (or Blender)

coffee beans   *water – freshly boiling*

Method, using a jug:

1. Grind the beans to the required degree of fineness in the coffee grinder (or blender).
2. Measure the ground coffee (2 tbs. to each pint (500 ml.) of water) into a warmed jug. Add the required amount of freshly boiling water and stir vigorously with a wooden spoon, then stand, covered, in a warm place for 4 minutes.
3. Draw the edge of the spoon across the surface to skim off the grounds floating on the top of the coffee, and stand 1 minute more.
4. Strain through a fine strainer into a warmed serving jug or into cups. Add cream or hot milk if desired.

To Make the Best Coffee

1. Always use fresh coffee beans.
2. If buying roasted beans, only buy a few days' supply at once, and store in an airtight tin.
3. Keep to the proportion of 2 heaped tbs. ground coffee to 1 pint (500 ml.) water.
4. Always use freshly boiled water drawn from the cold tap.
5. Drink as soon as it is made, as coffee loses its flavour by standing a long time.
6. Never boil the milk or the coffee.

Iced Coffee · Blender

Serves 3

1 pt. (500 ml.) very cold milk	2 rounded tbs. caster sugar
2 rounded tbs. instant coffee powder	5 drops vanilla essence
	2 tbs. crushed ice

FOR SERVING
whipped cream   grated chocolate

1. Blend the milk, coffee, sugar, vanilla and ice at fast speed until very frothy and the coffee has completely dissolved.
2. Serve in glasses with a dollop of whipped cream on top, sprinkled with finely grated chocolate.

Mint-Choc Milk (Hot or Cold) · Blender

Serves 3

1 pt. (500 ml.) milk (hot or chilled)	6 drops oil of peppermint, or more of peppermint essence
4 tbs. chocolate powder	

1. Blend all the ingredients at fast speed for a few seconds until the drink is frothy. Add the peppermint essence carefully, drop by drop, tasting in between because essences vary in concentration.

Quick Lemon · Blender

This drink is also excellent for use with reducing diets if a low-calorie sweetener is used instead of sugar. Makes 3 drinks.

1 lemon (preferably thin skinned)	1¼ pt. (600 ml.) water (or ¾ pt. (350 ml.) water with ½ pt. (250 ml.) crushed ice)
2 level tbs. caster sugar	(Use less water if the lemon is small)

1. Wash the lemon, cut into four and put in the blender.
2. Add the sugar and water and blend at fastest speed for 7 *seconds*

255

only. This is important as if left longer a bitter flavour will develop. For the same reason strain immediately.

3. Serve ice-cold with slices of lemon floating on top.

To Treat a Cold – This recipe can be followed using boiling water, and 2 tablespoons of honey to sweeten instead of sugar

Oranges and Lemons · Blender

Makes 6 drinks	*Makes 3 drinks*
2 *oranges*	1 *orange*
1 *large lemon*	1 *small lemon*
3 *oz. (75 g.) caster sugar*	1½ *oz. (40 g.) caster sugar*
2 *pt. (1 l.) water*	1 *pt. (½ l.) water*

or

1. With a potato peeler or sharp knife, pare the orange or yellow portion from the peel of the fruit. Put this rind in the blender.
2. Remove all the remaining peel and pith, then add the flesh of the oranges and lemon to the rind, together with the water and sugar, and blend at fast speed until the peel is chopped small.
3. Strain and serve in glasses with ice.

Orange Squash · Blender

Serves 2

2 *oranges*	1 *tbs. sugar*
1 *thick slice of lemon*	½ *pt. (250 ml.) water*

1. Peel one orange thinly, using a sharp knife or a potato peeler, and put the orange paring into the blender together with the peeled flesh, but not pith, of both the oranges, the sugar, lemon and water.
2. Blend at fast speed for about 30 seconds, until the peel is chopped.
3. Strain and serve with ice.

Strawberry Crush · Blender

This strawberry mixture is very popular with children when frozen into ice lolly moulds with sticks. Serves 4 drinks

$\frac{1}{4}$ pt. (125 ml.) orange juice –
from fresh fruit, tinned, or
concentrated frozen juice,
suitably diluted

6 oz. (150 g.) strawberries, hulled
1 level tbs. sugar
crushed ice

1. Blend the strawberries and orange juice with the sugar at fast speed for a few seconds until the berries are puréed.
2. Strain and chill.
3. When ready to serve, half-fill the glasses with crushed ice, then top up with the strawberry mixture, and serve with straws.

Tomato Juice · Blender

Serves 3

1 lb. (500 g.) ripe and red tomatoes
$\frac{1}{2}$ teasp. salt
pepper
juice of $\frac{1}{2}$ lemon

1 rounded teasp. sugar
minute sliver of a clove of
 garlic
Worcester sauce to taste

1. Blend all ingredients at fast speed until the tomatoes are completely broken up and the mixture is homogeneous – about 30 seconds.
2. Strain into a small saucepan through a nylon sieve to remove the pips and skins.
3. Bring to the boil and simmer for 1–2 minutes.
4. Cool, taste and add further salt or Worcester sauce if desired. Chill in the refrigerator and serve in glasses with a tiny sprig of mint floating on the top.

Quicker Method – but the flavour is not so good
1. Put all the ingredients in the blender – but omit the garlic.
2. Blend at fast speed as before, and strain into a jug which has been rubbed with cut garlic.
3. Correct the seasoning and serve as with first method.

Banana Milk Shake · Blender

Serves 2

2 ripe bananas
¾ pt. (375 ml.) milk

2 teasp. sugar
chocolate to grate on top

1. Blend the peeled bananas, milk and sugar at fast speed until the banana is completely liquidized, and the drink frothy (probably about 30 seconds).
2. Serve in glasses with plain chocolate grated on top.

Butterscotch Shake · Blender

1 large serving

½ pt. (250 ml.) milk
1 level tbs. butterscotch
  Instant Whip

2 level teasp. drinking
  chocolate

1. Blend all the ingredients at fast speed until the mixture is quite smooth, and frothy.
2. Pour into glasses and serve.

Mocha Milk Shake · Blender

1 large serving

½ pt. (250 ml.) milk
2 rounded teasp. instant
  coffee powder

2 rounded teasp. drinking
  chocolate powder
2 rounded teasp. caster sugar

1. Method as in previous recipe.

Hawaiian Iced Coffee · Blender

A most unusual, but very pleasant, drink for a hot day. Serves 6

1 pt. (500 ml.) chilled strong
  black coffee
½ pt. (250 ml.) chilled pineapple
  juice

7 oz. (225 g.) vanilla icecream
  (family sized block)

1. Blend all the ingredients at fast speed until the mixture is smooth and very frothy – but not longer.
2. Pour into tall glasses and serve while still really cold.

Lemon Milk Shake · Blender

Serves 4

1 *pt. (500 ml.) milk*	4 *scoops of vanilla icecream*
6 *tbs. lemon juice*	1 *tbs. sugar*

1. Blend the milk, sugar and icecream at fast speed.
2. At once pour the lemon juice through the hole in the lid and continue blending for a few seconds until the drink is very frothy.
3. Serve in tall glasses with a slice of lemon fixed to the rim.

N.B. This drink must be made immediately before serving as if left to stand, the milk separates.

Milky Orange Delight · Blender

Serves 3

1 *pt. (500 ml.) chilled milk*	*a little plain chocolate*
6 *level tbs. frozen*	
concentrated orange juice	

1. Blend the milk and frozen orange juice at fast speed for a few seconds until all the lumps of orange have disappeared, and the drink is frothy.
2. Serve immediately in tall glasses, sprinkling a little finely grated chocolate on the top of each.

Orange Egg Flip · Blender

A most palatable and nourishing drink, particularly suitable for an invalid. Serves 2

½ pt. (250 ml.) orange juice, fresh,   1 tbs. honey or sugar
   frozen or tinned   1 tbs. lemon juice
1 egg   3–4 ice cubes

1. Blend all the ingredients at fast speed for a short while, until the ice is well chopped and the drink frothy. In the smaller blenders the ice must be crushed first.

Rosehip Shake · Blender

Sweet, but very popular with children. Serves 4

1 pt. (500 ml.) milk   1 tbs. lemon juice
6 tbs. rosehip syrup   4 tbs. crushed ice

1. Blend the milk and ice at fast speed.
2. Pour through the hole in the lid the rosehip syrup, followed by the lemon juice, and continue blending until the drink is frothy.
3. Serve in glasses while still very cold and frothy.

Sherry Egg Nog · Blender

Serves 1

¼ pt. (125 ml.) cold milk   2 tbs. sherry
1 egg   1 teasp. sugar

1. Blend all the ingredients at fast speed until the mixture is smooth and frothy (probably about 30 seconds). Serve in a glass.

Strawberry or Raspberry Ice Cream Soda · Blender

This recipe can be successfully varied by omitting the icecream, but in this case 1–2 tablespoons of sugar must be blended in with the fruit. Serves 4

8 oz. (250 g.) *fresh or frozen* *strawberries or raspberries*	1 pt. (500 ml.) *fizzy lemonade* *or soda water*
2 *bricks or scoops vanilla* *icecream*	*ice*

1. Blend the fruit with the icecream and a little lemonade or soda water at slow speed for a short while until the fruit is puréed.
2. Pour into individual glasses, add ice to each and top up with the remaining lemonade or soda water.

Strawberry Milk Shake · Blender

Serves 2

4 oz. (100 g.) *strawberries hulled*	1 *scoop or 1 brickette vanilla*
½ pt. (250 ml.) *milk*	*or strawberry icecream*
1 *tbs. sugar* (1 oz.) (25 g.)	

1. Blend all ingredients at low speed for 5 seconds, then increase to fast for a further 10 seconds, or until the mixture is deeply frothy. Serve in glasses immediately.

High Protein Milk · Blender

A smooth, extra-nourishing and delicious drink for invalids. Particularly valuable if the patient cannot take solid foods. Serves 2

½ pt. (250 ml.) *milk*	*glucose or caster sugar to*
1 *egg*	*sweeten according to the*
½–1 oz. (15–25 g.) *dried low-* *fat milk powder*	*flavouring* *flavouring – see below*

1. Blend all the ingredients at fast speed for 10–15 seconds, until the drink is smooth and frothy.
2. Serve in glasses, ice-cold. This quantity may be divided into two parts, and each flavoured in a different way.

Suggestions for Flavouring

1. Blackcurrant syrup
2. Rosehip syrup
3. Concentrated frozen orange juice

} dropped in through the hole in the lid as the drink is blending. These flavours are particularly valuable as they add Vitamin C to the nutrients of the drink

4. Peppermint – a few drops of oil or essence
5. Milk shake syrups in various flavours
6. Coffee, 2 teasp. instant coffee powder dissolved in 1 tbs. boiling water.
7. Chocolate – 3 heaped teasp. drinking chocolate
8. Vanilla – a few drops of vanilla essence.

DRINKS FOR INVALIDS OR FOR SPECIFIC MEDICAL CONDITIONS

The blender is ideal for reconstituting any of the proprietary dried milks or other dried drinks which are on the market. They should be used in the quantities suggested on the packet. It is best to put the liquid into the goblet first to prevent the powder sticking round the bottom. If much of the food is being used it is easier to make up a day's supply at a time, and then stir in a variety of flavours as required during the day.

Here is one example:

Complan
A nutritionally well-balanced drink, high in protein and suitable for use in many illnesses both by children and by adults.

2 oz. (50 g.) Complan (3   flavouring
  heaped dsp.)   sugar if desired
½ pt. (250 ml.) water (hot or cold)

1. Blend the water and added Complan powder at fast speed until the drink is smooth and frothy.

2. Flavour. Either add the flavouring and blend in the jar, or stir into each cup as desired.
Suggested flavourings:
Vanilla
Coffee
Drinking chocolate
Fruit flavouring syrup
Marmite.

Complan with Fruit Juice
A most refreshing drink for an invalid, which can even be taken by a patient who is nauseated.

$\frac{1}{2}$ *pt. (250 ml.) fruit juice –*   1 *oz. (25 g.) Complan*
sweetened to taste

1. Blend the fruit juice, chilled from the refrigerator, and added Complan powder at fast speed. When serving add a lump or two of ice if necessary.

19

Baby Foods

ृ૨૦ૹ૨૦ૹ૨૦ૹ૨૦ૹ૨૦ૹ૨૦ૹ૨૦ૹ૨૦ૹ૨૦ૹ૨૦ૹ૨૦ૹ૨૦ૹ

Blender

The quantities given in the following recipes are very small and it is usually more convenient to blend a larger quantity and store some for use next day, especially when using one of the larger blenders. However, as has been said before (p. 56), great care must be taken that there is no opportunity for undesirable bacterial growth, and food for a baby should *never* be used if there is any question that it might have been stored longer than was safe.

Savoury

All should be rewarmed if necessary before feeding the baby.

Cheese and Potato Dinner

   1 *oz.* (25 g.) grated cheese   1 *medium tomato – without*
   2 *tbs. mashed or boiled potato*   *skin or pips*

Blend all the ingredients at slow speed, increasing to medium or fast if necessary, until quite smooth. Add a little milk or white sauce if it is too stodgy.

Fish Dinner

1 oz. (25 g.) cooked white fish
 – no skin or bones
1 tbs. cooked carrots
1 tbs. mashed or boiled potato

2 tbs. white or parsley sauce
or 1 tbs. milk + small knob
butter

Blend all the ingredients together at slow speed until they are quite smooth, adding a little more milk if necessary.

Beef Dinner

1 oz. (25 g.) beef (from stew,
 joint, etc.)
1 tbs. cooked peas

1 rounded tbs. mashed potato
2 tbs. gravy

Blend the peas in the gravy at slow speed, then add the meat cut across the grain into small pieces, and finally the potato. Blend until all is mixed well and the meat chopped fairly fine.

Liver Dinner

1 oz. (25 g.) cooked liver
 (lamb's, calf's, pig's or chicken's)
1 rasher grilled bacon
 (optional)

1 tbs. cooked spinach,
 sprouts or other vegetables
1 tbs. mashed or boiled potato
3 tbs. gravy or stock

Blend the gravy, roughly chopped liver and bacon (if used) at low speed to chop them, then add the vegetables and blend until all is smooth, adding more gravy if necessary.

Sweets

Apple Dessert

1 medium eating apple,
 peeled and cored
2 tbs. evaporated milk

1 teasp. sugar
1 teasp. lemon juice
 (optional)

Drop the quarters of apple on to the blades revolving at slow speed

and blend until they are chopped. Add the milk, sugar and juice and
increase to fast speed until the apple is very fine.

The addition of lemon juice is not strictly necessary except that it
prevents the apple starting to brown after a short while.

Banana Goo

4 tbs. rice pudding, semolina pudding or blancmange	sugar
1 small banana	2 teasp. rosehip syrup or concentrated orange juice

Break the banana into chunks and blend with the fruit juice and
the milk pudding at slow speed until smooth, adding sugar to taste

Fruit Dessert

2 tbs. tinned or stewed fruit (no pips)	2 teasp. dry baby cereal (Farex, Groats etc.)
2 tbs. syrup from tinned or Stewed fruit	sugar

Blend all the ingredients at slow speed until smooth. Fruit with
stones should first have these removed.

Peach or Pineapple Rice

2 rings of tinned pineapple or 2 peach halves	2 tbs. rice pudding or creamed rice

Cut the fruit into rough pieces and blend with the rice at slow speed
until the fruit is sufficiently broken down to suit the baby.

20

Preserves

JAM MAKING

The blender can be used to break down fruit, and especially its skins, so that the cooking time can be much reduced. This considerably improves the flavour and colour of the jam, although it will have more uniform appearance, with less large pieces of fruit than jam made by the conventional method. It is particularly useful for fruits that have tough skins, such as gooseberries, blackcurrants and plums.

Less water should be used in this method than in the conventional recipe as the fruit need only stew for a few minutes after blending.

The fruit (stoned if necessary) and water must be measured and then put in the blender together, in batches, at fast speed for a few seconds until the skins are fully broken down. Bring this purée to the boil and simmer for just a minute or two until any small pieces of skin remaining are quite soft.

Alternatively the fruit and water can be stewed together until half-cooked, and then blended. Then add the sugar and proceed with the jam in the normal way. The following blackcurrant jam recipe is just one example of the many possible using such a procedure.

Some jam recipes require the fruit to be sieved, as in seedless blackberry jam, and in this case the fruit can be blended and then passed through a strainer or the colander/sieve attachment to the mixer can be used.

Blackcurrant Jam · Blender

This recipe has a higher proportion of sugar than is usual, but blackcurrants are high in pectin, and this jam gives a good flavour and set while making the blackcurrants go as far as possible. Yield 3½ lb. (1½ kg. approx.)

1 lb. (½ kg.) blackcurrants   ¾ pt. (400 ml.) water
2 lb. (1 kg.) sugar

1. Wash and pick the blackcurrants from their stalks.
2. Blend in batches, with the water, switching on at fast speed for a few seconds until all the skins are broken up.
3. Put this purée into the preserving pan, bring slowly to the boil and simmer for 2 minutes.
4. Add the sugar and boil rapidly until the setting point is reached.
5. Pot in clean, dry, warm jars and cover while still warm.

Marmalade

The scope of this book does not allow a detailed explanation of all the methods and recipes for the making of marmalade, and therefore only three recipes are given to show how the mixer and its attachments can be used to save time and effort. The methods given in these recipes can be used for many other marmalades, using any of the citrus fruits.

In marmalade making, it is the cutting up of the peel which is the most laborious task and it is for this that the mixer attachments are most used. The peel can be chopped in the blender, although a small jar may mean refilling it a good many times to make a quantity of marmalade; it can also be minced in the mincer, and the peel can be shredded finely using the slicer/shredder. This is particularly useful for jelly marmalade recipes.

Apart from these uses of the mechanical aids of the mixer, the methods given in any marmalade recipes can be followed.

Blender Cut Marmalade (with Seville Oranges) · Blender

Makes 10 lb. (4½ kg.) approx.

> 3 lb. (1½ kg.) *seville oranges*   6 lb. (3 kg.) *sugar*
> 5 pt. (3 l.) *water*   1 *lemon*

1. Scald the oranges and lemon with boiling water and scrub well.
2. Cut the fruit into four and remove all the pips. Tie these in a muslin bag.
3. Put into the blender as much fruit as will one-third fill it, and pour in water up to this level out of the measured 5 pints (3 l.)
4. Put on the lid and blend at the fastest speed for a few seconds, just sufficient to chop the peel. The longer the blender works, the finer the cut of the marmalade.
5. Empty the jar into the preserving pan, and refill with a second load of fruit and water – continuing until all the fruit is chopped.
6. Put the bag of pips in the pan, together with any remaining water. Bring to the boil and cook gently until the peel is tender (about 2 hours).
7. Remove the bag of pips and squeeze it well into the pan.
8. Add the sugar and stir it well until it dissolves, then boil rapidly until the setting point of marmalade is reached.
9. Remove the scum, but let the marmalade cool slightly (about 15 minutes) so that the peel will not rise in the jars, then stir well, pot in clean, warm jars, and cover.

Minced Marmalade · Mincer Attachment (and Citrus Fruit Juice Extractor)

Makes 10 lb. (4½ kg.) approx.

> 2 lb. (1 kg.) *seville oranges*   ¼ lb. (100 g.) *lemon*
> ¾ lb. (375 g.) *sweet oranges*   (1 *large lemon*)
>   (2 *large oranges*)   5 pt. (3 l.) *water*
>   6 lb. (3 kg.) *sugar*

1. Scald the fruit with boiling water and scrub well.
2. Cut in half and squeeze out the juice, using the citrus juice

extractor if available. Tie the pips into a muslin bag, and put this, together with the juice, into the preserving pan.

3. If there is a lot of pith, remove this from the inside of the skins, and then mince the peel, using the mincer attachment fitted with its coarsest screen.

4. Cook the minced peel with the water and juice etc. in the preserving pan, gently simmering until it is soft – about 2 hours.

5. Squeeze the bag of pips and remove, then add the sugar and stir until it is dissolved.

6. Boil rapidly until the setting point is reached, remove the scum and allow the marmalade to cool for 10–15 minutes. Stir, pot in clean, warm jars, and cover.

Jelly Marmalade · Blender or Slicer/Shredder or Mincer

In jelly, as in ordinary marmalade, it is the slicing of the peel which takes the time, and this can be done quite satisfactorily by the slicer/shredder or the blender or the mincing attachments. However no domestic mixer can produce the thin, even slivers of peel which are found in commercial jelly marmalade, and if these are desired the peel must be very thinly sliced by hand with a sharp knife. This is very time-consuming and so it may be best to compromise by using one of the mixer attachments which will quickly produce peel cut into pieces, but of less uniform size and shape than those cut with a knife.

Yield 10 lb. ($4\frac{1}{2}$ kg. approx.)

4 lb. (2 kg.) *seville oranges*	6 lb. (3 kg.) *sugar*
4 *lemons or* 2 *teasp. citric acid*	9 pt. (5 l.) *water*

Method for Chopping Peel

There are at least four ways of chopping the peel, which should be as delicate in appearance in the finished marmalade as possible. They are all quite satisfactory but are given here in the author's order of preference:

a. Cut the oranges in half, remove the fruit from the skins, and as much pith as possible, and then shred with the coarsest blade of the slicer/shredder.

b. Using a potato peeler or a sharp knife, peel very thinly the orange portion from the skin. Put 5 oz. (125 g.) of this into the blender, together with 1 pint ($\frac{1}{2}$ l.) of the measured water, and blend at fastest speed until the peel is sufficiently finely chopped. Only a few seconds' chopping should give peel of attractive appearance, but it will be in pieces rather than in strips.

c. Cut the oranges in half, remove the fruit from the skins and as much pith as possible, and mince the peel with the mincing attachment, using the fine screen fitted to the mincer.

d. Cut the oranges in half, remove the fruit from the skins and as much pith as possible, and then shred with the finest blade fitted to the slicer/shredder attachment.

Method for Making Marmalade

1. Scald and scrub the oranges, then cut several in half and scoop out fruit if using methods (a), (c) or (d) above for slicing the peel, sufficient to give 6 oz. (150 g.) of shredded peel. If using method (b) peel off 5 oz. (125 g.) of the rind, very thinly; process the rind according to (a) (b), (c) or (d) and put it to cook in 2 pints (1 l.) of water. Simmer until tender in a closed pan – about $1\frac{1}{2}$–2 hours. Drain off the liquid.

2. All the remaining fruit must be put in the blender – the whole oranges cut into 4. Fill the jar one-third full, then add water from the measured 9 pints (5 l.), sufficient to cover the fruit. Blend at maximum speed for just a few seconds to chop the fruit. Empty out into the preserving pan and refill the jar with fruit – repeating until all the fruit is chopped.

3. Simmer this fruit pulp with the juice of the lemons for about 2 hours, then add the liquid drained from the peel, and strain through a scalded jelly bag, allowing to drip for 15 minutes.

4. Return the pulp to the preserving pan, add the remaining water from the 9 pints (5 l.), simmer for 20 minutes more, and strain again through the jelly bag.

5. Put all the drippings from the jelly bag into the preserving pan, together with the sugar.

6. Stir well to dissolve the sugar, then add the shredded cooked peel and boil rapidly until the setting point is reached.

7. Skim at once, but allow the marmalade to cool for 15 minutes, then stir, pot in clean, warm jars, and cover.

Preserved Apple Purée · Colander/Sieve or Blender

This is an excellent way of preserving apples, particularly windfalls, for future use. The pureé can be used for fools, flans, creams or apple snow.

cooking apples　　　　　　　*orange or lemon rind if*
sugar　　　　　　　　　　　*desired*

1. Wash the apples, and remove any bruised or diseased parts. Cut in quarters but do not peel or core.

2. Stew the apples with a small quantity of water, just sufficient to prevent them sticking, until quite tender. Thinly peeled lemon or orange rind can be included at this stage if desired.

3. Use either the colander/sieve or the blender to purée the fruit. The former will deal with a large quantity very quickly, but the latter is quite satisfactory for a smaller amount. In this case the fruit must be put in the blender in several batches, never filling the jar more than two-thirds full. Blend at fast speed until the purée is smooth. The contents of the jar must be passed through a nylon strainer to remove the pieces of core and pips, but it will be found that most of the peel has been ground so small as to pass unnoticed in the fruit pulp.

4. Return purée to the saucepan, add sufficient sugar to sweeten, and reheat slowly to boiling point.

5. Transfer, boiling, to hot, clean preserving jars and seal immediately with lids and rubber rings just previously dipped in boiling water.

6. Stand the sealed jars in a deep saucepan filled with hot water (and fitted with a false bottom to prevent the base of the glass jars from coming into contact with the saucepan), and bring to the boil – then keep at boiling point for 5 minutes.

7. Cool, and when quite cold test that a vacuum has been formed by lifting up each jar by the lid.
8. Alternatively the purée can be deep frozen.

Apple Chutney · Mincer Attachment

Yield 7 lb. approx.

3 lb. (1½ kg.) cooking apples –
weighed after preparation
½ lb. (250 g.) raisins (large ones,
stoned if possible)
¼ lb. (125 g.) onion
¼ lb. (125 g.) whole mustard seed

¼ oz. (5 g.) cayenne pepper (no
more)
3 oz. (75 g.) salt
2 oz. (50 g.) ground ginger
3 pt. (1½ l.) vinegar
1 lb. (500 g.) soft, light brown
sugar

1. Soak the mustard seed in the vinegar overnight.
2. Peel and core the apples and peel the onions.
3. Using the mincing attachment with the coarsest screen, mince the raisins, apples and onion. These latter two must be cut into suitably sized pieces to go down the funnel of the mincer.
4. Put all the ingredients in a preserving pan and heat gently until they are well cooked and soft – about 2 hours.
5. Bottle while hot into clean jars and cover with an airtight lid which will prevent the evaporation of the vinegar. If a metal screw-on lid is used, it must be well lacquered and a layer of cork or waxed board put inside, as the vinegar will attack metal.

Keep several months before using to allow the flavour to mature.

Apple and Mint Chutney · Slicer/Shredder or Mincer attachment (and Blender)

Yield 10 lb. (4½ kg.) approx.

4 lb. (2 kg.) cooking apples
1 lb. (½ kg.) onions
2 lb. (1 kg.) green tomatoes
1 lb. (½ kg.) demerara sugar
1 lb. (½ kg.) seedless raisins

2 pt. (1 l.) malt vinegar
1½ oz. (40 g.) mixed pickling spice
(tied in a muslin bag)
6 tbs. chopped mint
salt

273

1. Peel and core the apples, skin the onions and wash the tomatoes then either slice them on the coarsest cutter of the slicer/shredder or mince them using the largest screen.
2. Put all the ingredients except the mint into a large saucepan, and simmer slowly until the vegetables are cooked, and the chutney has the consistency of jam.
3. Meanwhile pick, wash and dry the mint, then drop the leaves on to the fast-revolving knives of the blender jar, to chop it finely.
4. Stir the mint into the chutney when it is cooked, remove the spice bag, and bottle while hot in clean, warm jars. Cover with an airtight cover, and keep several months before using to allow the flavour to mature.

Bottled Mint Sauce · Blender

    4 oz. (125 g.) *mint leaves*   ½ *lb.* (250 g.) *granulated sugar*
    ½ *pt.* (250 ml.) *vinegar*

1. Bring the vinegar and the sugar to the boil in a saucepan, stirring to ensure that all the sugar is dissolved.
2. Pick the mint leaves from the stalks, wash and dry. (If the mint is picked clean from the garden there is no need to wash.)
3. Blend the mint leaves, and the vinegar and sugar at fast speed until the mint is finely chopped.
4. Pour into clean jars and screw on the lids firmly.
5. This will keep well for some months and is ready for use when required. More vinegar can be added before serving if desired.

(A recipe for fresh Mint Sauce is given on p. 98.)

Index